Secure Connected Objects

Secure Connected Objects

Dominique Paret
Jean-Paul Huon

WILEY

First published 2017 in Great Britain and the United States by ISTE Ltd and John Wiley & Sons, Inc.

ISTE Ltd
27-37 St George's Road
London SW19 4EU
UK

www.iste.co.uk

John Wiley & Sons, Inc.
111 River Street
Hoboken, NJ 07030
USA

www.wiley.com

Library of Congress Control Number: 2017932154

British Library Cataloguing-in-Publication Data
A CIP record for this book is available from the British Library
ISBN 978-1-78630-059-1

Contents

Part 4C. From the Base Station to the Server   203

Chapter 14. Network Access Layer – IP.   205

14.1. IPv4   205
    14.1.1. Operation.   206
    14.1.2. Services provided   206
    14.1.3. Reliability   206
14.2. IPv6   207
    14.2.1. Differences between IPv6 and IPv4   207
    14.2.2. Problems of privacy and/or anonymity?.   209
14.3. 6LoWPAN   209
    14.3.1. Description of the technology   210
    14.3.2. Integration of an IPv6 packet into an IEEE 802.15.4 frame   210
    14.3.3. Autoconfiguration of an IP address   211
    14.3.4. Network supervision and management   211
    14.3.5. Constraints on "upper-layer" applications.   211
    14.3.6. Security.   212
    14.3.7. Routing.   212

Chapter 15. The Server   215

15.1. Conventional functions of a server in IoT   216

Chapter 16. Transport and Messaging Protocols.   219

16.1. Transport   219
    16.1.1. Operation.   220
    16.1.2. Structure of a TCP segment   220
16.2. "IoT messaging" technologies   221
    16.2.1. Main protocol parameters.   221
16.3. Protocols   225
16.4. HTTP – HyperText Transfer Protocol   226
16.5. HTTP/2   227
16.6. MQTT – Message Queuing Telemetry Transport   227
    16.6.1. Security in MQTT   229
16.7. CoAP – Constrained Application Protocol.   229
16.8. XMPP   230
16.9. DDS – Data Distribution Service   231
16.10. AMQP – Advanced Message Queuing Protocol   232
16.11. SMQ   233
16.12. JMS – Java Messaging Service   233
16.13. Other protocols   234

Foreword

To begin with, I must applaud Dominique Paret and Jean-Paul Huon for this excellent initiative to write a book on the Internet of Things (IoT). There is a wealth of literature on this topic, but not a day goes by when we do not see numerous successful cyberattacks, which could endanger the large-scale rollout of IoT technologies if we are not conscious and cautious of the danger they pose. As Europe is projected to become the second biggest IoT market in the world by 2030, this represents an unmissable opportunity!

This very thorough book is written both for readers wishing to familiarize themselves with the complex issues surrounding networking objects and for those who design these connective "things".

This book sets itself apart from the rest by: restating the fundamental elements, both software and hardware, of the technological building blocks, to describe service architectures; teaching the reader about the different protocols; making designers aware of the legal issues and the processing of sensitive data; and finally, discussing end-to-end security using an excellent technical basis.

Other points are highlighted in the discussion of numerous elements in the overall design of the IoT chain and the technical-economic realization of the so-called secure connected object.

Dominique and Jean-Paul have, for years, been recognized experts in the development of RFID technologies, contactless chip cards, NFC, IoT and software. The highly technical nature of the topics discussed herein must attest to their expertise.

EESTEL is proud to welcome these authors as members, to participate in the work of training, dissemination and security assessments, without which the electronic transaction market, and that of IoT in particular, could never develop.

Once again, bravo!

I hope that you, the reader, will enjoy this book and reap the benefits it has to offer.

Pierre CRÉGO

Preface

After a great deal of discussion on how to construct this essentially technical book, built around the concrete realization of secure connected Things in applications for the IoT (Internet of Things), we chose the following layout for the presentation:

– a general introduction to the world of IoT;

– a detailed description of the numerous aspects and problems connected to this discipline, which must be taken into account in undertaking any IoT project;

– a brick-by-brick description of the overall architecture of IoT solutions;

– the lengthy, detailed technical description of the various elements of the architecture is divided into four sub-parts:

- from the outside world to the Thing, inclusive,

- from the Thing to the base station, inclusive (the physical layer),

- from the base station to the server, inclusive (the IP/TCP layer and application layer),

- from the server to the outside world (the application layer);

– the concrete illustration of an IoT solution, using detailed examples and the true costs they bring with them.

Dominique PARET
Jean-Paul HUON
March 2017

Acknowledgements

As per usual, there are many people to whom thanks are due for their goodwill, for listening, for their remarks and constructive comments. Thus, to all those people, who know beyond a doubt who they are: a huge, warm and heartfelt thank you!

Now a few more specific acknowledgements and hat-tips to certain very long-standing friends:

– firstly to Jean-Yves Cadorel and Eric Devoyon (formerly of CRESITT, and then 3ZA) and Jean-Marc Vauguier co-founder of Z#BRE;

– secondly to Pierre Crégo, head of Mercury Technologies, founder and head of education at EESTEL, amongst other roles;

– and to a number of friends: Maître Nathalie Damiano, Jean-Claude Paillier, Claude Meggle, François Brion, Jean-Luc Garnier, members of the Association EESTEL, Christophe Huguet who is a networking expert from Exaprobe, Antony Passemard, Michael Garcia from AWS and many more.

All of these, in their own way, have provided us with many excellent examples as technical explanations, … and also with many shared golden moments.

Preamble

As a preamble to this book, let us start as we mean to go on, and show the "color" of the coming discussion.

First of all, this book is not intended to be (and is not) an encyclopedia of connected Things and IoT/IoE. There are thousands of articles about the subject online (some better than others), providing a framework for wild and wonderful flights of theoretical fancy, enormous and varied future markets of all kinds, stupendous commercial figures, etc. For our part, as we are not keen on unproductive redundancies, we have focused only on those subjects about which far fewer articles are available: that is, the daily operation, on the ground, of this domain, between concrete discussion of the Designs, Applications and Realization of secure connected Things – IoT/IoE. Even so, the discussion will be plenty extensive!

As each word of the title has been considered at length, it is worth giving a brief explanation of each term.

IoT/IoE – Today, there is a great deal of talk about the "IoT" – the Internet of Things. For our part, we wished to skip over the (immense but) restricted field of IoT ("Things, Objects") and move up to the level of the IoE – the Internet of *Everything* – i.e. absolutely everything, including animals, individuals, groups of individuals, and so on.

Things – This term serves as our starting point for the whole string of explanations… Thus, a "Thing" as meant here could also be called a "terminal"! In this book, when we speak of "Things", with a capital "T", the term includes everything that is found in everyday literature referred to as "devices", "elements", "nodes", "end devices", "endpoints", "terminals", etc. – in short, any "thing", be it large or small, which serves as a point of origin for data which we have to or wish to exploit.

Connected – Connected, certainly… but connected to what? How? Why? At what cost? Furthermore, Things may be simply connected to one another by any type of connection, and we speak of "Connected Things"; or else they may be connected via a specific type of link – e.g. via the Internet (which complicates matters somewhat), in which case we speak of "IoT or IoE"… but this is not a goal in its own right. Beware of confusion between styles! We must not mix up cabbage and carrots… but we have not precisely defined what is a cabbage and what is a carrot! Please, dear reader, take care to avoid unwarranted confusion of the terminology.

Secured – Here, there is no doubt; there is no alternative. A connected Thing must be secure, and that security must be rigorously established from end to end of the chain, including in Cloud storage if such a service is used; otherwise it is all for naught. (Be careful: that one sentence encapsulates 35 years of security of banking transactions and high-level industrial exchanges). Security is not a luxury, but an absolute necessity, in terms of the operation of the whole system and in terms of individuals' private lives, in today's world and tomorrow's, because there is too great a risk of piracy, hacking, phishing, etc. to which we are exposed.

Applications – Obviously, we cannot forget the vast domain of all kinds of applications.

Design – The aim of this book is to serve as a guide so readers forget nothing and avoid the pitfalls that could emerge in the process of designing secure connected Things.

Concrete realization – This is the true purpose and the very core of this book. It is all very well to speak about the Internet of Things; to discourse articulately on the subject (how many times have we seen and heard such speeches…?) but to concretely, physically create a connected Thing for commercial ends and successfully sell it in large quantities, at a reasoned and reasonable price is far better… Otherwise we may as well do nothing, without a lot of noise!

Here, then, is the express purpose of this book.

PART 1

Introduction – The Buzz about IoT and IoE

This first part is divided into a number of introductory chapters, always having a direct or semi-direct link to the Internet of Things – IoT.

By way of introduction to this book, Chapter 1 offers a brief overview of the relevant vocabulary, with a view to avoiding the misunderstandings which occur all too often in the field, and resolving the confusion between the terms "connected things", "communicating things" and devices which do actually form part of the "Internet of Things" *per se*.

For its part, Chapter 2 touches on the (overly) vast mode of IoT, the catchall surrounding the IoT, the "buzz" in the media, in the specialized or general press, etc., and the concrete reality, which consists of defining, designing, manufacturing, perfecting and industrializing a product, and in particular, successfully selling it!

To conclude this first part, Chapter 3 employs a concrete example to present a view of the technical-economic situation, with the "why" leading to the conception and design of a communicating thing that uses the Internet.

1

Introduction

This first part recaps fundamental and classic concepts of theories… but first, in order to clarify our approach, let us look at a little vocabulary and examine a few definitions of the "Who is Who" in the "IoX".

1.1. Definition of communicating- or connected Things

1.1.1. *Connected Things – Communicating Things*

What a marvellous term "Connected Thing" is, which conveys absolutely anything… and its opposite! How many people will delight in that name!

> "Thing" is easy: it is easy to imagine that the term covers everything from an extremely miniature Thing to an enormous ocean liner!
>
> "Connected" to what? How? Why? … etc. In this aspect, we are often still left searching for meaning!

Over the ages, connections have been established in different ways: in smoke signals, …, over wired connections, but today, all of this now seems somewhat retro to some people. The uni-directional or bi-directional, "wireless" or "contactless", connection is much more in fashion.

That said, let us keep things simple and open our eyes. Radio-frequency identification (RFID) has been in use for a number of years (decades, even); so too have contactless chip cards, NFC, Zigbee, Bluetooth BT & BLE, Wi-Fi, etc. and, much like Mr Jourdain in Molière's *The Bourgeois Gentleman* speaking prose all his life without even knowing it, we have been making "wireless" "Connected Things" –secure ones, even, and even highly secure!

An example from the public "automobile" market:

For 15 years, an electronic valve for cars has been a "Connected Thing" (using UHF), connected to the electronics of the car, but this is not an example of the IoT!

Thus, this current fashion is not truly groundbreaking, except for a certain faction of the press and avid "followers" of new words… even if those new words express the same things as the old ones!

1.1.2. *Definition of the IoT*

What exactly does the IoT consist of, and what is the IoE (i.e. the Internet of Everything)?

It is a physical network of Things (or "devices/objects") incorporating sensors, electronics, software and connectivity, enabling these Things to exchange data with an operator, a manufacturer, a service provider or other connected devices. Thus, it is based on a number of different things.

1.1.2.1. *Infrastructure of the IoT*

The IoT works under the auspices of the "ITU – the International Telecommunications Union – Global Standards Initiative (IoT-GSI)". For information, IoT-GSI covers connected devices and Things (e.g. personal computerized devices, portable or office computers, tablets and smartphones, etc.) via multiples communication protocols connecting the elements to one another, such as Bluetooth, ZigBee, Long-Range Wide-Area Networks such as LoRa, SIGFOX, etc.

1.1.2.2. *IoT devices (or nodes or elements or Things)*

IoT devices (elements) or indeed what we define generally as Things, often function without a human interface, generally using the energy supplied by a battery, and are usually devoted to a single task. They are generally described as "smart objects", or as "connected devices". As it is, there is a whole host of such devices! For example:

– electrodomestic networks which can be remotely monitored or controlled;

– sensors, industrial equipment and other integrated elements which are connected in networks;

– "Smart home" elements such as lighting, heating or ventilation units with remote management/control, access, etc.

– "wearables", fashion accessories or connected clothing, etc.

– etc.

This typically means that an IoT device falls into one or several of the following functional domains:

– Surveillance: teledetection and notification of operating conditions and use of other external environmental factors;

– Control: means that certain functions of the Thing can be remotely managed or customized;

– Automation: devices which can operate independently, capable of adapting to environmental or operation factors with minimal human interaction;

– Optimization: monitoring- and control functions meaning that the manufacturers of the Things can optimize their performances and effectiveness in real time, based on the history and/or instantaneous operational data;

– Preventative maintenance or diagnostics: these can also be carried out remotely.

1.1.3. *Internet of x*

Having barely had the time to gain familiarity with the Internet of Things, suddenly we are talking about the Internet of Everything – IoE. What is the difference between these two concepts? We shall answer this excellent question shortly, but first, let us take something of a purist stance, and call a spade a spade. To begin with, in order for there to be an "Internet of x", the "Internet" (and its structure) must be involved in the story – otherwise there could not be an IoT and certainly not an IoE; however, there are many, many Connected Things which operate with links other than the Internet... thus, it is important not to confuse cabbages and carrots*!!!

IoT, as the name indicates, implies that sooner or later we must use an Internet connection... but that is not always the case!

NOTE.–. *We shall refrain from defining what cabbages and carrots respectively are in this story!*

1.1.3.1. *Internet of Things - IoT*

The "Internet of Things" is often defined as being the network of physical Things containing "embedded" technology (integrated, onboard), so as to communicate, detect or interact with their internal states and/or the external environment. Figure 1.1 shows a non-exhaustive example of the functional chain of such a structure.

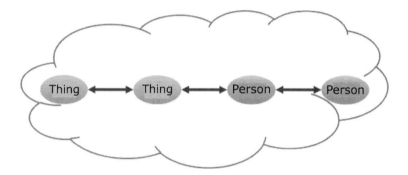

Figure 1.1. *Functional chain of IoT*

Often, by default, in the eyes of many, the Internet of Things is all so-called connected products, monitored by mobile applications: watches, weighing scales, bracelets, toothbrushes, refrigerators, etc., which often do not use the Internet at all, instead using other means of communication such as NFC, BLE or Wi-Fi, for example.

1.1.3.2. *Internet of Everything - IoE*

The Internet of Everything – IoE, for short – goes far beyond "Things" (Connected Things). In fact, this is an expression invented in 2015 and promulgated by Cisco – one of the world leaders in network infrastructure. There is every chance that in tomorrow's world, the Internet of Everything will become a reality, encapsulating not only the world of the Internet of Things, but also that of data, processes... and people (through their smartphones and social networks)! More broadly still, the Internet of Everything is based on the harvesting of the information that we share individually and collectively – that is, it operates at a much higher level than with simples Things in the Internet of Things. That data mining will be organized by private companies capable of processing enormous streams of data – known as "Big Data" (via the Internet) – and charged with turning those data to profit, selling them on either to advertising agencies or marketing networks, or to public-sector organizations wishing to optimize their services and territories, or indeed to public-interest private companies (transport operators, energy providers, works contractors, waste-management companies, etc.), and so on. In other words, the raw material used by this new industry will be our personal information, freely given, without us having any control over the use made of it... Of course, we must not neglect to mention the flip side of the coin: the danger of the servers hosting all these data being hacked!

The admirable goal of the Internet of Everything is to support numerous developments and improvements, such as smart homes, optimized control of energy consumption and natural-resource consumption, smart parking, more appropriate road tolls, etc. and also help improve administrative performances by enhancing agents' productivity and reducing operating expenditure. That, at least, is the dream...

Examples

The Internet of Everything makes it possible for cities to ultimately become "Smart Cities", and for public administrations to hinge their efforts on the following three axes:

– budget savings:

EXAMPLE.– sensors built into trash cans send a message to indicate that they need to be emptied. Such a system in Finland has already delivered a 40% saving on the waste collection budget.

– new revenues:

EXAMPLE.– in New York, urban screens operating 24/7 are used for surveillance in the city, dissemination of information, offering means of communication (e.g. Wi-Fi), but also generating revenue through advertising.

– advantages for citizens:

EXAMPLE.– "smart parking" employs an intelligent system to inform drivers of the number of free spaces left in the different parking lots in the city.

In Nice, this system has reduced traffic jams by 30%, increased parking revenue and reduced CO_2 emissions.

Having come to the end of these few introductory remarks about our near future, let us now turn our attention to the enormous world of IoT.

The (Overly) Vast World of IoT

2.1. 2011–2016: the craze for the term "Connected Thing"

Over the past five years, the media has been inundating us with news of Connected Things, in enormous tidal waves of hype for each and every successive one! What does this represent, and where are we to situate this book and its content within this quagmire of information?

2.1.1. *The catch-all*

Anything and everything! It is true that the dawn of connected Things and the generalized use of digital technology have led to the production of vast quantities of data, creating new opportunities to improve operational efficiency, to reinvent the customer experience and to create new services. Therefore, in all major fields of activity, IoT plans are being announced with a great deal of fanfare, with enticing slogans:

– Aeronautics: "air travel and airport security 2.0"

– Automobile: "when intelligence rhymes with performance"

– Energy: "draw value from the grid and rationalize your consumption"

– Commerce and large-scale distribution: "enhance supply-chain reliability whilst also improving customer service"

– Luxury: "new services for a demanding clientele"

– Health: "the beginnings of a revolution"

– Cities and collectives: "when the environment can communicate"

– Rail travel: "new opportunities"

– Sea travel: more modest, a sector only just coming to terms with the technology

– and all sorts of other industries, services, smart cities, insurance companies, distribution firms and transport operators have their own projects!

2.1.2. Fashion, buzz and "bubble"

Is this market for Connected Things a bubble, as we saw only a few years ago in other areas (e.g. property, dot-com businesses, and so on)? Can it last? What does our crystal ball say (see Figure 2.1)?

Figure 2.1. *Is the IoT market a short-lived buzz, or will it endure?*

2.1.2.1. What the crystal ball shows

Taking, as a starting point, the hypotheses of Cisco and Ericsson, and in the knowledge that between 2015 and 2021, the number of IoT-connected devices is projected to grow by 23% annually, peaking at almost 16 billion units out of a total of 28 billion connected products (taking account of PCs, portable computers, tablets, mobile telephones and landline phones), here are a few nuggets of information.

– in 2018, the number of IoT Things connected by non-cellular radio protocols should rise from 4.2 billion to 14.2 billion units;

– it is also predicted that the cellular IoT (with Things connected *via* mobile telephone technologies (2G, 3G, 4G, LTE-M, NB-IoT, 5G, etc.) will develop spectacularly, with 1.5 billion units in 2021, compared to 400 million in 2015 (as the peak throughput of the descending radio channels of the LTE networks run by mobile operators will surpass a gigabit per second and this will lead to the development of compatible mobile terminals and IoT Things, first in Japan, the United States, South Korea and China).

– One final point: in terms of the number of Things and IoT connections, Western Europe will lead the way, with 400% progression by 2021. This phenomenon will be due, notably, to the recent evolutions in legislation in the field of communicating energy meters, and to the EC's demand regarding the eCall initiative (distress call) for connected vehicles.

As our crystal ball has offered us the point of view elucidated above – which is merely one more projection amongst others – wisdom leads us to point out that the concept of the hype cycle has a well-known shape, which, whilst it is unequivocal, is not always too close to the mark, though not too far wide of it either!

2.1.3. *"Hype" cycle for innovations*

New technologies offer numerous admirable, wonderful ideas, but how are we to know whether or not they will achieve real commercial success? In addition, it is very difficult to estimate the financial risk that a company will have to endure (often over the course of several years of R&D) for the commercial launch of a new product on a market with no point of reference, as the product is a so-called disruptive innovation – a technological breakthrough.

Each year, the Gartner group, made up of specialist consultants in the prospective development of emerging technologies, offers its clients a view of the life cycles of their innovations, the different phases of adoption and maturity, to try and project when the product should (finally) become profitable!

Every summer, Gartner polishes off its crystal ball, and for the coming year, publishes its "Hype cycle" (registered trademark of Gartner) for the technological products currently in fashion. This helps everyone to gain an idea of how to position their product and glimpse its evolution over time, and thus enable companies to estimate the kind of sales effort they will need to implement alongside the development, with a view to planning the product's rollout.

Every innovation/technological product is believed to obey a hype cycle, made up of five key phases in terms of visibility and maturity (see Figure 2.2).

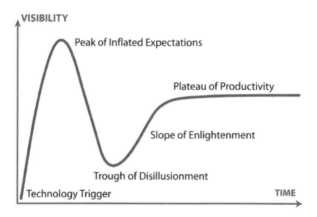

Figure 2.2. *Hype cycle (source: Gartner)*

– Phase 1: emergence of the idea: "Technology Trigger"

As at the start of any branch of activity, there are many innovative ideas around: good ones, bad ones, ones which are idealistic but not particularly constructive, etc. This creates a "buzz" and draws interest from the media. This is the stage where teams of future engineering students doing their final-year projects are itching to create their future "start-ups".

In general, at this stage, all we have are models/prototypes (POC – Proof of Concept), and the commercial viability of the products has not yet been proven.

– Phase 2: "Peak of Inflated Expectations"

The publicity created when the idea was launched has given rise to numerous emulating products. There are many new entrants to the race and numerous start-ups, SO/HOs, SMEs, SMIs, and this is the stage when a few "success stories" begin to flourish… but there is also a certain amount of "bad buzz".

It is at this moment when innovators need to take concrete action, and move on to real production to make the product available, because the public's expectations are high.

– Phase 3: "Trough of Disillusionment"

After this significant phase of hope in the market, we see a phase of depression, stemming from the fact that the products are not always available or do not live up to the expectations people had of them, or indeed because there are far too many disparate offers and solutions, the price is still a little too high and, because of the lack of norms for the market, there are too many protocols and standards and/or proprietary standards, little or no interoperability, etc.

At this stage, public interest takes a nosedive, and companies have to decide whether they are willing/able to invest to truly adapt the product to the demands of the "early adopters" of the market.

It is often at this stage when numerous start-ups fail, through lack of liquidity, funding, aid, a solid financial position. Thus, there are "crashes" and a few/many decomposed bodies of companies wash up on the shoreline.

– Phase 4: "Slope of Enlightenment"

The project begins to reach its final development phase. Companies come to have an increasingly good understanding of the market they are dealing with. It is a time when groups of complementary interests come together to form joint ventures; the best start-ups are bought up by larger companies/groups, either to develop and help these SMIs grow, or to bring their own products up to speed in the domain... or indeed to better be able to smother them in the longer term (this approach is deeply unkind, but it is done, and it is a very effective strategy!).

This is when the second or third generations of the product are released.

– Phase 5: "Plateau of Productivity"

Finally, a genuine market emerges; the technology begins to be more widely used, and it is finally adopted by the "cautious majority" (Rodgers' model states that the number of people adopting a new product obeys a Gaussian curve. Once the cautious majority has been won over, the product has reached half its level of salability).

Viability criteria begin to become clearer; the relevance of the innovation is more convincing, and profitability comes shining through. Hurrah! We are saved!

These five phases have different durations and amplitudes depending on the technologies and the markets in which they arise. Some products may reach the plateau of productivity in two years; others in ten; others still may become obsolete before ever reaching it!

With experience, Gartner has managed to define around a hundred reference curves for the technology sector: e-commerce, telemedicine, transport, software, etc. For instance, as regards the subject of interest to us here, Figure 2.3 shows the results of Gartner's crystal ball for 2015.

Figure 2.3. *Hype cycle in mid-2015 (source: Gartner - july 2015)*

In short, we see here the well-known industrial and economic projection, which overlaps with the hype cycle! Consider yourselves warned!

2.2. The true goal of this book

Let us return now to our initial question: What does this represent, and where are we to situate this book and its content within this quagmire of information? Elementary, my dear readers... allow me to explain!

The next part of this book describes the steps to be taken and respected so that your project avoids the trough of disillusionment (parts 2 and 3 of the hype cycle), so you can skip over that part and go directly from the phase of reflection on innovation (or innovation trigger, part 1) to the slope of enlightenment (part 4) – i.e. the way from innovation to a stage of healthy production, or indeed the move from the virtual to the real world!

Quite some challenge, is it not?

Thus, as we progress through this book, we shall offer you the path of reasoned wisdom, constructed on the basis of true integration of the worlds of legislation, technology, economics, ergonomics, etc.... rather than a boulevard of broken dreams!

3

Why a Connectable Thing?

As a prelude to part 2 of this book, pertaining to all the constraints one needs to manage and satisfy when designing a connected Thing, so as to lend some context to the discussion, let us give a concrete example of what defines the reason for developing a connectable Thing, what lies behind the desire to create it, which conditions it needs to satisfy, its aim, its usefulness, and so in time its salability, and hence its technical aspects and economic acceptability.

We generally perceive the Internet of Things only through a "Thing" capable of simplifying data retrieval, or fun, as was the case when connected bracelets began emerging. However, the changes wrought go far beyond a simple Thing, and are mainly seen in the impacts such devices have on economic models.

A "secure connected Thing" may come in a very wide range of forms, from a watch to a car, for example. To offer a concrete example, let us look at two cases: firstly home care for the elderly or handicapped, and secondly a connected car.

3.1. Examples of connectable things

The first concrete example we shall present is that of home care for the elderly, in a study performed in the French region of Le Loiret, which will serve as a reference point throughout this book.

3.1.1. *Home care for the elderly*

In France, local authorities are in charge of home care for the elderly, and disburse large sums of money to satisfy that need. The solution adopted needs to resolve a number of problems:

– the local authority must remain in close contact with the dependent people and their families, but at present, it is generally home-help organizations that are in direct contact with the citizens, with the authority merely providing the funding;

– the strategy must improve the elderly people's quality of life, and that of their families as well;

– there must be far better control of expenditure, and it is important to ensure the services provided are effective (the cost of such services runs to around €35 million per year for 10,000 dependent people).

The thinking in terms of an IoT design to take care of these issues has been to analyze and use data including financial data. This is a key point of the problem, because all too many IoT projects do not have a viable economic model, and therefore fail at the proof of concept (POC) stage, or the first tests. However, a successful solution is one which is implemented on the ground and is economically productive, as opposed to a technological demonstration with no future.

The angle of attack chosen to solve this problem is simplicity, and the desire to improve the lives of as many of the players involved as possible. With this in mind, the solution has to generate economic gains which outweigh the cost of its development and implementation. To deal with these challenges, the IoT-based solution employed by the company Z#bre, for example, is based on a device which reads a contactless badge (much like a contactless chip card), carried by all personnel who come into the home (support workers to help the person get up in the morning, meal providers, cleaners, nursing staff, etc.), and sends that information over a LPWAN (see Chapters 12 and 13). Thus:

– we have real-time knowledge of personnel's visits to the elderly people's homes;

– we can associate and adjust the different payments for the services actually provided by each staff member;

– we can provide families with real-time information about the progress of the services being provided.

Hence, faced with the issue of an ageing population, the local authority has been able to improve its interventions and develop additional services to serve the need for secure home help for people having lost their independence, and satisfy their families' expectations. Notably, this desire resulted in the setting up of a direct and privileged link between the local authorities, the beneficiaries of the service (around 10,000 in late 2016) and their families:

– via the communicating "Thing" – the box (see the example of the "Lysbox" made by Z#bre, shown in Figure 3.1), which uses NFC contactless technology to interact with the user/service provider. The box is installed in the home of the service receiver, and has the ability to evolve to include new services in the domains of security and home care;

– via a social portal made available to the recipients, their families and the aid-providing organizations, providing real-time information about rights, and about the home interventions and facilitating contact between all the actors involved.

Figure 3.1. *Example of an IoT connoctod Thing: the Lysbox, made by Z#bre*

The innovation behind this project integrated:

– for the first time, direct contact between the relevant departments at the local authority, the people receiving the help and those personnel physically providing it in their homes;

– the provision of a box, for free, to receivers of APA (Aide aux Personnes Agées – Aid for the Elderly), which is a first in France in terms of contactless technology for ordinary citizens;

– the use of the LTN-NB (low-throughput network-narrow band) "SIGFOX" (see details in Chapter 13) devoted to the Internet of Things, which has no impact in terms of public health (100 times less radiation than a cellphone) and is capable of operating on battery;

– a device which has a low cost thanks to low-throughput technology (low costs of telecoms);

– a service that offers a return on investment from the very first year, with the implementation of the effectiveness check.

Figure 3.2 illustrates the general, overall architecture of the system.

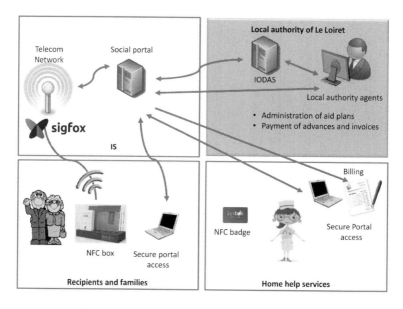

Figure 3.2. *Overall architecture of the system*

Ultimately, this project:

– was rolled out in the space of only six months to 10,000 beneficiaries;

– generates €3 million in savings each year for the local authority;

– has helped the families of the aged to stay informed, in real time, about the services provided to their loved ones;

– has improved the quality of the service, with service providers having access to all relevant information.

3.1.2. *In the automotive industry*

The second example, which is rather more generic, pertains to the world of the automobile, which has been massively affected by the major economic change due to the introduction of connectivity, because now a car must be viewed as a "secure connected Thing", whose connectivity significantly alters its use.

Previously, one vehicle could be differentiated from another by its bodywork and by the mechanical elements it had. Its electronics was not really part of the equation. Nowadays, though, many paradigms have utterly changed, and it is now the vehicles' electronics, and the OS they run, which set them apart. They are able to automate more and more functions – for example, improving safety by detecting obstacles, or simplifying driving with guidance systems or parking assistance.

Everyone knows that the next step is automation of actual driving. At present, this is limited to automated parking, or to cruise control on highways, but it will reach the next stage when full industrial production of autonomous vehicles hits the market.

In this context, automobile manufacturers are in danger of becoming nothing more than subcontractors specializing in the working of sheet metal… with the real value going to those who have connectivity and Cloud facilities capable of handling and supplying all the necessary data for a self-driving car (Google is one example, amongst others). The majority of manufacturers have begun to make the change, systematically connecting all their vehicles, whether or not customers have requested connectivity. The considerable mass of measurement data, for example, provides extremely precise readings (because they are taken on the fly, on the ground) of the topology of the roads, and the state of them (for instance, detecting the formation of potholes). All these data enable the automatic boxes to anticipate changes of speed and gear before reaching a turn.

Changes will continue in the way in which we do our shopping. Superstores will most likely be impacted by automated delivery, made possible by autonomous vehicles.

Through the lens of these few examples, we have seen the economic upset that will undoubtedly be caused by the Internet of Things.

Having supped this little aperitif, let us now move on to the hors-d'œuvres, which are the various types of constraints that must be overcome when undertaking an IoT project.

PART 2

Constraints Surrounding an IoT Project

Before embarking on any project, it is always good to know the path to tread before encountering dire disappointment. For our part, we cannot claim to be omniscient, but the benefit of our long experience leads us to precede the technical details with the following brief discussion, describing the majority of issues and questions to be resolved before starting any hardware or software in the IoT domain.

There are multiple constraints that need to be dealt with: financial ones, marketing ones, technical, industrial, regulatory and normative ones, safety issues and cost concerns, etc.

Until all these areas have been satisfactorily covered, be careful of the respective viabilities of your projects.

We have now built the framework for this absolutely necessary – indeed vital – part!

Aspects to be Taken into Consideration

This micro-chapter, in fact, serves as an introduction to the enormous second part of this book.

4.1. Aspects pertaining to the concrete realization of Connected Things

To give some concrete meaning to the creation of Connected Things, let us begin by listing the numerous aspects which pertain, either directly or indirectly, to the industrial manufacture of a communicating Thing, whether or not its connection is to the Internet. These aspects can be summed up in seven broad categories, which are absolutely necessary in all projects, and will be discussed at length in the coming chapters:

– financial aspects;

– marketing aspects;

  technical aspects;

– industrial aspects;

– regulatory and normative aspects;

– safety aspects;

– cost aspects.

In addition, each of these aspects is often subdivided into multiple sub-aspects. Let us briefly describe their content before continuing.

4.1.1. *Financial and marketing aspects*

The financial and marketing aspects category includes:

– commercial/cost aspects;

– economic aspects, the size of the user's wallet, etc.;

– marketing aspects, trying to find the best possible use for a technology, rather than a gimmick, etc.;

– ergonomic aspects, definitions of the users' needs and desires, etc.

4.1.2. *Technical and industrial aspects*

The same is true for the technical and industrial aspects, comprising the:

– technical aspects, specifications, etc.;

– energy aspects – consumption, battery life, etc.;

– industrial aspects, prototypes, series starter, full production, their costs, etc.

4.1.3. *Regulatory and normative aspects*

Likewise for the regulatory and normative aspects:

– regulatory aspects concerning RF emissions and pollution, health regulations (effects of wave radiation), private data, personal data, public-domain data, etc.;

– normative aspects, communication protocols, waste-management norms, etc.

4.1.4. *Security aspects*

The same goes for:

– data security aspects;

– privacy safety aspects;

– etc.

4.1.5. *Cost aspects*

Finally, we take a detailed look at:

– material costs;

– capital expenditure (CAPEX) on development, and operating expenditure (OPEX);

– and the sum of all costs (notated as Σ), giving a total cost, and telling us the overall industrial cost price of the Thing itself, and the industrial margin, with the establishment of a sales price.

Here, then, is the menu for the coming chapters, with the mandatory requirement to offer satisfactory choice: "cheese course plus dessert plus coffee plus liqueur", with no other form of possible sub-option!

Once again, the stage is set.

Thus, lights… camera… Action!

5

Financial and Marketing Aspects

5.1. Economic aspects

The economic aspect is an extremely important one. If we are to develop a product, sooner or later it must make money! How do we do this? To whom do we sell it?

If these two points are not clearly defined from the very start of your project, it is pointless to even begin! Therefore, they need to be carefully studied before doing anything at all in technical terms.

5.1.1. *Saleable / buyable*

Making a product with a view to selling it is all very well, but we still need to make sure that people will buy it. That sentence might seem banal and obvious, but unfortunately, there are many who forget it! It is here that we see the enormous difference between a "saleable" product and a "buyable" one. In this book, we shall only speak of products intended to be "buyable"!

5.1.1.1. *Multiple points to be studied*

What does a product need to make it buyable – i.e. to make a person actually reach for their wallet? We need to carefully define which fields of application and which potential market the product is to be designed.

The application is already in place

– is the product's purpose to essentially replace something which already exists? If so, it needs to be cheaper!

– is its function to replace an existing product and also to improve upon it in some way? Even so, the price needs to remain reasonable!

In both these cases, the keyword is: "replacement value", and its weighting to enter the arena and make money. If it cannot do that, then there is "no way"!

The application is innovating and/or represents a technological breakthrough

– is its function to replace and greatly improve the application?

– is it entirely new, because there is nothing like it out there?

Is it a fad/fashion?

Will it last? The price needs to be negotiated between the seller and the buyer.

In these two cases, the key question is: How many people are willing to pay to get it at that price?

Buyable

However obvious it may seem, sooner or later, the product (the Thing) needs to be "buyable" for a certain audience, at an acceptable price (e.g. sale of the factory-sealed product in a superstore), and it must be interoperable with other products, rather than (strictly proprietary) in its own little world. In parallel, do we think that the product will win a small part of the larger market, or a very small portion of a micro-market of sales?

ROI – Return on investment

This is another tricky point in terms of IoT. How do we estimate the return on investment (ROI), and calculate the amount of time it will take? In addition, we have to project the product's life span in a market as changeable as that of Communicating Things. Above all, it is the balance between the "use value" (perceived by the user) and the "value proposition" (product or solution put forward by the industrialist) which is important.

As often happens, to envisage the best possible solution and be sure of achieving it, we need to work backwards – in other words, we need to start with the goal in mind, and work back, step by step, to reach the beginning of the story.

Generally, ROI is calculated solely on the basis of the Thing itself. Indeed, in order to improve margins and/or reduce the sale price and shorten the length of time taken to achieve ROI, the usual solution is to try to drive down the cost price. The problem is that with this approach, the possibilities for new functions and innovations are reduced. That is exactly what happened in 2005, when the majority of mobile phone manufacturers focused solely on the cost price in order to reduce the sales price or increase their profits.

Another way of working is to start at the other end of the chain, and look for how to increase the use value for the consumer (the perceived value). In this area, Apple have consistently been one of the best, because the company were able to integrate functions with high use values into their smartphones (audio players, cameras, browsers, etc.). With the use value thus increased, Apple were able to sell their smartphones at twice the price of other products on the market. Thus, they were able to build their hardware using components with power that other cellphone manufacturers could only dream about (in particular, the processor had great computing power, enabling it to run the graphics screen and all the functions).

This example demonstrates that the best way of working is to start with the end goal in mind – i.e. to start with the consumer, identify what his/her expectations and desires are and create a product to fulfill them, without resorting to "cost cutting".

As we have just seen with this example, the quickest possible ROI does not necessarily mean making the cheapest product on the market, and we can see that the ROI is extremely closely linked to the use value perceived by the consumer. Unfortunately, at present, in IoT, many products are driven by technology. They are technically fantastic… but no-one is interested in them, because the use value they offer is not enough to cater for a sufficient level of consumer demand.

5.1.1.2. *In conclusion, it is always good to remember that…*

In order for a solution to interest everyone in the chain, everybody must make a little money out of it… If not, it goes down like a lead balloon!

5.2. Ergonomic aspects

The ergonomic aspects are another important point to consider: even if a product is technically excellent, poor design on an ergonomic level can see it dead in the water!

5.2.1. *Mechanical form and design vs ergonomics*

The shape, the design, the material, the box, the functional ergonomics* of a Thing must all be studied in detail. All of this involves, for instance, making wise choices in terms of form, esthetics, molds, cost of molds (sometimes quite considerable), manufacturing time, amounts of parts, etc.

– The term comes from the Greek: *ergon* ("work") and νόμος / *nómos* ("law, research"). Thus, ergonomics refers not to sleek design or attractive appearance, but instead the level of comfort when we work with a device!

In addition, in IoT, as we shall show later on in this book, practically all designs of Things require the presence of an antenna, and normally, no customer wants to see an antenna on the outside of a case – potentially very attractive and/or small – which is sometimes completely at odds with the technical, mechanical and ergonomic requirements!

Therefore, beware!

5.2.1.1. *Flexibility of use*

In addition to design, true ergonomics of use must be very carefully thought out (the presence or absence of buttons/keys on the Thing, the need for a manual, etc.), and of course, from the starting point of development, we must take account of the elderly and handicapped or people with reduced mobility, who may interact with the Thing.

Technical and Industrial Aspects

6.1. Technical aspects

Here, from a purely technical point of view, is a long list of the essential points to take into consideration when embarking upon an IoT project for industrial purposes. This set makes an enormous difference with POC (Proof of Concept), which is well known and is only a very small step away from industrialization, always keeping in mind that:

> Reference design 1 + Reference design 2 + ... = (may be) 1 POC
>
> but 1 POC
>
> cannot be, is not and never will be
>
> an industrial product!!

With this clearly established, we have crossed paths with innumerable unfortunates who believed that the above equation was sufficient to launch a product on the market! May God have mercy on their souls!

In short, having drawn these comparisons, let us now move on to the nitty gritty.

6.1.1. *Life cycle of a new product*

It is helpful to define a life cycle for a project (its division into phases, the time periods involved, etc.), which includes the phases of Innovation, definition of the clients' needs, etc.

6.1.2. *Techno-economic feasibility*

During the techno-economic feasibility phase, we look closely at the product's techno-functional specifications, from which we draw a complete overview, methodology and the feasibility tools to be put in place... which may involve a POC.

Similarly, we need to begin by looking simultaneously at the problems of sourcing, qualification, choice of suppliers/partners and, also, at calculating the budgets for R&D, Industrialization, Toolkits and cost price of the final product so as to sign off on the project's launch as a "GO" or "NO GO".

6.1.3. *Design*

Next comes the phase of active simultaneous development of "hardware" and "software", selections, management of normative constraints, evaluation of the "Design to Cost" relation, models, and technical evaluations and certifications thereof.

6.1.4. *Industrialization, manufacturing process and quality assurance*

This lengthy phase includes:

– firstly, the precise validation of the design, the construction of the processes of mechanical/plasturgic industrialization, electronic cards, assembly/tests, making of prototypes, qualifications/certifications and finally the launch of industrial pre-series and series manufacture;

– secondly, all stages of validation of the suppliers, prototypes and pre-series processes.

6.2. Energy aspects

In terms of technical aspects, we must not forget those aspects linked to the Thing's battery life, consequently its intrinsic energy consumption, and thus how it is supplied with energy! This is one of the key points in the world of communicating Things and IoT.

In summary, depending on the technical and technological designs of the Things and their application vocations, there are different angles on energy supply to the Things.

6.2.1. *Power supply to the Thing*

In IoT, the problem of energy supply to the Thing is not one which is easily solved. This goes way back to the days of the earliest TV remote controls, the first electronic watches and calculators, etc. The point, essentially, is that every technological era brings its own problems in this area.

6.2.1.1. *220V mains power supply*

Direct power supply from the 220V mains grid will often be the case with industrial Things, and thus energy supply should not represent too much of an issue. However, for portable, mobile Things, this is no longer a viable solution.

6.2.1.2. *Presence of a battery (rechargeable or otherwise) – a so-called "battery-assisted" system*

Battery-assisted systems are lightweight, mobile Things operating on battery power (in whatever format), whose quantity of energy is known (generally expressed in Amp hours (Ah), or more specifically in coulombs – see below), meaning a known battery life depending on the Thing's peak consumption and average consumption.

EXAMPLES.– watches, wearable technologies

6.2.1.3. *Energy harvesting or scavenging*

These energy-harvesting systems provide very small quantities of electrical current to (very) low-consumption electronic circuits, using energy sources present in the environment. Thus, essentially, they are "batteryless" systems where energy harvesting is the process whereby the energy needed for operation is drawn from external sources in infinitesimal quantities, and then stored to allow devices to operate on battery power (e.g. using super-capacitors C – known as gold capacitors – which are charged with a voltage V and give out a certain number of coulombs $Q = C\,V$. Examples are those used by wearable electronics, and wireless sensor networks).

Amongst these energy-harvesting systems, we could cite those, for example, whose power comes from:

– remote power supply produced by radiated electromagnetic fields (RFID, NFC, etc.);

– solar energy;

– wind energy;

– motion; kinetics;

– dynamo;

– vibratory energy;

– chemical energy;

– etc.

6.2.1.4. *Battery life and lifespan*

When designing a communicating Thing, battery life and lifespan are amongst the first subjects which need to be discussed with the person representing the end user (your buyer, the retailer who will sell the Thing, etc.). It is crucially important to reach an agreement on the length of time for which the Thing will operate without changing the batteries, and prevent any gross misrepresentations in its marketing. It is a seemingly trivial issue, but these discussions can go on for quite some time, and failure to have them can cost you dearly. To help you in conducting these discussions, below is a non-exhaustive list of examples of questions needing to be answered in this area.

Brief overview of the "silly" little questions to be answered

– Can the batteries easily be accessed and changed?

– Are the batteries single-use or rechargeable?

– Is the Thing disposable?

– Who changes the batteries: the individual user or a maintenance service?

– Are they easy to install?

– Are the batteries to be replaced for preventive purposes, rather than curative?

– How much will the service cost?

– Has the person carrying out the service been specifically trained or not?

– Which battery manufacturers provide contractual guarantees of their battery life?

– Who guarantees the duration of the battery life in the application?

– Are the batteries installed during manufacture or at the end of the production chain?

– Have measures been taken to allow for potential long-term storage in a warehouse?

– Are the batteries activated only when first used after an unknown period of storage?

– At that point, who activates them?

– How much do they cost?

– And so on.

Over to you…

Let us now look at the energy management technology.

6.2.1.5. *Quantification of energy*

As we all know, sleep is a wonderful thing – and the greater the proportion of time a Thing is in sleep mode, the less it consumes. Then, there is always the problem of whether someone has actually gone to sleep and is truly sleeping. The only known effective method to determine this is to wake him/her up and ask! (Who has never asked "Are you sleeping, sweetie?" and endured a tongue-lashing the next morning from the woken partner unable to get back to sleep!). The same is true in IoT! In short, we need to painstakingly determine the details and phases of the Thing's energy consumption, and above all, quantify them.

Duality between Coulombs and Ah

Shocking as some may find it, having worked for over twenty years in the field, we are not fond of the "Ampère hour (Ah)", typically given on battery casings! We remain faithful to the good old coulomb (symbol C) which, in the international system (SI), is the true unit of electrical charge. It is named after the French physicist Charles-Augustin Coulomb. To recap, the coulomb is the amount of electricity passing through the cross-section of a conductor traversed by a current whose intensity is 1 amp per second ($Q = i\,t$ being well known). Given the knowledge that the elementary charge of an electron $|e|$ is $\approx 1.602 \times 10^{-19}$C, a charge of 1 coulomb is equivalent to $6.24150962915265 \times 10^{18}$ elementary charges!

Why use the coulomb? Whilst it may appear complicated, it is, in fact, very simple!

In order to estimate the lifespan of a battery when used for its intended application, we first need to take the time to quantify, in micro-slices of application (μs by μs), all the quantities of electricity consumed by the different elements and the different functions of the Thing. Then we need to add these quantities up (μC by μC) over the course of all these periods of time, and then take account of the cyclic ratios δ of operation of each of the various components/elements (phases of wakefulness, activity, normal sleep mode or hibernation, verification of sleep mode activation and how to achieve it, complete shutdowns, awakening of only a portion of the functions, the presence of partial networks, etc.), in the hope of ultimately being able to find the total, integrate it by finding Σq and then average it over a second or an hour, and finally find that value Q in coulombs, express it in Ah, and use that to estimate the lifespan of the Thing and its battery, in days, months or years. This is long-winded, tricky and hard to do, but it is the only way to avoid any inaccuracy or inventing, and printing a lifespan value "off the top of your head" on the product documentation, and sometimes obtaining very unfavorable results!

A few examples

Rather than being vague, let us look at the concrete foundation of the issues, using an example which is illustrative but highly representative of real-world operational sequences, in Figure 6.1.

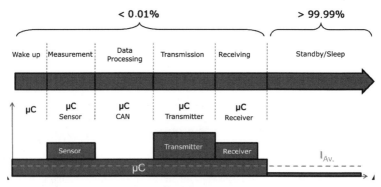

Operational sequences

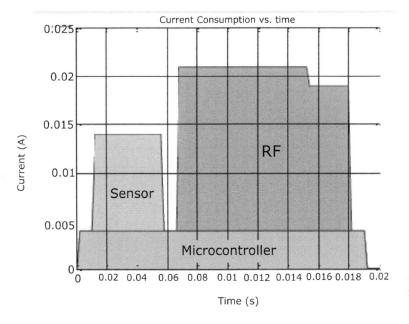

Figure 6.1. *Operational sequences of an Internet of Things system (source: the expert Renaud Briand, Toulouse/Bayonne)*

The second example is that of an old RFID device which was already a "communicating Thing" (nearly twenty years ago – check the date on the battery). It is an electronic valve used on a car wheel, working at UHF in direct relation with the vehicle's on-board computer – in fact, a remote pressure sensor, measuring the pressure and correcting its value as a function of temperature by way of a microcontroller – see Figure 6.2.

Figure 6.2. *Electronic valve for measuring tire pressure. For a color version of this figure, see www.iste.co.uk/paret/connectedobjects.zip*

The table in Table 6.1 shows an example of the amount of electricity consumed during the different phases of operation of the communicating Thing – the electronic valve – which need to be added up in order to determine which type of battery to use.

					Consumption	
Elements					**Standby**	**Operational**
Micro		conso (run @ 2MHz)	with E2prom			500 μA
		communication time				200 ms
		Q = i t	coulombs			100×10^{-6}
		duty cycle &acquis/day				
Sensor		conso			0.15 μA	300 μA
		acquisition time				100 ms
		Q = i t	coulombs			30×10^{-6}
		duty cycle &acquis/day				
e2prom	via I2C	conso				0 μA
		write time				100 ms
		Q = i t	coulombs			0×10^{-6}
		duty cycle &acquis/day				
Clock		conso				250 nA
		write time				
		Q = i t	coulombs			
		duty cycle &acquis/day				
Total		**Σ Q per day**	**coulombs**			$\mathbf{130 \times 10^{-6}}$
		in A.h				

Table 6.1. *Example of the amounts of electricity consumed during the different phases of the Thing's operation*

From this, it is easy to calculate the battery life.

Battery life = t = Σq / I t, in seconds

and, in the case of energy-harvesting devices:

Battery life = t = Σq / I = CV / I t, in seconds

EXAMPLE.– Remembering that 1 year = 365 × 24 × 60 × 60 = 31,536,000 seconds, with a 100 μF capacitor charged at 1V, i.e. $Q = 1 \times 10^{-4}$ coulomb, to achieve a lifespan of 1 year, the current, averaged as a function of the cyclic ratios, must be no greater than:

$$I\_ave = 1 \times 10^{-4} / 31, 53 \times 10^{+6} = 3.17 \times 10^{-12} = 3.17 \text{ pA}$$

6.3. Industrial aspects

As indicated, we shall now move on to the concrete realization of the Thing for commercial ends, after the "manipulations" and careful "tweaking" by students and other projects in engineering schools, the design references, the POCs everyone demands or offers, the failed functional prototypes of start-ups made with modules (Arduino, C° and other companies)... which all work on paper, but are, unfortunately, far from industrially viable!

One of the very first questions to ask yourself is the following: Am I technically and financially capable of bringing the industrial project to fruition alone, or do I need to subcontract all or part of the technical work, and have an industrial subcontractor – a partner by my side – and if so, for which parts of my project?

The answers to this question have (very) weighty consequences in terms of time, financial burdens and supports, and the ultimate viability of the project.

To help you, at the end of this book (Part 5), with a minutely detailed example, we offer a roadmap whose aim is to enable you to come at the project from the right angle. This guiding schema takes account, for example, of the quantities, production platforms, subcontracts for hardware and software, the mechanics (molds, etc.), SE security, Cloud computing, etc.

7

Regulatory and Normative Aspects

The goal of this chapter is to discuss the regulatory (and therefore mandatory) aspects, recommendations and norms (which are not obligatory but are highly advisable, notably with a view to interoperability with other devices), at the national, European and world level. It is true that when thinking about IoT, we need to design a product with worldwide scope; otherwise it is merely a drop in the ocean!

This already pours cold water on the excitement, as there is a whole host of regulations and worldwide norms to be satisfied, which vary depending on place of sale, of production, numerous certifications and different nuances of depth of those certifications, latent protectionism which sometimes (indeed often) force companies to produce their devices in the country in which they wish to sell them, and finally, we must be able to combat the various sentiments such as those often heard in the USA, saying that a product is not acceptable because it is *"not invented here"*!

Let us begin with the regulatory aspects and the recommendations.

7.1. Regulatory aspects and recommendations

Put briefly, a "regulation" is series of official documents/rules published by an organization attached to the "State" or to a "community of States" (such as the EU), which must be respected because of prescriptions, rules and regulations, laws, dispensations and/or decrees and other legal texts governing a social activity. The regulatory constraints governing IoT devices and the surrounding world are mainly environmental in nature, and generally pertain to four levels:

– respecting the limits on RF radiation/pollution – ERC 70 03 and the associated ETSI norms, FCC 47 part 15, etc.;

– "human exposure, SAR by electromagnetic fields";

– PIA – Privacy Impact Assessment – CEN EN 16 571

– GDPR (General Data Protection Regulation);

– waste management (integrated circuits and antennas of the targets/tags)

7.1.1. *Radiofrequency regulations*

All IoT systems which include RF, described in this book, ultimately have antennas which can emit radiofrequency waves. Numerous regulatory texts indicate, by way of the permitted values for emitted frequencies, bandwidths (WB – Wide Band or NB – Narrow Band), authorized radiated power/field levels, specific templates, duty cycles, constraints and restrictions (radiation, pollution, susceptibility, etc.) governing devices dedicated, in the broad sense of the term, to contactless/wireless applications (RFID, NFC, IoT, geolocation, etc.).

The problem of regulating the acceptable radiation and tolerated RF pollution levels is far from simple, given the diversity of the laws and exceptions present in all areas of the world and/or each country. Put simply, it is complex. There are a number of organizations (worldwide, American, European, French, etc.) which regulate the field and are in charge of drawing up parameters affecting IoT systems of the type SRD (Short Range Devices) and LR (Long Range) devices. These are:

At the global level:

The ITU – the International Telecommunications Union – with its Radiocommunication sector, the ITU-R.

In the USA:

The well-known FCC – U.S. Federal Communications Commission – which, under the aegis of the ANSI (American National Standards Institute), created the famous referential document "US Code of Federal Regulations (CFR) Title 47, Chapter I, Part 15, Radio Frequency Devices", which is the local bible for the regulations of interest to us here.

In Japan:

The specifications ARIB STD-T96 (2010.07.15) (H22.7.15) (Version 1.1): "950MHz-Band Telemeter, Telecontrol and Data Transmission Radio Equipment for Specified Low Power Radio Station" are binding.

In Europe:

The well-known recommendation ECC - ERC - REC 70 03 "Relating to the use of Short Range Devices (SRD)" from the ERO (European Regulation Organization) is gospel. Readers are strongly encouraged to obtain a copy of the latest version (from ero.dk).

In addition, the measuring and testing methods prescribed by ETSI – *"Electromagnetic compatibility and Radio spectrum Matters (ERM); - EN 300 - xxx - frequencies from 9 kHz to x GHz"* conform to the ERO recommendations.

In France:

Two organizations govern the frequency distributions that can be used for IoT, and their specific uses:

– ANFR – Agence Nationale des Fréquences (National Frequency Agency); and

– ARCEP – Autorité de Régulation des Communications Electroniques et des Postes (Electronic and Postal Communication Regulatory Authority),

which adhere, as closely as possible, to the European recommendations, and produce documents serving as the basis for the writing of French norms and regulations on "Short Range Devices – SRD" – "Non-Specific" applications, which cover many IoT applications.

7.1.1.1. *Constraints due to NFC radiation and pollution*

In RF applications for IoT, one of the other fundamental constraints is that the technology respects the levels of RF radiation and pollution prescribed by national and international legislation. Despite the fact that in RF, it is possible to use multiple frequencies, today, practically the entire world operates at around the same frequencies or frequency bands (13.56 MHz, 800–900 MHz and 2.4 GHz). At these frequencies, the regulations and norms on pollution are more or less harmonious throughout the world, although there are some minor variations from one region to another.

7.2. Health-related recommendations

Another necessary consideration pertains to human health.

Certain entities, associations, etc. have no weight with which to directly impose certain requirements on a State, but do have significant skills, meaning they are able to recommend certain values and criteria in their fields of expertise. Beyond that point, the governments are at liberty to accept, recommend, adopt, impose, etc. these values by means of laws or decrees. The below example explicitly illustrates this.

7.2.1. *Exposure of the human body to electromagnetic fields*

It is also necessary to take account of the health consequences stemming from the exposure of the human body to the electromagnetic fields given off by IoT Things – known simply as "human exposure".

The organization in charge of these issues is the "International Commission on Non-Ionizing Radiation Protection (ICNIRP)". All the same people also meet regularly as part of the WHO – the World Health Organization.

The ICNIRP has issued specific "recommendations" on maximum values (e.g. exposure for six minutes, for the head and torso) – notably a "Specific Absorption Rate – SAR" of over 2 W/kg per 10 g of human tissue for signals of up to 300 GHz. In the USA, the ANSI document from 1992 and that of the IEEE from 1999, for their part, specify 1.6 W/kg per 1 g. In general, it is "long-distance" systems which are most crucial in terms of obeying these recommendations, because they may need to radiate higher levels (EIRP – Effective Isotropic Radiated Power). Note that the content of these documents was taken into consideration when drafting the ISO standards on RFID, so systems which conform to these standards are also compliant with the recommendations on human exposure.

7.2.2. *Specific Absorption Rate (SAR)*

To be clear, in this domain, it is not difficult to show that the most representative parameter, the SAR, is equal to:

$$\text{SAR(rms)} = \frac{\sigma\,|\,E(\text{eff})\,|^2}{\rho} = \frac{J^2}{\rho\,\sigma} = \frac{(\sigma\,\omega\,R\,B/2)^2}{\rho\,\sigma}$$

where: ρ = density of human tissue in g/cm^3 = 1000 kg/m^3

σ = conductivity in S/m of human tissue = 0.51 S/m

ω = pulsation in rad/s

B = magnetic induction in tesla of the magnetic field radiated

R = constant 0.2

7.3. Societal regulations and individual freedoms (privacy)

The issue of privacy is a thorny one, and its regulation is a long story, which we shall attempt to tell as shortly as possible... but, given that RF systems work both with near-field and far-field, endless discussions can be had on the subject of individual freedoms.

7.3.1. *The various data needing to be protected*

Industrial data

Sensitive industrial data are usually protected by specific security systems (encryption, etc.), which we shall explain in detail in Chapter 8.

Personal data

The milestones in the history of discretion and security of personal data, whether sensitive or not, include:

– France's *Loi Informatique et Libertés* (on the protection of personal data), with the CNIL being set up to regulate these matters;

– Mandate 436 and PIA for RFID and IoT applications;

– General Data Protection Regulation – GDPR;

– and finally, "Privacy by design"

7.3.2. *Loi Informatique et Libertés*

Enacted on 6 January 1978, Article 1 of France's Act n° 78-17 (and its subsequent modifications), on information technology, files and liberties, states that "*Information technology should be at the service of every citizen. Its development shall take place in the context of international co-operation. It shall not violate human identity, human rights, privacy, or individual or public liberties.*" This says it all, in terms of the application! It is for this reason that at the time of the act, the French government established the *Commission nationale de l'informatique et des libertés – CNIL* (French Data Protection Authority) – whose aim is to guide professionals in conforming to the law, and help private citizens maintain control over their personal data and exercise their rights. The CNIL also analyzes the impact of technological innovations and emerging uses for privacy and liberties, and works in close collaboration with its European and international counterparts to achieve consistent, harmonious regulation.

7.3.3. *Mandate 436, PIA and RFID and IoT applications*

Mandate 436

When industrial applications for RFID first started to emerge in 2008, the European Commission in Brussels published its "Mandate 486" (see Figure 7.1), looking in detail at the problems raised by the issues of privacy, individual liberties and societal aspects of RFID, including NFC and IoT Things, which are simply particular branches of the discipline.

EUROPEAN COMMISSION
ENTERPRISE AND INDUSTRY DIRECTORATE-GENERAL

Innovation policy
ICT for Competitiveness and Innovation

Brussels, 8 December 2008
DG ENTR/D4

M 436 – EN

STANDARDISATION MANDATE
TO THE EUROPEAN STANDARDISATION ORGANISATIONS CEN, CENELEC AND ETSI
IN THE FIELD OF INFORMATION AND COMMUNICATION TECHNOLOGIES
APPLIED TO RADIO FREQUENCY IDENTIFICATION (RFID) AND SYSTEMS

Figure 7.1. *The famous "Mandate 486"*

PIA – Privacy Impact Assessment – CEN "EN 16 571"

Sooner or later, you will find it necessary, and indeed mandatory, to carry out a PIA (Privacy Impact Assessment) in accordance with European norm EN 16571:2014 (Information technology – RFID privacy impact assessment process, published by the CEN on 25 June 2014) – i.e. to quantify, in detail, all the risks linked to the distribution of the privacy impacts of your system, and send it to your local CNIL chapter for approval. Therefore, beware of the long and tortuous application process!

Below, for your information (and of course, for action), are a few extracts from its "scope".

"… on 12 May 2009, the European Commission published a recommendation (Mandate M436) regarding the application of the principles of respect for privacy and data protection in applications based on radio-frequency identification (RFID).

By virtue of this recommendation, a framework for evaluating the impact of RFID applications on personal data and privacy, adapted by corporate groups, must be submitted for approval to Working Group "Article 29" on data protection. This evaluation is commonly called a Privacy Impact Assessment – PIA. The framework for assessing the privacy impact of RFID applications is a response to that requirement.

The PIA process is based on an approach of risk management in terms of respect for privacy and data protection, hinging primarily on the implementation of the European Union's recommendation on RFID, and conforms to the EU's best practices and legal framework. It is designed to help RFID operators in the broadest sense to detect the privacy risks associated with an RFID application, assess their probability and document the measures taken to combat these risks. Such impacts (if any) may vary significantly depending on whether or not the RFID application handles personal data. The PIA framework gives RFID operators guidelines on risk assessment methods; it also proposes appropriate measures to effectively, concretely and reasonably limit any likely impact on privacy or data protection.

Finally, the PIA framework is sufficiently general to cover all RFID applications (including NFC, IoT, etc.), whilst being able to cater for sector- or application-specific aspects.

The PIA framework fits into the context of other norms on information protection, data management and operation, encouraging good governance in terms of data for RFID applications and others. The present framework could serve as the basis for the development of PIA models devoted specifically to a given industry, sector and/or application. Etc...."

Job done! The authors apologize for this lengthy legislative quote, but it really does say everything that needs to be said.

European norm CEN EN 16 571 gives a detailed description of the content, procedure and methodology to satisfactorily carry out a PIA. In Europe, France's *Centre National pour la RFID* (CNRFID), which contributed greatly to this field, has been appointed by Brussels to help companies fulfill their PIAs using specific software tools.

In RFID

Although the EC mandate only applies to EU Member States, EN 16571:2014 is reproduced by 37 national standards organizations. Hence, in principle, over 600 million citizens are protected by PIA for RFID. One would therefore expect these various interested parties to play an active role in promoting and implementing PIA and notifications to protect these citizens. What, though, is the reality of the situation?

– The regulatory bodies, the national data-protection authorities, appear not to be up to speed with the norms concerning PIAs and notification, but those organizations are nonetheless active in issuing "General Data Protection Regulations" (see details later on), which are peppered with references to PIAs.

– A certain number of RFID manufacturers design products which have optional functions to improve the protection of personal data.

– The problem lies mainly in the fact that at present, these functions are merely optional. The majority of defensive measures against the threats inherent in RFID have to be implemented in the systems by the designers, integrators or even the end users (RFID operators)… and many are ignorant of the risks and of what counter-measures are available.

– Users are obliged to carry out a PIA and inform the customer and the users of the RFID technology of the results.

– A non-scientific analysis put to retailers using RFID showed that, whilst some of them do apply the RFID logo, none seem to have provided notifications or implementations of the function of using "killbits" (bits which deactivate the tags, on demand).

– The actors associated with systems which reuse such tags – transport systems, contactless payment cards, employee badges, libraries, etc. – do not appear to have done much in the way of conforming to the norms in force.

The reality is that all the mechanisms have long been in place, to protect millions of citizens, but the naivety, ignorance and laziness of all the actors involved mean that the risks are still present. The "GDPR" – General Data Protection Regulation – as detailed below finally imposed a large degree of order on this madhouse! In addition, for its part, the GDPR does not require any legislation at national level; rather, it is a transnational regulation to which all member states are duty-bound to conform. Non-EU countries are also likely to adopt a similar approach.

In IoT

Many IoT systems are based on principles stemming from RFID or similar techniques, using tags, NFC cards, UHF communications, etc., and naturally fall under the umbrella of PIAs.

7.3.4. *GDPR – General Data Protection Regulation*

After more than six years of maturation in terms of personal data protection (with the integration of "privacy by design"), the European regulation, the GDPR, was ratified by the European Parliament and published on 4 May 2016 in the OJEU (Official Journal of the European Union – see Figure 7.2), for application within two years to the day – i.e. by 4 May 2018! It is a follow-up to EC directive 95/46, which was transposed into national legislation in the respective countries, and replaces the 20-year-old Data Protection Directive.

Figure 7.2. *Reproduction of text on the General Data Protection Regulation- GDPR*

During the drafting process, certain people stated or harbored the belief that there would be no legal obligation to comply with the GDPR. This is fundamentally wrong, because **the text of the GDPR is immediately applicable without the requirement of passing a law, and will become the Common Data Protection Act, to be imposed in all European countries by 2018.**

The GDPR is an enormous document (~150 pages), freely available. Readers are strongly encouraged to download it from http://ec.europa.eu/justice/dataprotection/reform/files/regulation_oj_en.pdf, and particularly to read it carefully, because a vast amount of data about physical persons, identified either directly or indirectly, will be uploaded by these wonderful connected Things. To a greater or lesser extent, these data can be considered **personal data**!

The GDPR does not reference specific norms, because the document itself defines the requirements that must be satisfied in order to correctly handle the data, and also the rules applicable with data are misused, including, at a very high level, the penalties incurred.

For information, it is helpful to cite the first paragraph of Article 33 – Data Protection Impact Assessment, in the Commission's initial proposition:

– Where processing operations present specific risks to the rights and freedoms of data subjects by virtue of their nature, their scope or their purposes, the controller or the processor acting on the controller's behalf shall carry out an assessment of the impact of the envisaged processing operations on the protection of personal data.

The Article 29 Working Group (comprising all the national data-protection authorities) published the following official guideline on what is necessary for IoT:

*– **Privacy Impact Assessments (PIAs) must be carried out before any new applications are launched in IoT.** The methodology followed in carrying out these PIAs must be based on the Privacy and Data Protection Impact Assessment Framework, whose WP.29 was adopted on 12 January 2011 for RFID applications.*

Responsibility of people and companies

The "Risk" department of large enterprises and other organizations handling enormous quantities of personal data need to consider the true scope and implications of the above regulation, which specifies that any violations of personal data must be reported to the national authority (Art. 33) and to the data's owners. Article 34, for its part, specifies that *"when a personal data breach is likely to lead to a high level of risk for a physical person's rights and freedoms, the processing controller shall communicate the personal data breach to the person affected as quickly as possible"*. However, there are exceptions to this rule, which particularly affect risk managers: "communication is not necessary if one of the following conditions is met:

– If the processing controller has implemented the appropriate technical and organizational protective measures, [...] such as encryption.

– The processing controller has taken ulterior measures meaning that the high risk to the rights and freedoms of the individuals discussed in paragraph 1 is no longer likely to materialize;"

Finally, if that communication "would require a disproportionate effort". In such cases, for instance, it is usual to resort to a "public communication", such as a press release.

The text of the GDPR also prescribes the amount of *financial sanctions which can be incurred in case of failure to comply with these regulations: €20 million, or 4% of the company's total annual turnover*, which is no laughing matter for anybody! (For instance, for Google, that amount could run to millions of dollars!). The text also deals with the burden of proof (Art. 24 – responsibility of the processing controller), noting that it is up to the (nominative) **processing controller** (even less of a laughing matter for some!), who must keep a regulation up to date and carry out impact analyses. Note, finally, that the right to be forgotten is expressly mentioned (art. 17).

To conclude, this regulation creates a position of DPO (Data Protection Officer – see section 4), who, beside his/her specific legal faculties, must have proven knowledge in computer science. The AFCDP (Association Française des Correspondants à la Protection des Données à Caractère Personnel – French DPO Association) is fighting, in this regard, for a so-called "grandfather" clause, which would encourage the transformation of CILs (Correspondants Informatique et Libertés – Computing and Freedom Officers, as instituted by the law of 6 August 2004) into DPOs. In short, this regulation stipulates a large number of measures which risk managers of large corporations are scrutinizing closely, considering the scope of the European regulation, and beginning to organize and set their houses in order to be ready for 25 May 2018!

7.3.5. Privacy by design

Obviously, the ultimate goal is not to wait until the end of the project to think about the PIA, but instead to consider these issues throughout the development process. This is what is known as "Privacy by design" – a term which emerged in the early 1990s in Canada. The privacy security chain must be examined, verified, verifiable and guaranteed from end to end.

The same team which worked on the development of EN 16 571 has, from the very start, been working on Privacy by Design. Work on PIA is to have an impact on other systems. It also shows how using the RFID PIA process can gradually lead to improved privacy.

Example of "Privacy by design"

The design of an IoT solution is generally based on that of a series of platforms, starting at the Thing, going to the Cloud and then returning to the user. If security and data protection is one of the critical criteria, the data are first encrypted locally by the device and then fed back to the central system. This architecture represents the vast majority of systems in place today.

This approach is based on the postulate that the encryption keys used are adequately protected both locally and in the central system. Unfortunately, in order to access those data, we of course need to decrypt them, and therefore, the keys have to be accessible.

Let us take the example of a medical terminal, collecting personal measurements. The first technical solution to protect the data is:

– to generate encryption keys in the Cloud;

– to securely inject some of the data into the measuring device;

– to use them to protect the information:

- locally,

- during transport,

- during storage in the Cloud.

The drawback to this approach is that, technically, the encrypted data and the decryption keys are present in the central system… and are therefore theoretically vulnerable to attack… particularly if the keys are not properly protected.

In the alternative to a "Privacy by Design" approach, the measuring device generates its own keys and protects its own data. They can be consulted locally, but even if a backup copy of the data is uploaded and the central system is "hacked", it will be impossible to decrypt the data. This approach offers excellent security… to the detriment of functional ease, as the readings can only be consulted locally.

This example demonstrates the need for prior analysis of:

– the data being protected;

– the respective levels of security for those data;

– the need for them to be accessible (local, central, remote, etc.).

The objective is to define the best possible compromise, given that the ideal solution, serving all of these antinomic criteria, can rarely be achieved.

A few additional remarks

To conclude our discussion on privacy, here are, generally in the form of questions remaining to be answered, a few general remarks which also need to be taken into consideration:

– the significant presence of numerous social networks (e.g. Facebook), where people make a great song and dance of their private details and acts on the Net casts great doubt over whether users actually want privacy. Thus, is the concept of privacy outdated for the younger generations?

– as a corollary to the above remark, could it be that privacy is only an issue for "doddering old fools"?

– does the use of the Net mean that its use value far outweighs the concerns it entails in terms of privacy?

– in terms of privacy, what are we to make of the fact that in the USA, the "patriot act" is binding, giving the government access to passwords and data, negating any possible discretion?

– etc.

7.4. Environmental regulations and recycling

Whenever we talk about IoT, the question of recycling the Things (which may be very numerous indeed) comes up sooner or later. The silicon in the integrated circuit is small, and we have long known how to recycle such chips, but what are we to do with the antennas and other elements of the Things which, in time, will become an increasingly prevalent source of waste?

7.4.1. *Electronic waste treatment*

Electrical and electronic equipment (EEE) often contains substances or components which are harmful to the environment, but there is excellent potential for recycling of the materials of which these devices are made (ferrous and non-ferrous metals, rare metals, plastics and so on). For example, in France, the Ministry of Ecology, Sustainable Development and Energy is in charge of regulating Waste

Electrical and Electronic Equipment (WEEE). These environmental issues have led to the establishment of a management chain (collection and recycling) specific to such WEEE, based on the principle of extended responsibility of the producers of such equipment.

7.4.2. *Regulation and organization of the chain*

The directives pertaining to waste electrical and electronic equipment and to the dangerous substances contained therein define the conditions for the entry of EEE onto the market, and set of the framework for WEEE management. In brief, they establish the following main principles:

– distinction between household equipment and professional equipment;

– a complete ban on the use of six hazardous substances in EEE;

– selective collection of WEEE;

– selective and systematic treatment of the hazardous substances and components in EEE;

– set objectives in terms of reuse/recycling and value creation from WEEE;

– extended responsibility of producers for the management of the WEEE from the equipment they sell.

The latest legislation in the pipeline deals with:

– the means of treatment of the waste electrical and electronic equipment relating to the composition of the electrical and electronic equipment and the elimination of the waste created by that equipment.

– the conditions of implementation of obligations to collect incumbent upon distributors of used electrical and electronic equipment;

– the conditions that must be met by an agent, in the sense of the environmental code, to ensure the obligations incumbent on the producer who gave him/her the mandate are met.

7.4.3. *Labeling of electrical and electronic equipment*

European Norm EN 50419 specifies the labeling of electrical and electronic equipment (including IoT Things), which applies as long as the device in question is not an integral part of another kind of device. The norm gives a non-exhaustive list of products falling into each category, which serves to clearly identify the producer of that device and certify that the device was placed on the market after August

2005. The definition of a technological means of identifying the producer, such as a barcode, an electronic data support or a microchip, is not covered by this norm.

7.5. Normative aspects

Although the IoT market is still in its infancy, even at this stage, should we be working on writing norms and standards to structure the market, or ought we to allow the ecosystem to develop by itself?

To facilitate the emergence of IoT, two approaches can be envisaged in terms of establishing norms:

– firstly, to say that innovation must be encouraged, leaving the field open for initiatives to flourish;

– secondly, to acknowledge from the start that the lack of standardization can lead to the fragmentation of the ecosystem.

From the normative point of view, this means that either we need to take action upstream, as a precursor to guide the market's development, or else, once the market is already established, do a little spring cleaning of the (overly numerous) proprietary protocols which are then present.

Note that, unlike with the contactless chip card market where the ISO 14 443 /x standards have guided and facilitated the rollout of applications and a high degree of interoperability between them, in the market of IoT applications, we are closer to the second scenario than the first – i.e. the introduction of the standardization phase after the first sallies in the field, and the obligation to deal with the standard that is eventually enforced.

Let us briefly examine where we stand.

7.5.1. *ISO/AFNOR*

At the ISO, in JTC 1, the Working Group WG 10 (and its counterpart at AFNOR, the French standardization body) is devoted to the Internet of Things. To date, the working group's activities have mainly focused on general ideas of architectures and theoretical and academic aspects of security and privacy which are part of the fundaments of the system. The first publications are available – namely:

ISO 30141 Internet of Things reference architecture

ISO/IEC 30141 – 1 Part 1: General Overview

ISO/IEC 30141 – 2 Part 2: Conceptual Model

ISO/IEC 30141 – 3 Part 3: Reference Architecture

ISO/IEC 30141 – 4 Part 4: Security and Privacy

In terms of the concrete reality of IoT applications, only a TR (Technical Report) is in the pipeline, regarding "use cases" and, in parallel to all this, ISO/IEC JTC1/SC 27, which deals with "IT security techniques", is looking at issues of security in IoT.

7.5.2. *IEEE*

In relation with the ISO's WG 10, the working group IEEE P2413 is in the process of drafting a standard setting out the "Architectural Framework for the Internet of Things (IoT)", including descriptions of numerous domains of IoT, definitions of omissions from those IoT domains, and identifying common points between the different domains. At time of writing, the following are available:

Informative references

IEEE 802.15.4-2011: "IEEE Standard for Local and metropolitan area networks – Part 15.4: Low-Rate Wireless Personal Area Networks (LR-WPANs)".

7.5.3. *ETSI*

For its part, in 2012, ETSI – the European Telecommunications Standards Institute – decided to write standards in the field of IoT, focusing on "LTNs – Low-Throughput Networks" – generalizing two principles used in NB (narrow-band) transmission solutions (on SIGFOX bases) and to the spreading of DSSS spectra (on LoRA-Semtech bases). This includes, firstly, the GS LTN set of documents:

GS LTN 001 Use Cases for Low Throughput Networks

GS LTN 002 Functional Architecture

GS LTN 003 Protocols and Interfaces

and secondly:

– ETSI TS 102 690: "Machine-to-Machine communications (M2M); Functional architecture".

– ETSI TS 102 921: "Machine-to-Machine communications (M2M); mIa, dIa and mId interfaces".

There are also other normative references to be taken into account. For example,

– GB/T 15629.15-2010: "Information technology – Telecommunications and information exchange between local systems and metropolitan area networks – Specific requirements – Part 15.4: Wireless medium access control and physical layer (PHY) specification for low rate wireless personal area networks".

In summary

At the time of writing, there is nothing truly concrete in place in terms of standardization for IoT (lower/physical layers, protocols, etc.)... and it will be a long time before we are able to design systems that are truly interoperable with different networks... but we are slowly getting there, and there is no harm in dreaming!

8

Security Aspects

First of all, before we look at security aspects relating to IoT and the creation of connected Things, let us examine one of the numerous "official" definitions of security – for example, that given by ETSI:

– *"Security is the ability to prevent fraud as well as facilitating the protection of data, integrity and confidentiality."*

Take care not to confuse "security" with "dependability/operational safety"!!

Let us turn now to the heart of the matter!

8.1. Security aspects

This is no groundbreaking revelation: the debate about security, which we outline below and which cannot be ignored, is vast, and represents one of the greatest fears regarding IoT, which is projected to have between 25 and 80 billion connected Things in the world by 2020 (Source: IDATE) (look again at Chapter 3).

Illustrating these fears, Figure 8.1 comes from a survey conducted in 2016 on a profile of IoT application developers and the way in which they build their projects (survey conducted in partnership with the IEEE, the members of the European research project Agile-IoT and the Eclipse IoT working group of the Eclipse Foundation).

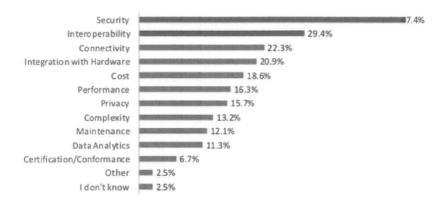

Figure 8.1. *Fears of app developers (Survey conducted in partnership with IEEE, Agile-IoT, Eclipse IoT)*

Indeed, security tops the list of developers concerns, closely followed by problems of interoperability, given the now vast proliferation of initiatives and standards relating to IoT. Unfortunately, today, there is still a major security problem, which will continue to be in the foreground over the next few years, remaining difficult to solve and, indubitably, requiring new initiatives from the industrial world.

8.1.1. *The weak links*

As long ago as six or seven years, based on our lengthy experience in the field of contact and contactless smart cards (each of us has over 20 years' experience in this domain!), we were convinced that, firstly, security in the world of IoT was going to become a major issue, and secondly, in the complete IoT chain, the connected Thing would inevitably be the least secure, in comparison to the gateways and tools present in the Cloud.

In fact, even today, the security of Things from the world of the Internet is very often improperly taken into account, if at all. How many Things are truly secure in terms of preventing or at least limiting, this new area of potential piracy? This subject is everywhere on the agenda, not because of increased awareness in the industry, but mainly because of the negative media coverage suffered by manufacturers in the event of problems, and its impact in terms of image and cost (an example from the automobile industry is Fiat Chrysler, with the Jeep Cherokee).

Let us draw up a (non-exhaustive) list of the fundamental problems of the classic weak links in the chain of IoT elements that still allow hackers the freedom to attack.

Reasons for "non-security"

– there is no security in the field of the Internet of Things because no plans for security were laid at the advent of the discipline;

– the question of security has never really been raised;

– the philosophy of security was not incorporated originally, and the way in which the security protocols are designed means that they are difficult to implement once the Things are already in production.

Major points that are difficult to resolve

– there is no consensus on the implementation of security in connected Things;

– there are connected Things on the market which are not necessarily "securable";

– there is no way to download an update or perform downloads of security patches (…we cannot easily upgrade a refrigerator or an IP camera!).

The observation

– today, we are realizing that we cannot wind the clock back, and that it is extremely complicated to implement this security retrospectively;

– manufacturers of common consumer products ("wearables", watches, bracelets, toys, etc.), anxious to keep their production costs down, avoid adding security features.

– passwords given upon purchase or created by the user are very rarely changed

– Etc.

Existence of structural weaknesses in terms of security

– there is a lack of security in Network Services;

– the Web interface is not secure;

– the Cloud interface is not (or hardly) secure;

– likewise, the mobile interface is not secure;

– there is insufficient authentication/authorization;

– the transport encryption lacks consistency;

– a whole host of issues need to be resolved concerning confidentiality;

– the security setup is insufficient;

– the insecurities of software/firmware are "embedded" in the components;

– there is an overarching lack of physical security.

Finally, on the other hand

– as a matter of course, hackers are interested in the whole chain; they seek out and identify the weak points/links that will allow them to make money;

– for a hacker, it is more worthwhile to capture data from the connected Thing, stored on The Cloud, than to hack the Thing itself. Therefore, hackers are increasingly focusing their efforts on these data-storage facilities;

– to address the issue of data protection, it is necessary – indeed, crucial – to know where the data go, on the Internet. By which channels? Where are they stored on The Cloud? In which Cloud? In which country? Who put them there? Etc.

Having conducted this analysis, we shall now consider some possible solutions!

8.1.2. *Possible solutions*

In order to avoid these weak links, there are some basic solutions.

To be secure

– it is important to know your enemy!

– this will bring about solutions, rather than problems;

– evidently, though, it comes at a cost.

We need to define a security target

In order to do so, we must:

– know the requirements;

– evaluate the risks and consequences (designer and user);

– know how to respond in the event of a problem;

– know how to and what to communicate with consumers/users.

– determine the price to be paid.

8.1.3. *Definition and choice of security target*

Before going into detail about the security techniques using for IoT communicating Things and devices, it is often desirable to first establish what we call the "security target" – the goal for which we are aiming. This target relates to two important groups of factors:

– the parameters that we want to secure (the branches of the target);

– the levels of security that we want to achieve for each of them (the levels on the rings of the target, so we can also create a spider graph showing the surface covered by the security target).

Figure 8.2 offers a simplified example of a security target, and although it looks simple, even this takes a great deal of time to establish!

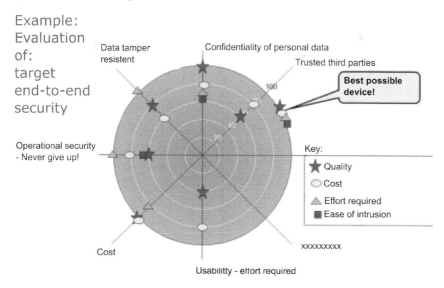

Figure 8.2. *Simplified educational example of security target*

The second stage is deciding whether and how all this is feasible and how much it will cost, constantly keeping the following few simple and pragmatic questions in mind:

– is it worthwhile?

– does the whole chain ensure end-to-end security?

– is there a weak link remaining in the chain, and if so, where is it?

8.1.4. *Concepts of security levels applied in IoT*

When the words "security of connected Things and IoT" are brought up, the idea of a security level very soon follows. Let us give some initial consideration to these levels.

No security

It is as well to begin with this one! This is the "lowest common denominator" in the equation… but the truth is that many simple IoT applications do not really need security. Messages are transmitted in "plain text", because the information transported does not contain sensitive material and, in the worst case scenario, it could be altered without causing a disaster.

With security

Here, we come to a delicate matter often mentioned in the same breath as sales patter. Thus, let us examine this area.

To secure messages transmitted between connected Things, data encryption will often be used… but, *by the same principle and the mathematical theory of encryption* (AES, RSA, ECC, etc.), the levels of security can range from total to absolutely nothing. Let us explain.

"Paper house" version of security

This describes the scenario where a very strong, ultra-secure barrier is placed across the door of a traditional Japanese house, whose walls are made of paper (see Figure 8.3).

Figure 8.3. *"Paper house" security*

Regardless of the barrier, anyone wishing to gain entrance can simply walk through the walls!! Unfortunately, this is indicative of the approach of many people in IoT who, very proud of themselves, implement cryptographic unit software in their application codes, thinking that this is sufficient! Any cryptography expert (in the area of smart cards, etc.) will make very short work of breaking the codes using the simplest of tools.

Therefore, the simple version, though cheap, must be discounted as an option!

"Sandcastle" version

Sandcastle security is a mechanism which is marketed as magnificent, whereas it really is not. This version, present in (too) many commercial circuits, is made up of a microcontroller incorporating a "soft" cryptographic computer, somewhat toughened and secured at the hardware level. This version is evidently better than the previous one, which was utterly worthless… but is nevertheless incapable of dealing with all kinds of attack. Generally, security systems of this kind only cover some of the best-known – perhaps the five or six most common of these – which might discourage amateurs, but certainly not experienced/professional hackers!

Thus, this version is a "castle… yes, but made of sand" (see Figure 8.4), and furthermore, it often borders on being a security sales "fib".

Figure 8.4. *"Sandcastle" security*

"Fortified Castle" with genuine "Secure Elements"

Finally, we step up our game, building a "first-class" version. Here, we return to the good old methods and techniques of the Middle Ages: those of fortified castles. We build a veritable fortress around our cryptographic calculator, deep in the darkest depths of buried layers of hardware, with multiple drawbridges, flooded moats, puzzle-like mazes, jail cells, oubliettes, (near) impenetrable dungeons, etc., – at last, everything that is needed to truly deter the most daring and the bravest of today's attackers… plus those from centuries to come! This ranges from counter-attack, defense, etc. to ultimate self-destruction and "scorched-earth policy", with the lemma: No, you will not take me. If die I must then die I shall, but I shall never give up my secrets! (See Figure 8.5 and further on in this chapter for all the details).

Figure 8.5. *"Fortified castle" security*

After these medieval and lyrical flights of fancy, we return to cold, hard, technical discussion.

This last principle is called the construction of a veritable "Secure Element". Of course, this requires a great deal of experience in terms of security, with full knowledge of weaknesses and extensive knowledge of chip technology, and of course this has a price, but it is the only solution to succeed in implementing a genuinely secure solution. It is worth noting that this Secure Element can be an entity either directly built into the chip of a microcontroller (all circuits used for smartcard applications are made in this way) or an external entity.

For reasons of lack of knowledge and sometimes cost (although usually, cost is no object when we are passionate about something!), today, few IoT solutions are set up to the level of security which will, in the near future, very soon become a necessity, based on the quality of the data transported which will be increasingly sensitive, fragile and critical.

Now that you are well enough informed to understand and implement the security of your IoT-connected Thing, it is up to you to choose where your loyalties lie!

8.1.5. *True security – the "Secure Element"*

The "Secure Element" – the true fortified castle – is that which incorporates all conceivable hard and soft techniques. At the time of writing, there are just over a hundred security hardware features in an integrated circuit of this type to block external attacks and guarantee system security. The same is not true of imitation Secure Elements, which only include four or five of these defenses. As highlighted above, the Secure Element can either be a single specific circuit or built into a microcontroller.

EXAMPLE.– SE - Hardware Security

In order to clarify our ideas, let us briefly discuss a practical example of a commercial Secure Element circuit.

In addition to being made with submicron technology of 90nm with glue logic in CMOS, the circuit incorporates hardware measurements and features to protect itself against all form of leaks and provide the highest level of resilience against attacks. For example, we can cite:

– scrambled encryption (see Figure 8.6 a) to d)):

  - of the CPU,

  - of the ROM, RAM and EEPROM,

    - dynamic RAM encryption, allowing random scrambling after each power up

    of the client ROM, making the component unique for each application

– security-enhanced sensors for detecting:

  - temperatures that are too high or too low,

  - voltage that is too high or too low,

  - Single Fault Injection (SFI) attacks,

  - attacks using light (visible or otherwise), injecting additional energy into the EEPROM memories to interfere with the content,

    - to offer dedicated security against the reverse engineering of hardware. Their design is based on handshaking and an asynchronous communication protocol in the CPU,

- leakage current analysis attacks, using a Triple-DES coprocessor with a high level of resistance to vital DPA leaks,

– active shielding technology and an OS controlled by security functions – in particular:

- protection of code access performed with Secure Fetch technology, which protects memory content as well as the operation of extraction of codes from the ROM, RAM and EEPROM. More specifically, this technology:

- considerably increases the probability of detecting fault injection attacks,

- offers increased protection against attacks with a high spatial resolution,

- considerably increases both the material hardware security of the chip against certain classes and scenarios of attack with long and short light pulses (be it single or multiple pulses) and laser attacks,

- facilitates the development of highly secure software applications for the clients/users

- Etc.

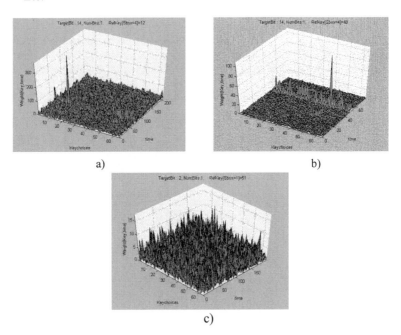

a)   b)

c)

Figures 8.6 a, b, c. *Depending on the physical implementations (Asynchronous CPU a), synchronous CPU b), and with the addition of a true SE c),it becomes impossible to identify the sensitive computational areas in the integrated circuit*

Exemple: SE - Hardware Security

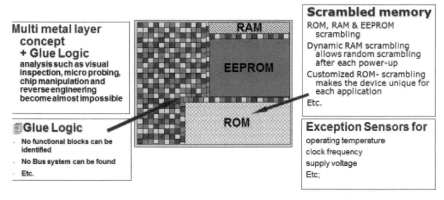

Multi metal layer concept + Glue Logic
analysis such as visual inspection, micro probing, chip manipulation and reverse engineering become almost impossible

Glue Logic
- No functional blocks can be identified
- No Bus system can be found
- Etc.

Scrambled memory
ROM, RAM & EEPROM scrambling

Dynamic RAM scrambling allows random scrambling after each power-up

Customized ROM- scrambling makes the device unique for each application

Etc.

Exception Sensors for
operating temperature

clock frequency

supply voltage

Etc;

Figure 8.6.d). *Puzzling of Topology of transistors and integrated circuit functions*

Evidently, all of this is the ultimate goal of integration but (only) requires many years of experience. In short, there are not many genuine providers of components of this type. In mono-chip integrated circuits, these true Secure Elements have been being made for many years by the few pioneers mainly in the market of smartcards, bank cards, electronic security ID cards, passports, visas, ID cards, etc. (Examples include NXP, Infineon, STm, Atmel and a few others), security depending!

"Standalone" versions have also started to appear on the market over the last few years to satisfy genuine secure IoT applications.

All of these mono-chip or standalone integrated circuits are accompanied by EAL certified safety levels in agreement with the Common Criteria (example, EAL 5+, see later on).

Obviously, it is absolutely necessary to have an SE of the same EAL level for a given security target in order to guarantee the end-to-end security (functional, privacy, etc.) of your system... otherwise it will, sooner or later, end in disaster.

Therefore, the same results will not be achieved with a simple microcontroller with a simple cryptographic device. We must open our eyes from time to time! You have been warned, so there are no excuses ...

8.1.6. *Cryptography*

Cryptography – the art of communicating with encrypted data, and their decoding to protect information – is one of the cornerstones of IoT security and is implemented with hardware and software technologies. Without going into a lesson on cryptographic security, which is not the aim of this book, let us take a quick look at cryptographic methods that can be used in conjunction with IoT connected Things.

Let us start by recalling the main aims.

8.1.6.1. *Main aims of cryptographic security*

In the context of connected Things and IoT, the main aim of cryptography is to be able to provide guarantees relating mainly to the security of identification, authentication, integrity, confidentiality and non-repudiation as messages are exchanged between Things.

Identification

Let us simply give an example of exchange of identification:

Identification: Who are you?

Login: FANTOMAS

It is simple: it allows you to make an initial sweep of the unknowns, but this is not enough!

Authentication

Authentication is the process which checks and confirms the identity of a remote Thing or an element on the network, to ensure that only authorized Things are connected to the network. Public key infrastructure (PKI) authentication is one of the most commonly used solutions, and uses digital certificates to establish the identity of a device.

EXAMPLE.–

....

Authentication: Prove it!

Password: id IoT …

EXAMPLE.–

Telephone: Hello, François; Barack speaking (identification)

Response: Oh yes? Use the red phone! (authentication request) (but unfortunately, I only have an iPhone 6 => Fatal Error! I am an impostor: the red phone is a Samsung and I have been trumped!)

Within the Internet of Things, the user must verify themselves... but so too must the Thing!

Integrity

Integrity is the maintenance of the consistency, accuracy and reliability of data over their entire life-cycle to ensure the message is not modified between sending and receiving and that it has not been altered by those unauthorized to do so. A common method of protecting data integrity is to create and implement a hash function (see below) on the data received and compare it with the original message.

Confidentiality

Similar to privacy, confidentiality prevents an unauthorized user or device from obtaining sensitive information, whilst ensuring that it is actually received by the user or the IoT element. The techniques of data encryption are frequently used to ensure confidentiality. A common example is TLS (Transport Layer Security), formerly SSL (Secure Sockets Layer): a security protocol for messages transmitted over the Internet, compatible with a large number of Internet protocols.

Non-repudiation

The term "non-repudiation" refers to the notion of a deal or contract between two parties and the idea that:

– one of them cannot deny sending the message (and it is possible to prove that they are indeed the sender);

– and the other cannot deny having received the message;

– and therefore, neither is able to deny that the transaction really took place.

8.1.7. *Symmetric and asymmetric encryption*

In cryptography, it is well known that two types of algorithms are mainly used: symmetrical and asymmetrical. To recap:

8.1.7.1. *Symmetric algorithms*

Symmetric cryptosystems, otherwise known as "secret key" or "private key" systems, are generally used to ensure confidentiality.

Symmetric algorithms share a unique secret key (essentially a password) which, when used with a cipher, allows the encryption and decryption of information communicated between the two parties. For example, Alice and Bob must possess the same key k to be able to talk to each other. The strength/power and the effectiveness of this cipher depend largely on the level of the secret and the strength (or length) of the key.

Examples of symmetric algorithms:

– the Triple Data Encryption Standard (3DES);

– the Advanced Encryption Standard (AES);

– the International Data Encryption Algorithm (IDEA);

– the Rivest Cipher 5 (RC5)

– etc.

These algorithms are relatively effective in terms of speed and computation power, but the management of the keys (security of exchanges and storage of keys) is critical because if an unauthorized person gains access to the secret key, then the communication is no longer protected.

8.1.7.2. *Asymmetric algorithms*

Asymmetric algorithms use a combination of "a pair of keys (one public and one private)", and are normally used to provide authentication and for the exchange of keys in symmetric-key algorithms.

Only the "public key" should be exchanged between the two communicators and is not kept secret (…thus, it is a public key). The message is encrypted using the "public key", but can only be decrypted with the private key.

– Alice has a pair of keys: one public, the other private;

– anyone can send Alice messages by encrypting them with her public key;

– only Alice can decrypt them by using her private key.

8.1.7.3. *… Some comparisons*

Asymmetric algorithms are mathematically more powerful than symmetric algorithms, but do not pose the same problems with key management.

Generally speaking, for the same type of key, asymmetric algorithms (e.g. RSA – Rivest-Shamir-Adelman, or EC – elliptic curve) are normally less secure than symmetric algorithms, requiring a longer encryption key in order to supply the same level of security as symmetric algorithms.

For example, a 1024-bit asymmetric key would ensure the same level of security as an 80-bit symmetric key – see Table 8.1.

Symmetric	Asymmetric	
	ECC	DH/DSA/RSA
80	163	1024
112	233	2048
128	283	3072
192	409	7680
256	571	15360
etc.		

Table 8.1. *Comparison of symmetric and asymmetric keys*

8.1.7.4. *Hash function*

In cryptography, we often use the hash function, which is a one-way operation used to digitally sign and verify the integrity of the data transmitted.

In order to be effective, a hash function must have the following qualities and be:

– easy to compute (any given message can be represented by a fixed-length hash);

– non-reversible (it must be practically impossible to generate the original message from the hash);

– unalterable (it must be virtually impossible to modify the original message without also altering the hash);

– unique (practically impossible for two different messages to generate the same hash).

Hash Example 1: A recipe consists of meat cut up into small pieces, potatoes and mixed spices. Once cooked, it is not easy to separate the ingredients used to recreate the initial hash!

Hash example 2: A pot of yellow paint and one of blue paint are poured simultaneously into a container and then quickly mixed to make green. It is then not easy to separate the ingredients used to return to the original colors!

The typical uses for a hash include digital signatures and verification of passwords (a hash is a shorter representation of a long password, which provides a superior level of security because it does not require full disclosure of the bits in a long password).

8.1.7.5. The numerous available cryptography techniques

There are a multitude of methods available to create cryptographic units – for example:

– proprietary cryptography;

– standardized cryptographies, which are among the most common;

For example, at the ISO

DES, 3DES, AES

RSA – modular exponentiation

ECC – ECDH elliptic curves

Table 8.2, by way of example, shows the "Crypto Suites" standardized by the ISO.

ISO/IEC 29167 – Crypto Suites

29167-	Cipher	Type	Keys	Functions	Status	By Country
01	Security services	-	-	-	published	AT: ASI (CISC)
10	AES-128	Block	Symmetric	TA	FDIS-Ballot	AT: ASI (NXP)
AMD1	AES-128 (additional functions)				WD	AT: ASI (NXP)
11	PRESENT-80	Block	Symmetric	TA	published	AT: ASI (NXP)
12	ECC-DH	Block	PK	TA	FDIS-Ballot	AT: ASI (NXP)
13	Grain-128A	Stream	Symmetric	TA, MA, AM, SM	FDIS-Ballot	CH: SNV (EM)
14	AES-OFB	Bk/Strm	Symmetric	TA, MA, (SM?)	FDIS-Ballot	KOR: KATS (ETRI)
15	XOR	Stream?	Symmetric	TA, MA, (SM?)	CD	CH: Chinese NC
16	ECDSA-ECDH	Block	PK	MA, AM, SM	DIS-Ballot	CH: Chinese NC
17	cryptoGPS	Block	PK	TA	DIS-Ballot	FR: AFNOR (Orange)
18	Hb2-128 (Hummingbird 2)	Block			Withdrawn	US: ANSI (Revere)
19	RAMON (Rabin Montgommery)	Block	PK + Symmetric	Ramon: TA, AES: MA, AM, SM	DIS-Ballot	DE: DIN (G&D)
20	Algebraic Eraser	Block	PK	TA (+??)	WD	US: ANSI (Secure RF)
xx	SIMON	Block	?	?	discussion	?
xx	SPECK	Block	?	?	Discussion	?

Functions: TA = tag authentication, MA = mutual authentication, AM = authenticated messaging, SM = secure messaging

Table 8.2. *"Crypto Suites" standardized by the ISO*

8.1.8. *Consumer Things, IoT, security... and the Cloud*

Thus, why write a few paragraphs particularly about IoT Things from the consumer market? Because the "consumer" market is a specific world, and one which is extremely attractive in view of the volumes of IoT-connected Things in play, but also because consumer security demand is very specific, and it is unstable ground upon which one must venture with infinite precaution!

8.1.8.1. *What do we mean by consumer electronics?*

In its ordinary sense, the term "consumer electronics" covers:

– "White goods"... large household electrical appliances, fridges, washing machines, dishwashers, etc.;

– "Brown goods"... radios, hi-fis, televisions, etc.;

– "Small household electrical appliances" or "small brown goods"... hairdryers, razors, healthcare products, etc.;

– "Grey goods"... telephony: cordless phones, mobiles, smartphones; IT: PCs, tablets, etc.; gadgets: wearables, watches, bracelets;

– Cars,

...and their respective price ranges!

8.1.8.2. *Conditions for public adoption of IoT*

The conditions for public adoption of IoT require:

– desirable features and applications to have, whether they are a replacement or original;

– the retail price displayed to be affordable!

– interoperability with other brands;

– "security" to be guaranteed at all levels (end to end)

– privacy to be ensured;

...and of course, aspects such as health, ethics, standardization, regulations, societal and environmental concerns, etc. must all be satisfied!

8.1.8.3. *What do we mean by consumer security?*

Consumer security is a form of security, obviously, but at what cost? It is necessary:

– to ensure that the Thing itself is secure (however small and cheap it may be) with a compatible cryptographic unit and if possible a genuine SE;

– that the chain from the Thing to the networks to processing, etc., be "tamper resistant", from end to end;

– that all privacy management issues and other issues relating to one's private life be regulated (otherwise, beware the dithyrambic reviews in newspapers and harsh criticism from consumer associations;

– that privacy should preferably be implemented by design;

– that there should a trusted third party;

– that dependability (not to be confused with security) be ensured by a "never give up" strategy with potential fallback positions to carry out and guarantee a minimum safe operation (otherwise, watch out for repercussions for your corporate image in the press or by word of mouth);

– everything must properly "mesh" technically with long-distance communication problems, low speed and low use;

...and of course, on top of that, it must be "cheap" so that the product is affordable for the consumer!

This leads us directly to a discussion about the price of components, and the component that is the main integrated circuit and its silicon chip!

8.1.8.4. *Let us talk a little about silicon chips*

It is well known that with complexity and technology of wafers (the ones currently manufactured are around 10 or 12 inches in diameter - see Figure 8.7), the price of a silicon chip depends on its surface area ($x.y$ mm^2) and in our case, with security, it will be necessary to ensure that the surface of the cryptographic unit is as small as possible in relation to the functional surface area, which gives us a "relative" price per computation unit.

EXAMPLES.–

an RFID UHF circuit (ISO 18000-6) = 0.4 mm × 0.4 mm

an SOC circuit = 2 mm × 2 mm

a Combo circuit = 4 mm × 4 mm...

Figure 8.7. *Batch of wafers*

To give readers a concrete idea, here is an example of a (small) ISO cryptographic unit, known as a "GPS" (Girault-Poupard-Stern) unit:

Performances:

Total duration of authentication:	188 ms
Computation time and transmission of response from module:	28.8 ms
Time to compute unit's response:	14.2 ms
Total:	~250 ms

Space of silicon required:

6000 logic gates, of which, 2600 are for the cryptographic unit!

Surface area = 0.05 mm² with 180 nm technology

CC level: EAL??

Some hard facts! Figure 8.8 presents a different example of an integrated circuit, highlighting the relative surface area necessary for cryptography (a few % of the total surface area).

Here, once again, we are talking about the cryptographic function, its silicon surface, its power, etc. and optimization of its cost! It is here that we begin to think differently!

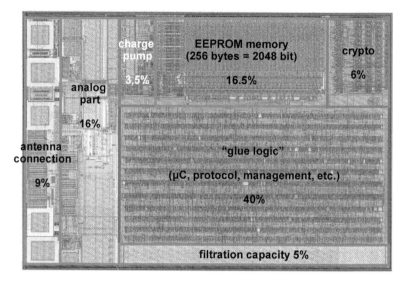

Figure 8.8. *Example of an integrated circuit, highlighting the relative surface area necessary for cryptography*

8.1.8.5. *Mathematical homomorphic encryption functions*

This is an old subject that is making a comeback. If your parents and grandparents have reverently kept their old schoolbooks on set theory, vector space, groups, bodies, rings etc. this is the time to take them out for some fresh air!

The reason for this revival? ... Technical, but of course, economical, my dear Watson!

Let us briefly come back down to Earth, and explain.

If we hope to one day inundate the consumer market with small communicative connected Things, they must not be expensive, meaning that the integrated components (circuits) cannot be expensive; therefore, the size of the silicon crystal must be small; therefore, the security part (the physical part of the cryptographic element) must be microscopic, and must not take up more space than the Thing's main function!

What are we to do, then? It is very simple: reduce that part to a minimum and send the advanced computations off to be done elsewhere... in some distant Cloud... and Bob's your uncle!

To help us better understand and be practical, let us look at a simple example.

EXAMPLE.–

Alice has two numbers, a = 5 and b = 6, but, for example, unfortunately, she does not have the power required to calculate (a × b) = c. What can she do? She could remotely send these two numbers directly to a supercomputer, but this information is crucial to her and she does not want it falling into the hands of an attacker.

Possible solution:

Using a small homomorphic asymmetric cryptographic unit, and her public key, Alice will calculate the two numbers a = 5 and b = 6, which gives two new encoded numbers (for example): a becomes a* = 261 145 and b becomes b* = 230 852.

Alice now transmits these two encoded numbers, a* and b*, as well as her public key, to a data center (for example, on the Cloud, for a price of course!) where the "supercomputer" can be found. The supercomputer calculates the homomorphic product c* of the two encoded numbers given which, for it, has no meaning. This product of a* × b* = 261 145 × 230 852 gives, for example, c* = 18 042 009.

The processing center transmits the result c* = 18 042 009 back to Alice, who decodes it locally with her private key to find 30.

…and that is where the wonder lies! If we can show that (a × b = c) and that (a* × b* = c*), it is because the asymmetric cryptographic function used is the *same form* of entry in the unencrypted version as in the encrypted version, so this function is *homomorphic*! (For further details, look over your 400 pages of handouts from the 1960s and 1970s!).

Let us briefly examine what we can expect as a result.

NOTE.–

There are several drawbacks to the key!

…

– the area of silicon from the asymmetric cryptographic function needs to be small (which is often the case);

– the public keys must be sufficiently long to provide the desired security for the application, but not be too long so as to have a short and appropriate calculation time (many people are working on this at the moment!);

– the round trip – *there, computation, back* – must not take a long time, so the application is viable! (this, too, is the subject of much current research);

– we must consider and/or define perhaps two types of Things: one that does and one that does not have the time to complete their tasks in the allotted computation time for a given EAL level and given consumption;

– we also have to be sure of the security level in the Cloud!

8.1.8.6. *Coming back to the Thing*

Often for reasons of cost (notably the cost price) and for acceptance of the retail price on the market, the overall design of the Thing is/has to be simplified and the security of the consumer Things becomes/is the weak link in the whole chain; as such, the end-to-end security is broken... which, somewhat trivially but clearly, "messes everything up"!

8.1.8.7. *In conclusion*

In view of the adoption of Secure IoT-connected Things by the general public, we can draw the following conclusions:

– there must be a Secure Element present;

– the cryptographic unit should be cheap (e.g. a homomorphic unit);

– the area of silicon dedicated to the cryptographic unit should be very small;

– the EAL value should be high;

– security should be consistent all along the chain;

– security/job security/respect of privacy must be ensured at all times.

8.2. Judging the quality of security

Obviously, once we have done all of this, it has to be assessed by independent organizations able to issue certificates and approval – e.g. ANSSI in France – Agence nationale de la sécurité des systèmes d'information (National Agency for the Security of Information and Systems) defines:

– CSPN – First-Level Security Certification

This certification allows a basic level of confidence in the security of a product, quickly and relatively cheaply

– CC - Common Criteria

The Common Criteria define different levels of assessment, thus offering higher or lower levels of assurance in the security of the product: the EAL (Evaluation Assurance Level).

EXAMPLES.– EAL4, EAL5+, etc.

8.3. Some thoughts about security, privacy and IoT

With the encryption methods described above, one could believe in a world which could become increasingly more protected in the area of privacy. However, the revolution of connected Things is coming…!

The problem hinges on the widespread adoption of encryption. There are those "for" and those "against", each with very good arguments. Now, we seem to be seeing the emergence of a victor in this battle: the "pro-encryption" side, because encryption is becoming the norm as regards applications or operating systems… but this also poses problems and concerns when it comes into the hands of terrorist organizations!

Needless to say, this debate is burning all the more fiercely with every passing day. This is the subject of the metaphor "going dark", which might indicate a certain amount of discretion and protection on Internet networks. In the report "Don't panic", published by the Berkman Center for Internet and Society at Harvard University (regular civilians, cyber-security researchers, former members of the US government, legal experts etc.), some extremely interesting conclusions are found on this subject. To sum up:

– end-to-end encryption and other connected technologies will ultimately not be widely used in the future, given that the economic models of numerous businesses rely on the data themselves;

– the software ecosystem will become increasingly fragmented. Instead of a democratization of encryption, we will bear witness to standardization and fuller collaboration between publishers;

– IoT is going to change the face of intelligence operations. The authors anticipate that millions/billions of pieces of data can be intercepted in real time;

– metadata are not encrypted, and this should not change any time soon, because current systems need these data to be clear in order to process them, which provides a mountain of accessible and useful data.

The debate must/should naturally turn towards the way in which we protect our privacy and private data in the future, but it must also take account of the evolution of technology; it must be remembered that encryption is not the only possible solution or a miracle cure.

These thoughts on IoT are therefore very interesting insofar as it can also be said that "the inability to monitor an encrypted channel could be remedied by the possibility of monitoring any person remotely, through other channels or networks". Authors in this field often mention the ubiquity of systems and IoT, which, eventually, will collect so much data that they can be retrieved and used at one point or another in the chain.

8.4. Vulnerabilities and attacks in the IoT chain

Threats exist on all levels of IoT architectures, and there are potential vulnerabilities, which can be exploited by certain malevolent people (cracking weak passwords, using malware such as viruses, Trojans, etc.)

To guarantee companies the appropriate level of security for their IoT-connected devices and infrastructures, it is necessary to carry out risk analysis and implement suitable defensive measures. Obviously, the levels of guarantee implemented should correspond to the permitted risk levels and the likelihood of their occurring. For IoT, the guaranteed security levels are generally defined in all the software present throughout the whole chain, through the design of the different boards, through the choice and application of chips (integrated circuits) and finally, depending largely on the potential access that an intruder can have to attack the different elements mentioned above.

The vulnerable points and corresponding attacks in IoT, in hardware and/or software, are generally summarized according to the fields in Table 8.3.

	level	software	board	integrated circuit
Attacks				
software		protocols weak crypto implementation weak password malware viruses Trojan horses	software	software
cost		low		
accessibility		easy	average	complex
hardware			non-invasive debug port	physically invasive: laser, FIB reverse engineering
cost			average	High
accessibility		easy	average	Complex

Table 8.3. *Vulnerable points and attacks in IOT, in hardware and/or software*

8.4.1. *Attacks on the software layer*

Attacks on software layers of boards, Things or chips, aiming to exploit IoT security flaws, generally involve network attacks in situations where the assailant cannot directly physically access the Thing or the infrastructure. These attacks, which are generally software-based, take time and have a relatively low cost.

8.4.1.1. *Software attacks*

Network

By taking control of a gateway or router, an attacked can intercept/steal data transmitted between IoT Things and back-end data-management systems, or even disseminate false content to the Things or back-end infrastructures.

Application

Attackers can try to take control of the IoT application, by controlling the Things and other devices and/or the back-end systems.

8.4.2. *Attacks on the board or Thing*

Attacks on printed circuit boards or Things require physical access to the boards or to the Thing, with somewhat specialized equipment, and can be more expensive than the previous type of attack. Generally, these attacks combine software and hardware, often connecting to a debug port on a board/Thing in order to download malicious software or to install a sniffer to log packets transmitted. Consequently, the attackers often attempt to exploit test mode features on the board to provide a possible basis for new attacks, and they exploit the fact that in the industry, systems often have well-known default passwords which are rarely changed (e.g. username "admin" and password "admin")!

Boards or Things

At sensor or Thing level, an assailant can try to take control of the Thing or insert unauthorized Things into the IoT architecture (for example, using the well-known "man-in-the-middle" kind of attack). Gateways, routers or IoT Things that communicate within or outside an IoT architecture are also potentially vulnerable to an attack of this type.

8.4.3. *Attacks on the integrated circuits*

Attacks at the integrated circuit level generally consist of software attacks and physically invasive attacks, in which the assailant has direct access to the Thing or the infrastructure. The attackers can attempt to take control of a Thing by targeting its microprocessor or one of the neighboring integrated circuits (ICs). Historically, in particular, the protection and security checks in ICs have tended to be quite weak. These attacks often involve highly specialized equipment which is expensive and not easily affordable to just anyone... but it is often available in industrial research laboratories and universities, where ill-intentioned, unscrupulous and corrupt people sometimes hang around.

For general knowledge, a (non-exhaustive) list of these attacks is given in the following paragraphs.

8.4.3.1. *Hardware attacks*

Laser attacks

The aim of laser attacks is to generate a false error code (pause/error runtime value or memory code change) by using a laser to inject an enormous amount of energy onto a very small area of the chip (for example, changing a Boolean value of False to True in a code).

FIB (focused ion beam) attacks

An attack using a focused ion beam – FIB   is normally used for debugging the chip, but can be used maliciously to carry out reverse engineering from the physical implementation of the chip, to subsequently extract information and/or bypass the security mechanisms. This is expertly handled, but we already knew that!

8.4.4. Security standards

On account of the wide range of IoT devices and the rapid emergence of new elements on the market, there is not currently any standard that describes, in detail, the potential attacks on IoT or its vulnerabilities. Nevertheless, certain standards do exist, and can provide good references of IoT vulnerabilities – for example:

– the Common Weakness Enumeration (CWE), which lists and describes software weaknesses in architecture and design;

– the Common Attack Pattern Enumeration and Classification (CAPEC) document which serves as a resource for the identification and understanding of attack methods;

– The Federal Information Processing Standard (FIPS) 140-2 U.S., which looks at security administration and accreditation standards for cryptographic units.

– the well-known "Common Criteria" which is the shared norm for the international criteria (ISO/IEC 15408), mentioned previously in the context of certification of computer security developed for the smart card industry.

We have now come to the end of this second part of this book, which gave a broad overview of the numerous aspects that need to be borne in mind and taken into account when progressing from idea to creation of a project on secured connected Things in IoT.

We now move on to Part 3, returning to the numerous technical meanders at the heart of the subject of the Thing and associated networks.

Overall Architecture of the IoT Chain

Following Part 2 of this book, which we said was the "hors d'œuvre", let us now move on to the "entrées", examining the numerous architectural and technical facets of the subject of Things and their associated networks.

Before getting to the true meat of this third part, as outlined above, so that we have the right bones for the construction of an IoT system architecture, we shall begin by devoting a short chapter to recapping the communication models which apply to this field.

9

Communication Models in IoT

Before describing the architectures of the Things and IoT networks, for clarity of understanding, it is necessary to briefly recap (or unveil, for those who are new to the domain of IoT) the standard communication models that are ISO, OSI and Internet protocols.

9.1. Communication models in IoT

The simpler the form of communication used by a connected Thing, the more complex may be that of a connected Thing communicating via the Internet as part of the IoT. Let us therefore recap the OSI and TCP/IP communication models.

9.1.1. *OSI model*

The OSI model (standing for Open System Interconnections), drawn from the (old) Chapter 7 of ISO 7498-1, comprises a communication architecture divided into seven layers (see Table 9.1).

Each layer handles a certain number of problems pertaining to data transmission, and provides specific services to the upper layers:

– the higher layers, which are closest to the user, handle more abstract data, using services provided by the lower layers;

– the lower layers format the data received from the higher layers so that they can be transmitted on a physical support.

	PDU	Layers	Functions
Upper layers	Data	7. Application	Network service access point
		6. Presentation	Handles the encryption and decryption of data, converts the machine data into data that can be manipulated by any other machine
		5. Session	Inter-host communication, handles the sessions between the different applications
	Segment/ Datagram	4. Transport	End-to-end connection, connectability and flow control. The idea of a port comes into play here.
So-called lower layers – hardware	Packet	3. Network	Determines the path taken by the data and logical addressing
	Frame	2. Data link	Physical addressing (MAC address)
	Bit	1. Physical	Transmission of signals in digital or analog form

Note: In this table, Protocol Data Unit (PDU) is the unit of measurement of the data exchanged over a computer network.

Table 9.1. *Open System Interconnections (OSI) model*

9.1.1.1. *Description of the OSI model*

Let us look at each layer of the model, from bottom to top. Each layer must fulfill the following functions (see Figure 9.1):

– the "physical" layer is in charge of actual transmission of the signals between the interlocutors. Its service is limited to the transmission and receiving of a bit or a continuous bitstream;

– the "data link" layer handles the communications between two machines that are directly connected to one another, or are connected to a device which emulates a direct connection;

– the "network" layer takes care of communications step by step, generally between machines, routing and addressing the packets;

– the "transport" layer manages end-to-end communications between processes (the programs being executed);

– the "session" layer is responsible for synchronizing the exchanges and "transactions". It is the session layer which establishes and ends the session;

– the "presentation" layer is charged with the coding of the application data – more specifically, converting between data handled by the application and bitstreams that can actually be transmitted;

– the "application" layer is the network service access point. It has no specific service of its own, falling within the scope of the norm.

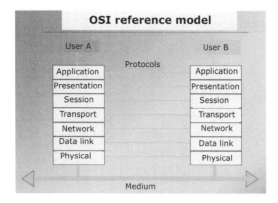

Figure 9.1. *Functions of the OSI model*

In such an architecture, an "entity" of level (N+1) sends data to the level (N) entity, in the form of a (N+1)-PDU which will, in turn, be encapsulated in an (N)-PDU. For example, during a communication between two elements, the data flow coming from the transport layer – level 4 in the OSI model – (or, for instance, in IoT, TCP segments) is encapsulated into packets as it passes to the level of the network layer (or, in IoT, for example, Internet Protocol *IP*). These packets are then transmitted to the data link layer – level 2 in the OSI model – and encapsulated into frames (e.g. by Ethernet). See Figure 9.2 for an example.

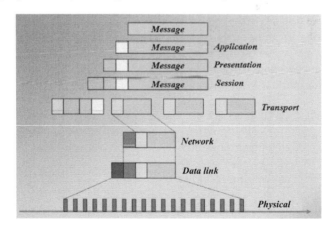

Figure 9.2. *Encapsulation of the different frames*

On the receiver side, each entity analyzes the protocol envelope corresponding to its layer and passes the data on to the next layer up. In addition, certain functions may be present in several layers, such as transmission error detection, correction of those errors and data flow control.

These layers are sometimes divided into two groups.

– the four lower layers, simply called the "low layers", are primarily communication-oriented and are often provided by an operating system;

– the upper three layers, called the "top/high layers", are mainly application-oriented and, as is the case in IoT, tend to manifest in the form of libraries or specific programs.

Furthermore, the lower layers are normally transparent for the data being transported, whilst the upper layers may not be – particularly the presentation layer. In the world of the Internet, these last three layers are rarely distinguished from one another. This being the case, all the functions of these layers are considered to be integral parts of the application protocol.

9.1.2. *TCP/IP model*

The software protocols used for the Internet and IoT are conventions setting the structure of the information exchanges necessary to the transfer of the content of application for the end user. Notably, they identify the interfaces (and therefore the Things), and help ensure receipt of the sent data and of interoperability.

The Internet also works on a layer-based model, quite similar to the OSI model. Elements belonging to the same layers use a communication protocol to exchange information with one another. Additionally, protocols are sets of rules which define a language used for communication between multiple elements. They are defined by open-access standards – documents known as RFCs: Requests For Comments.

The basic set of TCP/IP protocols is used for data transfer on the Internet. This label comes from the names of the protocols: – TCP – Transmission Control Protocol – and IP – Internet Protocol.

The referential document is RFC 1122.

The TCP/IP model of the Internet (which ultimately contains only four layers) was developed to deal with a practical problem. The OSI model described above (which is easier to understand) corresponds to a more theoretical approach, and can be used to describe the TCP/IP set of Internet protocols but, as the TCP/IP and OSI sets of protocols do not correspond exactly with one another, all the definitions of the layers in TCP/IP are/may be subject to (lengthy) debates.

9.1.2.1. *TCP/IP layers*

The term ("stack") is often employed for TCP/IP, but not in the sense of a computing "stack", which is the basic tool of evolved programming languages.

As the OSI model does not have enough levels in its lower layers to represent reality, it was necessary to add a further layer of interconnection of networks (IP – Internet Protocol) between the Transport and Network layers of the OSI model, as indicated by Figure 9.3.

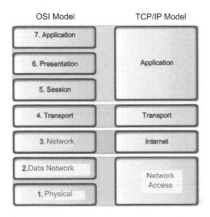

Figure 9.3. *Comparison of the OSI and TCP/IP models*

The protocols specific to a particular type of network, operating above the data link layer, should belong to the network layer. As we shall see later on, the ARP and STP protocols (which provide redundant paths within a network whilst avoiding loops) are two examples of this. However, they are local protocols which operate below the network interconnection function. Often, confusion is sown when we place these two groups of protocols (not to mention those operating above the network interconnection protocol, such as ICMP) in the same layer.

Figure 9.4 shows the position, in the OSI model, of the very numerous usual protocols encountered in Internet solutions.

	Layers in the OSI model	Examples of protocols/programs used for the layer in question as a function of the intended applications
7	Application	e.g. **HTTP**, HTTPS, Gopher, SMTP, SNMP, FTP, Telnet, NFS
6	Presentation	e.g. ASCII, Unicode, MIME, XDR, ASN.1, SMB, AFP
5	Session	e.g. ISO 8327 / CCITT X.225, RPC, Netbios, ASP
4	Transport	e.g. **TCP**, UDP, SCTP, SPX, ATP
3	Network	e.g. **IP (IPv4 or IPv6)**, ICMP, IGMP, X.25, CLNP, ARP, RARP, OSPF, RIP, IPX, DDP
2	Data link	e.g. **Ethernet**, Token Ring, PPP, HDLC, Frame relay, RNIS (ISDN), ATM, **Wi-Fi**, **Bluetooth**, **ZigBee**, irDA (Infrared Data Association)
1	Physical	e.g. signal encoding techniques (electronic, radio, laser, etc.) for transmission of the information over the physical networks (hardwired, optical, radioelectric networks, etc.)

Figure 9.4. *Usual protocols encountered in the OSI model and in Internet solutions (bold font indicates those most commonly used in IoT)*

Typically, in the TCP/IP model, the top three layers of the OSI model (Application, Presentation and Session, in the table in Figure 9.4) are considered to form a single "Application" layer. As TCP/IP does not have a unified session layer to support the higher layers, these functions are generally fulfilled (or ignored) by each application.

A simplified version of the TCP/IP layers is shown in Figure 9.5.

	Layers in the TCP/IP model	Examples of protocols/programs used for the layer in question as a function of the intended applications
5	Application "layer 7"	e.g. **HTTP**, FTP, DNS (routing protocols such as RIP, which operate above UDP, can also be considered to form part of the application layer)
4	Transport	e.g. **TCP**, UDP, SCTP (routing protocols such as OSPF, which operate above IP, can also be considered to be part of the transport layer)
3	Network	For TCP/IP, this is **IP** (the required protocols such as ICMP and IGMP operate above IP, but can nonetheless be considered to belong to the network layer; ARP does not operate above IP),
2	Data link	e.g. **Ethernet**, Token Ring, etc.
1	Physical	e.g. the local loop (transmission by modulation on analog lines: RTC telephone lines, digital connections, ADSL, etc.), the major arteries of communication (transmission by multiplexing, switching, etc.), radiocommunication networks (radio, wireless telephony, satellite, etc.)

Figure 9.5. *Simplified version of the TCP/IP layers*

A different and more common approach to the model is to consider a simplified two-layer model – our old friend, TCP/IP. Indeed, IP has no connection with the physical network, and, it is not an "application layer", but they are "applications" which rely on a transport layer (represented, for example, by TCP or UDP – User Datagram Protocol). This representation is more closely faithful to the concepts of IP. Thus, we should have (see Figure 9.6).

usual concept TCP / IP number and name of the layer			Examples
	applications		....
2	transport TCP	Transport layer	**TCP, UDP**, DCCP, **SCTP**, RSVP ...
1	Internet IP	Internet layer	IP, IPv4, **IPv6** ICMP, ICMPv6 ECN, IGMP, IPsec, ...
	network access	Link layer	ARP, NDP, OSPF, Tunnels L2TP, PPP, MAC, Ethernet DSL, ISDN, FDDI, ...

Figure 9.6. *The famous two-layer simplified TCP/IP model*

In this model, TCP introduces the idea of a session, but TCP is on the Transport level in a model based on the OSI. The fact that the OSI model was created first also accounts for certain inconsistencies, such as the implementation of a routing protocol above UDP.

Remarks:

– RIP is implemented on UDP, whereas OSPF, which emerged after the OSI model, is directly based on IP;

– DHCP is also implemented on UDP at the "application" level, but it is the role of the network layer to provide a configuration for level 3.

Each of the protocols has its own functions and, together, they provide a range of resources capable of catering for the diverse needs on the Internet.

9.1.2.2. *Main protocols used in TCP/IP*

In the TCP/IP model, the main protocols used are as follows, classified by the layer to which they belong:

Physical layer

This layer describes the physical characteristics of the communication, such as the conventions specific to the nature of the media used, for cabled communications, fiber-optic links or RF connections, and all the associated details, such as connectors, types of coding or switching, levels of signals, wavelengths, synchronization and maximum distances.

Examples of protocols used in IoT: NFC, Wi-Fi, SIGFOX, LoRA, etc.

Data link layer

This layer specifies how the packets are transported over the physical layer, and in particular the format of the frames (i.e. the sequences of specific bits which mark the start and end of the packets). For example, the headers of the Ethernet frames contain fields indicating which machine(s) on the network a packet is intended to reach.

Examples of protocols in the data link layer: Ethernet, Wireless Ethernet, SLIP, Token Ring and ATM, etc.

This layer is subdivided by the OSI model into two sublayers: MAC and LLC.

Network layer

By its original definition, this layer solves the problem of routing of packets through a single network.

Examples of this type of protocols: X.25, and ARPANET's ICP (Initial Connection Protocol).

Two scenarios may arise in terms of the routing of data:

– when there is no pre-established path between two terminals needing to communicate with one another, the protocol is said to be a "non-oriented connection";

– on the other hand, the path the data will follow may be established when the connection begins, and in that case the protocol is known as "oriented connection".

With the dawn of the idea of interconnection of networks, further functions have been added to this layer – in particular, the transfer of data from a source network to a destination network. This generally implies the notion of routing the packets through a network of networks, known as the Internet.

In the set of protocols used by the Internet, IP handles the routing of packets from a source to a destination, and also supports other protocols, such as ICMP (used to transfer diagnostic messages linked to IP transmissions) and IGMP (used to handle multicast data). The ICMP and IGMP protocols are situated above IP, but perform functions of the network layer... which, once again, illustrates the incompatibility between the Internet and OSI models.

The IP network layer can transfer data for numerous higher-level protocols. These protocols are identified by a unique "IP Protocol Number".

– ICMP and IGMP are protocols no. 1 and 2, respectively.

– IP (Internet Protocol), version 4, also known as IPv4, is a network protocol which defines the mode of elementary exchange between elements forming part of the network, by assigning those elements a unique address on the network.

– IPv6 (Internet Protocol version 6) is a network protocol with no connection to layer 3 of the OSI model which, following the exhaustion of available IPv4 addresses, facilitates an increasing number of users (or Things) – see specific paragraphs later on.

Transport layer

In the overarching TCP/IP protocol suite, the protocols for the transport layer also determine to which application each data packet needs to be delivered. They can also solve problems such as those of the reliability of the exchanges (for instance, "have the data arrived properly at their destination?") and ensure that the data arrive in the correct order.

The dynamic routing protocols which are actually situated in this TCP layer (as they operate above IP) are generally considered to belong to the network layer.

Example: OSPF (IP protocol number 89).

– UDP – User Datagram Protocol – (IP protocol number 17) is a simple, "non-oriented connection", "non-reliable" protocol – which does not mean that it is particularly unreliable, but rather that it does not check that the packets have arrived at their destination, and does not guarantee the order in which they arrive. If an application needs such guarantees, it must obtain them for itself, or else use TCP (see the next paragraph). UDP is generally used for applications based on simple question-and-answer mechanisms such as DNS requests, for which the extra cost inherent in establishing a reliable connection would be disproportionate in relation to the need.

– TCP (IP protocol number 6) is a "reliable" transport protocol, responsible for establishing a connection and controlling the "oriented-connection" transmission mentioned earlier, which provides a reliable bitstream, ensuring that the addressee has actually received the data at the other end, without any alterations and in the correct order, retransmitting in case of loss and eliminating any duplicate data. It also handles "urgent" data which need to be processed out of the correct order. TCP attempts to deliver all data correctly and in sequence – this is its goal and its main advantage over UDP, although it may actually be a disadvantage in terms of real-time transfer or routing of feeds, with a high level of losses in the network layer.

To draw a preliminary conclusion on this matter, TCP and UDP are both used by numerous IoT applications depending on the requirements. Applications located at a given network address are distinguished by their TCP or UDP port number. By convention, known port numbers are associated with certain specific applications.

Mentioned previously, here are two more (for the road):

– RTP (Real-Time Protocol) is a protocol operating with UDP or TCP, specializing in the transport of data with "real-time" constraints. Typically, it is used to transport videos so that the pictures and sound can be synchronized directly without having to be stored previously;

– SCTP (Stream Control Transmission Protocol), defined in RFC 4960 and 3286, provides services similar to TCP, ensuring reliability, correct reordering of sequences, and congestion control. Whilst TCP is byte-oriented, SCTP handles "frames" (short sequences). One of the major advances which SCTP represents is the possibility for multi-target communications, which one end of the connection is made up of multiple IP addresses.

Application layer

Applications generally operate above TCP or UDP, and are often associated with a specific port. It is in this "application" layer that we find most "network" programs, particularly for IoT applications.

9.1.3. *By way of conclusion*

As a conclusion to this chapter, Figures 9.7(a) and (b) graphically represent the essence of the above paragraphs, and indicate the classic data flow paths in Internet protocols operating in each of the different layers of the TCP/IP model presented above.

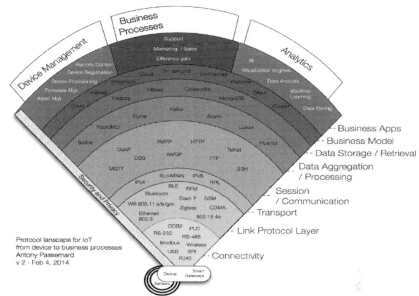

Note: the TCP layer is not clearly shown here; it is just above the IP layer

Figure 9.7a. *Protocol landscape for IoT from devices to business process (Antony Passemard – V2 - 2014. For a color version of this figure, see www.iste.co.uk/paret/connectedobjects.zip*

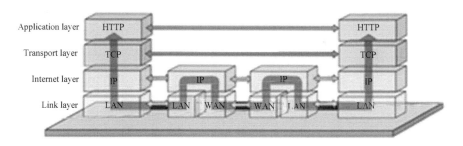

Figure 9.7b. *Data flow of Internet Protocol Suite*

Overall Architecture of an IoT System

The authors wish to thank their longstanding friends and collaborators, Jean-Yves Cadorel (CEO of 3ZA and Professor at PolyTech Orléans), Eric Devoyon (technical director at 3ZA), Pierre Crégo (CEO of Mercury Technologies) Jean-Luc Garnier of EESTEL, and Christophe Huguet, for their enlightened contributions to this chapter.

10.1. Overall architecture of a CT and IoT solution

Following this wide-reaching exploration of the numerous generic aspects of the protocols strictly necessary to understand design, concrete realization and applications, in the nebulous Internet of Things, we can now look at defining the overall architecture of a "connected Thing" (CT)-based or "pure IoT" solution, where the Thing itself is merely the small visible part of an immense iceberg below the surface!

First, though, we need to recap the goal, the purpose of an IoT application:

– to harvest raw data or slightly processed data from multiple sources (e.g. sets of digital or analog sensors), far removed from one another and communicating little or not at all with each other;

– to assemble, sort, work through, etc. all these data centrally in specific orders;

– to vent and send the worked data to the end users in question, in accordance with their needs.

Simples!

10.1.1. *Description of the complete chain*

Like Russian dolls, the ecosystem of the connected Thing and IoT has a great many facets, all fitting within one another, and in order for this system to work with different actors, there are many different branches of activity (e.g. maintenance teams, logistics teams to deliver and install the Thing in its intended place, training users, etc.)... In fact, there are lots of different professions involved, in addition to those who physically design and create the Thing itself.

Therefore, we shall offer this lengthy and detailed description – lengthy, yes, but absolutely necessary in order to properly describe our Secure Communicating Thing. Before all else, though, we have to define the connected Thing itself, the limits of its functions, and determine where it stops. In order to do this, we need to answer a few simple questions:

– is the connected Thing simple, with no Internet connection?

– is the connected Thing simple, but connected to the Internet?

– is the connected Thing a subset of an overarching connected solution (with a life cycle, logistics, the Cloud, etc.)?

– and so on.

With this done, we can design an architecture for the Secure Communicating Thing or IoT.

10.2. From a more technological point of view

Important note.–

In the coming sections, we shall, at great length, break down all the different links in the IoT chain, techniques, problems to be solved, technical aspects that must be in place, etc., which will serve as a guide through this book, and a guiding framework throughout the explanations given in the coming chapters.

10.2.1. *Architecture and overview of an IoT chain*

Figure 10.1 shows a highly representative overview of the architecture of the concrete whole chain of IoT communications, consisting of sensors and Things, smart devices and gateways, back-end datacenters and services, and finally, users.

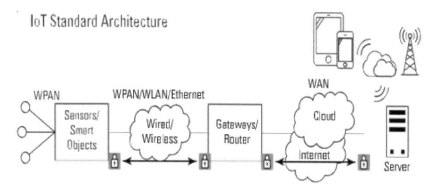

Figure 10.1. *Highly representative overview of the architecture of the standard IoT chain (source: Inside Secure)*

Numerous cases and subcases (infinitely numerous!), scenarios and use cases can be envisaged in IoT, and obviously, they cannot all be discussed in this book (...they are discussed in all regular journals!). Thus, so as not to mire the reader in this marshland of complex issues, here we offer a more in-depth examination of the solutions which are very general, but can easily be adapted to readers' own concrete solutions.

Figure 10.2 shows a wider-reaching overview of the enormous scale of the "mess", with all its possibilities and possible choices of solutions... and these are only the most frequent and likely scenarios (far from the only ones)! Just like the famous Route of Santiago de Compostela, we have already said that all roads lead to the Cloud, though they may come from different places! The same is true here.

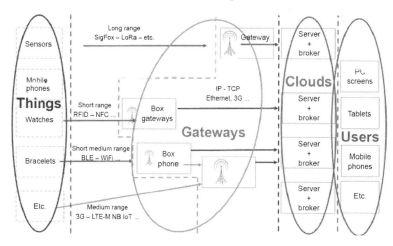

Figure 10.2. *Possibilities and possible choices of IoT solutions ... and these are not the only ones – just the most commonly encountered*

This figure shows neither what we expect from each block nor the physical divisions of the concrete elements making up the overall chain, but it does offer a simplified representation of this initial description of the general scope of the Thing's possibilities for connection, its architecture, a conventional device-to-device structure of the IoT network, which emphasizes the main elements and the four main entities and zones of interest – namely:

– the Things zone;

– the Base station/Gateway zone;

– the Cloud Servers zone;

– and the User zone with its command tools.

10.2.1.1. *The "Things" zone*

Let us begin by examining the left-hand side of Figure 10.3, labeled "Things".

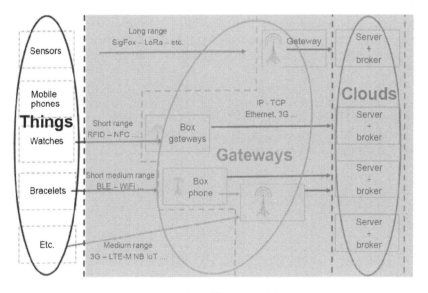

Figure 10.3. *"Things" zone*

Things are the elements in the network in which the creation and/or detection of the basic information and/or (pre-)checks are carried out. They are sometimes designed without the need for a direct Internet connection, and are usually deported, depending on the RF connections, either short distances (from a few centimeters to a few meters) or long distances (several kilometers).

The description of the secure connected Thing itself can be divided into two distinct parts.

Physical makeup of the Thing

In the Thing zone, we first find a part which is not concretely represented in the figure, running from the user (the outside world) to the Thing – i.e. the way in which a "user" communicates with the Thing (pressing a button, scanning an RFID badge, an NFC telephone, etc., a temperature/pressure sensor, etc.).

In more concrete terms, we shall then speak about what hardware the Thing must physically contain in order to work (sensors, A/D converters, etc.), its local intelligence (microcontroller, etc.), its security (SE), and so on.

Means of communication to access a base station

In this section, we shall discuss the means of communication that a Thing must employ to connect with a base station/gateway, depending on the distances between them (Short Range, Medium Range, Long Range), and on the type of communication networks it wants to use for these first relays (BTE, Zigbee, Wi-Fi, SIGFOX, LoRA, GSM, LTE-M NB IoT, etc.):

– one part of this Things bubble pertains to communicating Things which are already wireless (historically for x reason), operating with known, industrial protocols (BLE, Zigbee, etc.). In such cases there can be no question of changing the protocols used, and therefore we need to continue using the same protocol but take it to the next level, by creating one or more gateways between the different specific facets of these Things and the Internet;

– another part pertains to Things that are often small and simple (as is the case, for example, with simple sensors), which need to be able to communicate wirelessly, of their own accord. This part composed of "portable devices" (mobile telephones, tablets, watches, bracelets, clothing, wearables, etc.) must again be subdivided into multiple parts:

- Things communicating with one another over very short distances:

i) the typical example is of Things using NFC (Near-Field Communication), where the communication distance is around ten centimeters at most (e.g. with an access pass, a watch synchronizing with a phone, a bracelet for monitoring sporting activity, etc.).

- Things communicating at medium distances:

i) to achieve communication over a distance of several meters, tens of meters, certain Things communicate using BLE, Wi-Fi, Zigbee or similar protocols. The advantage of Bluetooth is that it is very widespread;

– Finally, communicating Things that must/can transmit and communicate some/a little data, in an epistolary manner, over long distances, either via conventional telephone connections such as GSM, or via radio relay antennas, proprietary or otherwise (often working at around 400, 800, 900MHz, ... for propagation, it must be so!), or via a "network operator", designed to harvest data and/or able to either process such data directly (proprietary networks, e.g. SIGFOX,) or transfer them via a public operator public (e.g. open networks such as LoRa, Orange, Bouygues and others) via the Internet to a Cloud (be it private or public) for processing (see Figure 10.4).

Figure 10.4. *Physical example of a Thing*

This long chapter will ultimately refer to Chapter 18, which presents an example of the concrete realization of an application.

10.2.2. *The "base station/gateway"*

Let us now look at the central zone in Figure 10.5, labeled "base station/ gateway".

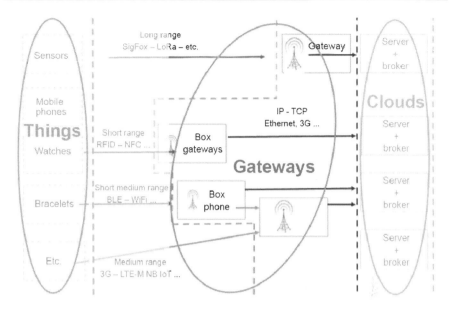

Figure 10.5. *"Base station/Gateway" zone*

In all the cases mentioned above, the relay from the Thing to the Cloud, generally using an Internet connection, is formed by an intermediary gateway known simply as a "Box" (domestic Livebox and Freebox are fairly conventional at this stage, routers, etc.), which receives the messages from the Things and handles the management and conversions of protocols (network, transport, session protocols, etc.), serves as a relay, links and then transfers the data to a harvesting network, either via a system of terrestrial connections based on Ethernet networks, for example, or via a GSM-type cellular telephone connection, or indeed via any other type of wireless telecommunication system (see Figure 10.6).

Usually, these gateways are connected to a network server by standard IP connections. On the gateway-server path, the data use one or more standard protocols (see the next few chapters), but can also be connected to public telecom networks (Orange, etc.) or private ones (EDF, etc.). It should be noted that in view of how similar certain networks are to a cellular network, gateways can often be co-installed locally with a pre-existing cellular base station. Hence, certain existing infrastructures are (almost) able to use the communicative capacities that are unused in the harvesting network.

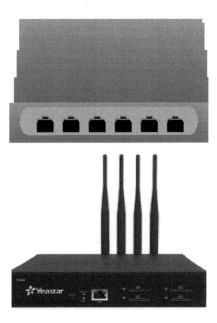

Figure 10.6. *Physical example of base station/Gateway*

The gateway is divided into three distinct parts.

10.2.2.1. *Physical makeup of the gateway*

This point pertains to the gateway's mechanical and physical form; its electronic content; what it does and its purpose; to whom it belongs; who its true proprietor is; where it is physically; its local intelligence; its security; etc.

10.2.2.2. *Means of communication necessary to access a server*

This point pertains to the possibilities of types of communication network that can be used, depending on the distances between the gateways and servers (Short, Medium, Long Range) and the types of hardwired (IP) or RF networks we want to reach.

10.2.2.3. *Protocols for communication with the server (IP + TCP layer, OSI)*

When managing communication between two elements, the data sent from the transport layer – level 4 of the OSI model – (e.g. *TCP* segments) are encapsulated into packets as they pass through the network layer (e.g. by *IP*). These packets are then passed onto the data link layer – level 2 of the OSI model – and encapsulated into new frames – e.g. Ethernet (see Figure 10.7). It is at this level that we encounter IP and TCP.

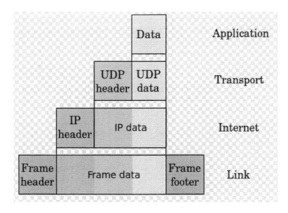

Figure 10.7. *Example of a function managed by a gateway (case of a UDP application)*

10.2.3. *The "Cloud" zone*

Let us now examine the right-hand side of Figure 10.8, bearing the label "Clouds".

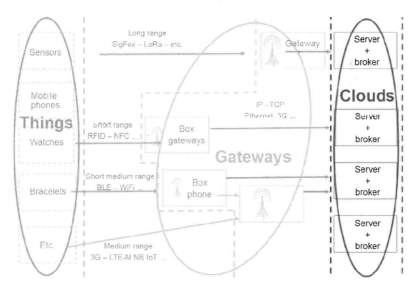

Figure 10.8. *"Cloud" zone*

Thanks to gateways, we come to the server devoted to the application, often situated in the Cloud. The role of the network server (application layer of the OSI model) is to manage the network; take measurements so as to eliminate duplicate packets; organize acknowledgements; adapt data throughput rates (data rates; simply); release the data to the users; etc. Figure 10.9 illustrates the typical physical form of a server.

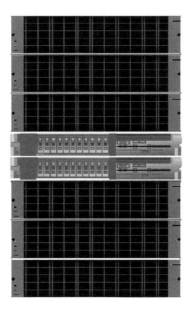

Figure 10.9. *Example of a server*

Later on, we shall examine what a server is; what it contains; what it can do; how we communicate with it; the command languages and protocols (HTTP, MQTP, CoAP, etc.); how to control it; what we use to control it; where it is; what the safety measures are; the Cloud architecture(s); the release of the data to the users via a broker; service providers such as AWS; etc.

10.2.4. The "User" zone

To conclude this brief initial view of the IoT chain, let us now examine the right-hand side of Figure 10.10, labeled "Users".

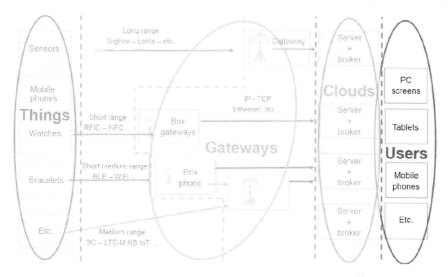

Figure 10.10. *"User" zone*

Prior to Chapter 17, in which we shall offer a more detailed examination of the relations existing between the server and the various users, and how information is sent back to the users and through which communication channels, let us briefly discuss the functions of this zone, which contains the "man–machine interfaces" (MMIs) used – screens, PCs, mobile phones, etc.), the operating systems (OS) that can be used (Linux, Microsoft, etc.) and how, in certain architectures, the whole of the network described above may be almost transparent, and how it is possible, using a single remote computer, to control the actions of the Things or to harvest or release their data to/from the different providers.

To the various providers and managers of the IoT network

To whom are the data sent back? What are these data? Which communication channels are used? We shall now look at these questions and more.

To the final initial client

Finally, we look at the particular channel by which the end user receives, or does not receive, useful information.

Table 10.1 offers a single table covering all the above paragraphs more succinctly.

The Thing collecting digital or analog data
The connected Thing itself is able to harvest data, possibly process them/refine them/polish them a little, and finally is able to transmit the information in the form of hardwired connections (less and less in today's world) or RF connections (on the rise). These Things could be, say, sensors, detectors, etc., whose purpose is to measure and collect data (e.g. temperature, humidity, presence, a camera, etc.). Note: Although they are not actually represented in the above figures, the individual Things have power management units (PMUs) so that they activate and deactivate to save on processing power and batteries.

RF connections
These are the connecting links which must exist so that the Thing can communicate, by way of **communication protocols**, over short and medium distances (e.g. NFC, BTLE, Zigbee, Wi-Fi) or long distances (e.g. SIGFOX, LoRA, GSM).

Internet relay
The Internet relay is a host processor (for example, in the form of a gatebox/box), which serves as an initial relay and the nerve center and functional heart of the device.

Back-office connections
These are connections to a "back office" via the Internet, using **messaging protocols** with a hardwired connection (ADSL, Ethernet, etc.) or an RF connection (GSM, etc.)

Front office
Memory: Memory work and storage memory (flash), data storage and/or code request, processing of data collected from the different Things

Return of the data to the various specific authorized people within their remit
In return or via a

Network manager	To professionals	End users via the Internet	
		Man–Machine Interface (keyboard/screen)	GSM

Security throughout the whole system

Table 10.1. *Overall summary table*

10.3. The very numerous protocols involved

As mentioned a little earlier on, a very general view of the IoT can be expressed as follows:

– the Things must/can communicate with one another (Device to Device – D2D);

– the data from the Things must be harvested and sent to the server infrastructure (Device to Server – D2S);

– the server infrastructure is designed to be able to share the data coming from the Things between different users ("share device data" – S2S) and possibly provide an answer to the Things/devices based on specific analysis programs.

Figure 10.11 shows the main protocols involved and their respective positions within the global architecture of IoT applications.

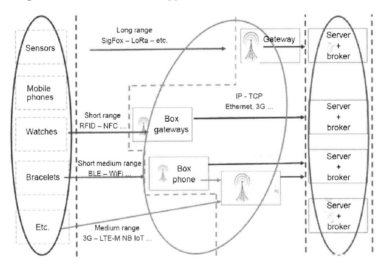

Figure 10.11. *Main protocols employed in IoT*

In this context, still just an overview, the protocols used can be described as follows:

– a protocol to collect data from the Thing and communicate them to servers (D2S) (e.g. MQTT, etc.);

– a protocol to connect Things/people, which is a particular case of the D2S model, because the people are connected to servers (e.g. XMPP, etc.);

– a rapid bus protocol for integration of smart machines (D2D) (e.g. DDS, etc.);

– a queue management protocol designed to connect servers to one another (S2S) (e.g. AMQP, etc.).

Numerous implementations of these protocols have been widely adopted in the field. Of course, amongst these, there are numerous similarities and complementary aspects, and it is perfectly understandable to be confused, because they often occupy essentially the same positions! In fact, all claim to be IoT protocols which can connect to thousands of devices… and while this may not be entirely true, it is not completely false either!

Throughout the above successive descriptions of these solutions, we have, hypocritically, without a clear explanation, drawn our electronic block diagrams of the hardware and defined the areas and outlined the software used by our Things, and at the same time inventoried the cost of the development and industrialization of our solutions, as will be detailed in Chapter 19!

Table 10.2 shows a summary of the protocols frequently used in IoT.

Protocols frequently used in IoT							
	From the Thing to the base station	From the base station to the Cloud		In the cloud			
		Internet layer	Transport layer	Operation	Applications	Reply to addressee	WEB service
SR	RFID	IP	TCP	OS	AWS	TCP IP	Apache
	NFC	IPV6	MQTT	Linux	AZURE	GSM	
	BLE	6LoPAN	HTPP	MS	MS	HTPP	
MR	Wi-Fi	etc.	etc.		broker		
	ZigBee						
	…						
LR	LoRa		GSM				
	SIGFOX		CoAp				
	…						
	GSM		GSM				

Table 10.2. *Overview of the protocols frequently used in IoT*

The people affected by all these entities

To conclude this chapter, let us now examine an additional point which is very important in understanding this new activity: that of the intrinsic quality of the people who are or should be concretely involved in the development of an IoT structure.

Actors participating in the IoT chain	
The *designers and manufacturers of Things* to be connected, *manufacturers of components* (semiconductor foundries, sensor manufacturers, etc.) and electronic modules.	Security: The actors in the area of computer security, who are present at all levels of the chain, from the design of the Thing to the service provision. In the best cases, these actors from the world of security work in close collaboration with all the actors in the value chain. Some, though, are absorbed by the actors.
RF links	
The *developers of onboard software* providing the Things with connectivity over short, medium or long distances by means of hardware components and *communication protocols*.	
Internet relay and back-office connections	
The *network operators and network equipment manufacturers*, forging the connection between the Things and the services available in the Cloud using *messaging protocols*: – businesses created with IoT, developing their own dedicated networks; – historical electronic communications operators, who already had networks and traditional equipment suppliers, which they adapt for new uses devoted to IoT; – *new actors* who are traditionally less involved in electronic communications, making their network infrastructures available to use new communications technologies (e.g. power network management).	
Back office and front office	
Conventional Cloud operators, who mainly take care of the design, and production in a *programming language*, of a software application for the storage and processing of raw data (e.g. OVH), as well as the function of broker, and producing a front-office operating system (proprietary or shared in the Cloud – examples include AWS, Microsoft Azure, etc.). In this particular field, the historical players of the Internet and servers are experiencing competition from new actors rolling out their own computer infrastructures (Amazon, Google, Apple etc.).	
In parallel		
The publishers and providers of software interfaces, or middleware, used to establish communication between the different Things.	The integrators conventionally found in the world of computing, orchestrating all of the aforementioned building blocks by assembling the different physical layers – Things and sensors – to design the final product, and then link it via the networks to the Cloud, from whence it is managed and where its data are stored and analyzed before being exploited with a view to future services.	The usual publishers of digital platforms, service providers and data aggregators, who exploit the user data generated by the Things to serve the users' needs.

Table 10.3. *Actors working together in an IoT chain*

In order to be able to offer end users (businesses, local authorities, private individuals) tangible applications which they can integrate into their daily activities, a multitude of actors, from different sectors but working together, must be considered in the IoT chain. A document published in July 2016 by France's *Arcep* (*Laying the groundwork for the IoT revolution – A roadmap for the issues*, white Paper) gives a fairly complete list of those actors, which we have summarized below in the form of the table presented in Table 10.3.

Now that we have laid out this general scheme of things, let us move on to the finer details.

PART 4

Detailed Description of the IoT Chain

Having devoured the hors d'œuvres (part 2) and entrées (part 3), we now serve up this fourth part, containing the main master dishes and, as the extensive domain of IoT represents a massive feast, there are a great many on the menu!

This long and detailed description of the IoT chain thus contains an important ordered succession (in the direction of the path taken by the information/data) of the different links making up the whole chain.

This part, which follows the path of the original signal – i.e. the data sent by the Thing – is split into four distinct but complementary sub-parts, recapped below:

4A   From the outside world to the Thing

– Chapter 11 – From the outside world to the Thing

– Chapter 12 – The secure connected Thing

4B   From the Thing to the base station

– Chapter 13 – Communication tools to access a base station

4C   From the base station to the server

– Chapter 14 – The network access layer – IP

– Chapter 15 – The server

– Chapter 16 – Transport and messaging protocols

4D   From the Cloud server to the various users

– Chapter 17 – Cloud computing and Fog networking

And now, dear friends, to work!

From the User (The Outside World) to the Thing

11

From the Outside World to the Thing

In this short chapter, we shall discuss the way in which a "user" communicates with the Thing (by pressing a button, presenting an RFID badge, via an NFC telephone, temperature sensors, pressure, etc.).

11.1. Connection of the Thing to the outside world

Sooner or later, we need to communicate with the Thing and provide it with data:

– using sensors (whether or not built into the Thing);

– using wired connections; or

– using RF connections.

11.1.1. *Using sensors*

Sensors to detect physical values – for which the recorded data are mainly analog – (temperatures, pressures, magnetic fields or inductions, positions, etc.) are often directly built into the Thing in the form of standalone integrated circuits or directly embedded on the Thing's single chip.

Because of these analog physical values, the input circuits for the Things are frequently equipped with A/D (analog/digital) converters, which consume as little energy as possible, to turn them into digital data. In addition, some of these initial raw data require corrective computations to be fine-tuned, refined, into exploitable data which are supplied to the network (for instance, a pressure value, corrected on the basis of the temperature). This means that the presence of (small) local microcontrollers is almost obligatory.

11.1.2. *Using wired connections*

Wired connections are often used in industrial connected Things (M2M), in which the data they need to transmit reach the Thing via conventional fieldbuses – e.g. CAN, LonWork, M_bus, etc.

EXAMPLES.– Applications of workshop machines set up in networks issuing periodic reports to remote management units.

11.1.3. *Using RF links*

RF links are very commonly employed in the case of so-called "wearable" communicating (small) Things, which seek a local mini base station/gateway with uplink directly to the Internet.

EXAMPLE.– a watch communicating with BLE looking to connect to a smartphone serving as a gateway.

This is also the case where the user communicates with the connected Thing with RFID badges, NFC contactless cards, BLE, to report an action, a presence, the sending of data, etc.

APPLICATIONS.– secure verification of access rights, use rights, etc.

In these cases, the communication distances in air are relatively short (around ten centimeters, for a watch and a mobile), or very short (a few centimeters for an NFC badge).

Let us give a few details on communications of this type.

11.1.4. *Very Short Range (<10 cm)*

These very short range RF connections – around ten centimeters maximum – between the "outside world" and the Thing may be of various types, such as NFC, RFID, etc.

11.1.4.1. *NFC at very short distances (~10 centimeters)*

NFC is well known for its applications and its use in all smartphones on the market. Its possibilities to be used with IoT are many, both direct and indirect (see the 1000+ technical pages previously written on the subject in numerous NFC books by Dominique Paret, published by Dunod and ISTE).

For example, we can cite an "NCF and IoT" application, able to connect any existing system to the Internet, by combining NFC and a link to the onboard microcontroller whose purpose is to benefit from shared, ergonomic man–machine interfaces and provide non-connected Things with a gateway to the Internet.

Example

The French solution IoTize from Keolabs, in combination with STMicroelectronics, Gemalto and ISEN and LIG-INP Labs, consists of connecting an NFC module (an integrated circuit and an NFC antenna, associated with a microcontroller) with the existing microcontroller of the device we wish to connect to the Internet via its debug port. This gives us the possibility to establish a direct wireless link between the processor of the system to be connected (using its debug port) and an NFC-compatible smartphone. NFC connectivity is therefore added to the other types of radio communication: Bluetooth, Wi-Fi, SIGFOX, ISM bands, etc.

The originality of this approach lies in the fact that the RF connection is made without modification of the firmware installed on the hardware of the system being connected to the Internet. On the side of smartphones with NFC connectivity, the application interface is developed by the user via an API. It is then possible to exploit the usage data of the analyzed system via the data extracted from the memory of the onboard microcontroller, and much like a Thing having a "native" Internet connection, to exploit application services installed in the Cloud. These modules adapt to existing applications with no alteration to the hardware or software, by the simple setting up and editing of an HTML file (see Figure 11.1).

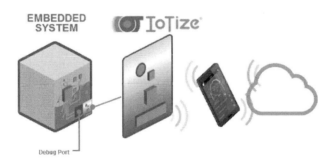

Figure 11.1. *Example of IoT/NFC applications. For a color version of this figure, see www.iste.co.uk/paret/connectedobjects.zip*

11.1.4.2. *Short-range RFID UHF (a few meters)*

Strange as it may seem to a number of readers, anyone beyond a certain age will tell you that the Internet of Things arose years ago, with connected/communicating Things which, at the time, were simply called RFID devices! However, then, RFID was (and indeed still is) performed at different frequencies: in LF at 125 kHz, HF at 13.56 MHz, UHF at 433 MHz and 860–960 MHz, at 2.45 GHz and in SHF at 5.8 GHz, and all the communication protocols are covered by the following ISO standards in the 18000 series:

– 18000-2 in LF at 125 kHz – batteryless passive tags;

– 18000-3 in HF at 13.56 MHz – batteryless passive tags;

– 18000-4 at 2.45 GHz;

– 18000-5 in SHF at 5.8 GHz;

– 18000-6 in UHF at 860–960 MHz – batteryless passive tags already operating with the FHSS and DSSS techniques, widely used thereafter in IoT, variants of which support sensors, A/D and D/A converters and encryption units.

This standard was introduced into the area of IoT by GS1, AIM and the RAIN RFID Alliance;

– 18000-7 in UHF at 433 MHz – active **and** battery-assisted tags.

This solution – an "almost connected Thing" (in fact, the ancestor of the connected Thing) was originally advanced by the American company SAVI Technology, which later went on to launch the "*Dash 7 Alliance*", sparking its rise in the area of IoT. Unlike most RFID technologies, ISO 18000 -7 (DASH7) allows for direct communication from Thing to Thing which, combined with the long range and the advantages of propagation of the signal at 433MHz, makes it an easy solution for most wireless sensors in so-called "mesh" networks. Dash 7 also covers sensors, encryption, IPv6 and other characteristics.

NOTE.– some of the batteryless tags mentioned above are also capable of drawing power by energy harvesting.

11.1.5. *Short range SR Wide band (tens of meters)*

Sometimes, for certain applications, it is necessary and mandatory that the reporting of an action, of a presence, of the sending of data to the Thing, can only be done at a distance of a few meters. In this case, the "outside world", to make itself understood to the Thing, can communicate with it using, say, the BLE protocol, defined below.

11.1.5.1. *BLE – Bluetooth Low Energy*

Bluetooth is probably the most widespread short/medium-range wireless communication technology, given that it is built into billions of mobile phones, headsets and millions of portable computers on the market, etc. The Bluetooth Low Energy (BLE) version is defined as the "low energy-consumption" part of the specification of the Bluetooth v4.0 standard, and included and improved in the latest version v5.0. For this, BLE uses different techniques to ensure very low energy consumption, whose main characteristics (highly useful in IoT) are:

– operation in the ISM band, between 2.4 and 2.483 GHz, without the need for a license;

– use of different frequency-hopping spread-spectrums – FHSS – employing 40 channels of 2 MHz width to achieve better performances over long distances, in combination with adaptive FHSS technique to prevent interference;

– bearer modulation of the type GFSK – Gaussian Frequency Shift Keying;

– emitted power of 0 dBm (1mW), which facilitates a typical operating distance (in air) of around 50 meters;

– a maximum throughput of 1Mbit/s with a net data rate of 260 kbits/s;

– improved reliability of the link by verification of the 32-bit message integrity, with a 24-bit CRC – cyclic redundancy check;

– an Advanced Encryption Standard (AES) encryption unit, with a 128-bit key (note: this is not a Secure Element; it is merely an encryption unit!);

– peer-to-peer (P2P) and star network possibilities;

– latency of around 6ms;

– a new data protocol, creating transmissions with small cyclic ratios – i.e. sending salvos of very short transmissions between long periods of inactivity;

– the aforementioned very short duty cycle means we can use sleep modes with extremely low consumption, so the device can operate for many years on just a button cell.

Table 11.1 shows the performances of BLE in comparison to the old version of BT.

Technical specification	Classic *Bluetooth* technology	*Bluetooth* low energy technology
Radio frequency	2.4GHz	2.4GHz
Distance/Range	~10-100 meters	~10-100 meters
Symbol rate	1-3Mbps	1Mbps
Application throughput	0.7 – 2.1Mbps	305kbps
Nodes/Active slaves	7	Unlimited
Security	56 to 128 bit	128-bit AES
Robustness	FHSS	FHSS
Latency (from not connected state to send data)	100+ ms	<6ms
Government regulation	Worldwide	Worldwide
Certification body	Bluetooth SIG	Bluetooth SIG
Voice capable	Yes	No
Network topology	Point-to-point, scatternet	Point-to-point, star
Power consumption	1 (reference value)	0.01 to 0.5 (use case dependent)
Service discover	Yes	Yes
Profile concept	Yes	Yes
Primary use cases	Mobile phones, headsets, stereo audio, automotive, PCs etc.	Mobile phones, gaming, PCs, sport & fitness, medical, automotive, industrial, automation, home electronics etc.

Table 11.1. *Main properties of BLE in comparison to standard BT*

11.1.5.2. *Zigbee and others*

Without wishing to denigrate other solutions in favor of BLE, there are many other industrial solutions, such as Zigbee connections, which establish a short/medium-range link before being relayed by other communication protocols.

Unfortunately, though, this book is not intended to be an encyclopedia of the genre, and we shall leave this discussion there.

12

The Secure Connected Thing

This subject has already been broached in the previous chapters, so this one will be very brief, simply offering a number of additions to the discussion.

Connected Things are the elements of a network where basic information is detected and analyzed. In principle, they are sometimes designed without the need for an Internet connection, but in today's world, the fashion is such that they are increasingly frequently deported, and must provide an Internet connection, either at short distances from a few centimeters to a few meters, or over long distances including several kilometers.

Let us start by speaking of the physical makeup of the Thing.

12.1. Physical constitution of the Thing

Let us take a brief look at the content of a Thing. We shall start with the hardware, which is generally made up of the following elements.

12.1.1. *Sensors*

Falling under the enormously broad umbrella term "sensors", we find all sorts of elements – e.g. capable of measuring "analog" physical values, detecting the opening/closing of elements in "on/off mode", the presence of people or animals using radiofrequency waves, etc. On this matter, we are limited only by our imagination!

12.1.2. *Local intelligence – microcontroller*

As previously mentioned, with the data thus captured, whether they are analog or digital (1 or 0 – on/off), we are sometimes/often forced to carry out local processing, optimizations, refinements of those initial data before they can be sent via the Internet to the data-harvesting network.

Let us illustrate these points using two examples.

Example 1

Frequently, it is necessary to have A/D converters available, because very often, the physical data measured are naturally analog (temperature, pressure, etc.) and, to render them usable in real terms, it is necessary to locally have a computational unit in the microcontroller to refine the measured data. For example, when dealing with a measure of pressure, it is always important to correlate and correct it with the ambient temperature, which requires the presence of two sensors: one for pressure and one for temperature, and a computing unit able to run an algorithm to correct the pressure measurement as a function of the ambient temperature.

Example 2

So as not to transmit needlessly, and consume data that give nothing to the system, and at the same time to consider saving on the Thing's energy consumption, it is helpful to only send those data which are deemed pertinent to the network, to avoid the presence of duplicate information, etc.

Here again, we need to locally process the initial data.

In the two small examples above, which are highly representative of daily life, we must seek and hope to find the "little", cheap microcontroller which has sufficient computation power, whose associated computation will not "drain" the Thing's energy reserves, and will have no impact on its dimensions, weight, volume, esthetics, etc. as a function of the battery used locally.

12.1.3. *Security (SE) …*

Security or no security: *that is the big question*! Should we or should we not integrate security into a Thing, and if so, what kind?

Of course, the answer depends on the intended application, the desired security target and the financial resources we want to invest in relation to that target… and we refer you to Chapter 8, which gives all the details!

This being the case, if you have followed the discussion in the previous chapters, you must understand that we are increasingly facing major problems in terms of security, sensitive data (industrial or otherwise), personal data, CNIL and GDPR, etc. and that for a long time, we have advocated true security, achieved with true Secure Elements. Obviously, this comes at a cost, but we get nothing for nothing!

12.1.3.1. *Means of communication*

The last, very important part making up a connected Thing is linked to its twofold communicative abilities – first to communicate with the surrounding world, and secondly to communicate with the base stations/Internet gateways.

With the surrounding world

Very often, the Thing is equipped with specific integrated circuits (in mono-chip version with the microcontroller), capable of handling short-range and/or medium-range NFC/BLE communications, as these two means of communication are very widely employed in the worlds of smartphones, wearables, PCs, etc.

With the base stations

For reasons of cost and consumption, often, the applications in Things turn to base stations/Internet gateways using LR (long-range) communications, low-throughput networks (LTNs), Low Power networks using solutions such as SIGFOX, LoRa, etc. for which numerous solutions are available on the market, from integrated circuit manufacturers. It should be noted that for certain IoT applications requiring higher throughputs, new solutions such as LTE-M, NB-IoT, etc. are beginning to emerge.

All these communication solutions from Things to the base stations/gateways will be discussed in the next chapter.

Finally, to close off this short chapter, note now that Part 5 is given over to a concrete and detailed example of a secure connected Thing.

From the Thing to the Base Station

Important preliminary remarks

In the coming, very long chapter, we describe the numerous radiofrequency protocols encountered in IoT solutions. First, though, we want to clarify why, after lengthy reflection and animated discussions, we have chosen a specific and preferential order in this long presentation.

– to begin with, all the figures and block diagrams presented in the previous chapters, and in this one as well, are read from left to right, following the origins of the signals and their steps;

– in these diagrams, the Things, which are the starting points of the chain are therefore on the far left, and then we work our way back toward the base stations – gateway – boxes, the Internet, the back offices, the Cloud, the front office… and finally return to the customers.

Thus, we have deemed it wiser to present the assorted protocols at the different steps of the signal and their successive encapsulations in the chain in that order

13

Means of Communication to Access a Base Station

Certain new needs of the Internet of Things (low data rates, long distances, low consumptions), which essentially run counter to the performances of conventional mobile networks, have led to the emergence of new techniques and technologies for mobile connectivity. These deliver very low levels of energy consumption and costs of Things, and are often grouped together under the generic term "LPWAN – Low Power Wide Area Network".

13.1. Possible network connectivity technologies

Today, there are a very large number of possible techniques and technologies to respond to and cover the multitude of network connectivity needs of the IoT, both in hardwired and radiofrequency connections – notably LTN LPWANs with LoRa, SIGFOX, Qowisio, etc., each having a proprietary, non-standard solution for addressing, localization, security, commissioning, etc. This is often the case because the severe constraints of LPWAN do not allow for the use of conventional management techniques.

In addition, in France, the historical mobile operators (Orange, Bouygues, SFR, etc.) have not yet breathed their last. Under the auspices of the GSMA, many of them have recently launched the "Mobile IoT Initiative" aimed at speeding up the commercial availability of a technology known as "LTE - Long Term Evolution", appropriate for the rollout of the frequency bands which they own, and which are only accessible under license. LTE-M is a variant of LTE designed to respond to the needs of M2M and IoT. Finally, the world of Wi-Fi has also put forward its own solution.

Table 13.1 shows the most common connectivity technologies.

	Types of networks	Range / rate	Names	Options	Examples
Wired			DSL		
			fiber optic		
			cable		
			CPL		carrier current
			CAN, etc.		earth bus
Wireless	**WPAN**	short range	NFC		NFC Forum
	WLAN	short range	BlueTooth		BT LE
		medium range	Zigbee		
			Thread		
			Z Wave		
			Li Fi		
			Wi-Fi		
	MAN **WAN**	long range low throughput	LPWAN LTN	LTN NB	SIGFOX, Qowisio,
				LTN DSSS	LoRa, Ingenu,
		long range high throughput	LPWAN WB	3GPP	2G, 3G, 4G
		low throughput	NB	3GPP LPWAN	LTE-M NB-IoT EC-GSM

Table 13.1. *Most common connectivity technologies*

Figure 13.1 indicates their usual relative positions in terms of the "data rate to distance" ratio.

In this chapter, we shall restrict our explanations to those which are currently popular in IoT, meaning that here, we shall focus solely on RF networks. Within that class, though, there are two very distinct domains: "non-operated" networks and "operated" networks.

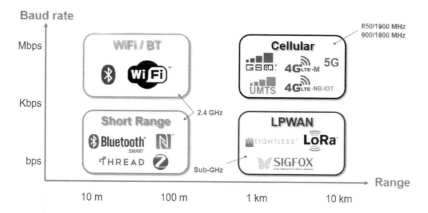

Figure 13.1. *"Data rate/distance" ratios for the most common connectivity technologies*

13.1.1. *Local or ultra-local non-operated RF networks*

For wireless uses, short-range RF, for (W)PAN (Personal Area Network) or (W)LAN (Local Area Network) connections, the technologies Wi-Fi, Bluetooth Low Energy, Zigbee10, Thread11, z-Wave, NFC and Li-fi (with the frequencies in the range of visible light) are used. In the eyes of the regulatory authorities (e.g. the AnFR in France), all these connections function in "free" bands, said to be "non-operated".

Generally, the local networks used, particularly by private individuals, are non-operated. In this case, it is the end user who becomes responsible for the configuration and proper operation of his/her local network by making the acquisition of the network equipment (routers linked/integrated into an Internet box, for example). Although they are perfectly well suited to domestic or individual use, these networks offer very limited mobility. In addition, these technologies (W)LAN and (W)PAN provide little or no extended connectivity on a national or international scale, unlike a MAN (Metropolitan Area Network) or WAN (Wide Area Network). These different categories of network, which partially overlap geographically, serve different needs, and in IoT, they offer or can offer possibilities for linkup and complementarity with other networks.

13.1.2. *Extended-deployment operated RF networks*

Of the wireless RF technologies employed over long distances, known as "extended networks", such as MANs or WANs, we can cite the following as main examples:

– conventional cellular networks (3GPP): 2G, 3G, 4G, … (and 5G in the near future), most of which are deployed on frequencies on exclusive authorizations, paid for to the State (licenses). We then speak of operated networks; notable examples are the historical cellular mobile operators, which are almost exclusively deployed with these 3GPP technologies;

– LPWAN-type solutions for (certain) IoT applications via cellular networks (3GPP) are undergoing standardization at the time of writing: these include LTE-M, NB-IoT and EC-GSM, which have not yet really been rolled out;

– when the networks LoRa, Qowisio, Ingenu, Weightless-N, Wireless M-BUS, etc. (see details later on) are based on and/or use an operator for the implementation and operation of their networks on a larger scale (which is usually necessary), these LPWANs (Low Power Wide Area Networks) then become operated.

13.1.3. *Is there space for all these technologies?*

We have just listed a very great number of forms of technology (look again at Table 13.1), but is there room for all these technologies to coexist? This is a good question indeed!! In view of the extremely broad range of applications for IoT, the answer is a definite yes. How will they be distributed in relation to one another, though? Only time will tell, because the future depends as much on cutting-edge technology as it does on marketing, politics, etc. Below is simply a mini-list of the questions which must be addressed on a daily basis:

– In the future, who will the actors in LPWAN be?

– How will they be able to defend against the onslaught of LTE and Wi-Fi?

– How will tenured actors in the telecom industry react?

– How might they prevent their own fragmentation?

– Etc.

13.2. Medium-range MR Wide-band (hundreds of meters)

Multiple standards are available for Medium Range – MR (order of magnitude of 100 meters) in Wide band – and undoubtedly, Wi-Fi is the most widely used.

13.2.1. *Wi-Fi*

Wi-Fi is a set of wireless communication protocols governed by the standards of the group IEEE 802.11 (ISO/IEC 8802-11), describing the characteristics of a WLAN – Wireless LAN, Wi-Fi.

A Wi-Fi network uses RF to link various communicating Things in order to establish a connection and facilitate high-throughput data transmission between them:

– 11 Mbit/s theoretical or 6 Mbit/s actual in 802.11b;

– 54 Mbit/s theoretical or around 25 Mbit/s actual in 802.11a or 802.11g;

– 600 Mbit/s theoretical for 802.11n;

– and 1.3 Gbit/s theoretical for 802.11ac.

The "indoor" operating range can reach several tens of meters (generally between twenty and fifty meters). We can thus establish an Internet-connected Wi-Fi network in a zone with a high concentration of users (private homes, offices, a station, an airport, a hotel, a train, etc.). These zones or access points are called Wi-Fi terminals, Wi-Fi access points, or indeed "hot spots".

The standard 802.11, mentioned earlier, defines the lower layers of the OSI model for a wireless connection – i.e.:

– the physical layer – there are four types of modulation of the radioelectric waves and the characteristics of the signaling for data transmission: FHSS, DSSS, OFDM and Infrared;

– the data link layer – the interface between the bus of the Thing and the physical layer (notably an access method similar to that used in the Ethernet standard and the communication rules between the different stations) is, as usual, made up of two sub-layers:

- Media Access Control, or 802.11 MAC;

- Logical Link Control, or 802.2 LLC.

It is possible to use an IP-based transport protocol on an 802.11 network, in the same way as on an Ethernet network.

13.2.1.1. *Networking modes*

"Infrastructure" mode

This mode of operation enables us to connect Things equipped with Wi-Fi cards with one another via one or more Access Points (APs) which act as concentrators (e.g. a repeater or switch in an Ethernet network).

"Ad hoc" mode

This operational mode is ideal for quickly and directly connecting or interconnecting Things with Wi-Fi cards, without using additional hardware such as an AP (example: file exchange between mobile phones on a train, on the street, in a café, etc.).

"Bridge" mode

This mode serves to connect multiple access points to extend a wired network – e.g. between two buildings. The connection is made at the level of layer 2 in the OSI model. One access point – generally the one which distributes the Internet access – has to operate as a "Root Bridge", and the others connect to it in "Bridge" mode and then retransmit the connection over their Ethernet interface.

"Range-extender" mode

Finally, range-extender mode can be used to boost a Wi-Fi signal over a greater distance. This technology can cover a large number of practical applications. It can be used with IPv4, or IPv6, and allows for the development of new distributed algorithms.

13.3. Long-range (LR – tens of kilometers)

13.3.1. *NB, UNB, WB, UWB, FHSS, DSSS and RF regulations*

What a rag-tag bunch of acronyms… but they are highly strategic!

The usual approach is to find frequencies within the radio spectrum, if possible free to access without a license, which correspond to our desired applications and on which it is permissible to transmit. Thus, as we have done many times in the past, for over twenty years in the fields of RFID, contactless chip cards, NFC, UWB geolocation, Bluetooth, etc., we once again need to conduct a detailed examination of what is facilitated by the different RF regulations in force nationwide and, of course, worldwide if we want to sell our product irrespective of geographical boundaries!

It should be noted that the whole of the RF spectrum and the bands associated with it are ultimately regulated by States, whose respective administrations manage the applications pertaining to communicating Things considered "SRDs –Short Range Devices" (e.g. the FCC in the USA, ARIB in Asia, the ERC in Europe, and in France the AnFR – *Agence Nationale des FRéquences*, which delegates responsibility to Arcep – *Autorité de regulation des communications électroniques et des postes*).

In addition, with these SRDs, e.g. in Europe in ERC 70-03 and its annexes, there are bands reserved for the use of "specific SRDs", – attributed therefore to particular applications (e.g. RFID, HF microphones, etc.) and "non-specific SRD uses": in these ranges, there are a few bands which are free to use, without paying a license fee. Often, these have functional constraints pertaining mainly to the bandwidth: "UNB – Ultra Narrow Band", "NB – Narrow Band", "WB – Wide Band", "UWB – Ultra Wide Band", with or without the possibility of "direct-sequence spread spectrum – DSSS" or "frequency-hop spread spectrum – FHSS" to extend the bandwidth, effective radiated power (ERP) or effective isotropic radiated power (EIRP) depending on the frequency bands, the occupation time (duty cycle), and a whole host of further small points which need to be carefully considered.

...In short, like it or not, we must live with it!

QUESTION.– Are these constraints compatible and solvable with all or most of the features and performances we expect of IoT-connected Things?

ANSWER.– Yes, the shoe will more or less fit... but often we need to make use of a shoehorn!!

The aim of the game, then, is to find how we can create numerous technical tricks to get the most out of these constraints so as to satisfy the range of our IoT applications! Furthermore, in the same way that many (if not all) roads lead to Rome, many solutions may serve, each with performances appropriate for the aims desired and/or manifested, depending on the technical, commercial, political (etc.) views put forward by the protagonists. This is what makes our profession so marvellous!

Having laid down these essential foundations, let us now give a few details to help refine readers' understanding.

13.3.2. *Regulators and regulations*

Obviously, well-intentioned people have taken the situation in hand. These people are the "Regulators", who establish regulations at national, regional and even worldwide level.

13.3.2.1. *Throughout the world*

Without going into too much detail, the ITU decided to divide our beautiful blue planet into three RF regions – see Figure 13.2.

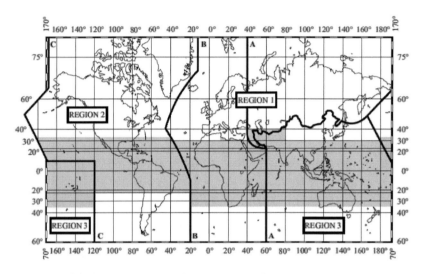

Figure 13.2. *Division of the world into Regions by the ITU*

To recap, Figure 13.3 is indicative (as at the start of 2017) of the majority of frequencies and frequency bands and their associated power levels (in dBm ERP) on which RF communications can be used in the main regions of the globe.

NOTE.– we must keep a very close eye on the variations in values of the frequencies in this table, because in view of the worldwide explosion of IoT, the ITU, having received a great many requests to standardize these values, is in the process of drawing up new, more uniform frequency plans, particularly in the 902–928 MHz band.

Countries	Frequency band review	Max. output power
EU	868 MHz	14 dBm
USA	915 MHz	20 dBm
Korea	900 MHz	14 dBm
Japan	920 MHz	
Malaysia	862 to 875 MHz	20 dBm
Philippines	868 MHz	
Vietnam	920 to 925 MHz	
India	865 to 867 MHz	
Singapore	922 MHz	
Thailand	920 to 925 MHz	
Indonesia	922 MHz	
ANZ	915 to 928 MHz	
Taiwan	920 to 925 MHz	
China	470 to 510 MHz	17 dBm

Figure 13.3. *Main frequency bands that can be used in IoT (document from ARCEP)*

13.3.2.2. *In Europe*

Let us look at Europe, where the ECC recommendation ERC 70-03 describes an SRD as being "a short-range radiofrequency transmitter used in telecommunications for transmission of data unlikely to cause harmful scrambling to other radio equipment". In the case of IoT, generally, the effective radiated power (ERP) authorized for SRDs is limited, being 25–100 mW depending on the frequency bands used (see below), which limits their usable range to a few hundred meters or kilometers, and the user does not need to hold a license.

Table 13.2 gives an overview of the ISM bands that can be used in accordance with ECC Rec. 70-03 and its multiple annexes, specifying different use cases – e.g. for the application of short-range wireless devices such as wattmeters and other remote tools, RFID, radio-controlled models, fire alarms, security alarms and distress alarms, vehicle radar, wireless microphones and listening devices, signing panels and signals (including command signs), remote garage door keys and car keys, barcode reading, motion detection and many more examples.

The European Commission, through the CEPT and ETSI, requires the attribution of several device bands for these purposes, and limits the parameters linked to their use, issuing directives to prevent RF interference.

Frequency bands allocation in Rec. 70-03		
Annex 1. Non-specific short-range devices		
Frequency bands	**Band**	**Notes**
6765–6795 kHz	ISM	
13.553–13.567 MHz	ISM	RFID
26.957–27.283 MHz	ISM	Citizens' Band
40.660–40.700 MHz	ISM	
138.20–138.45 MHz		
433.050–434.790 MHz	ISM	LPD433 (70-centimeter band)
863–870 MHz		See below for details
2400.0–2483.5 MHz	ISM	13-centimeter band
5725–5875 MHz	ISM	5-centimeter band
24.00–24.25 GHz	ISM	1.2-centimeter band
61.0–61.5 GHz	ISM	
etc.		

Table 13.2. *ISM bands that can be used in accordance with ECC Rec. 70-03*

In France, the main bands used without a license are (see Table 13.3):

Bands	Applications	Performances
169 MHz	Reserved for telemeasurement and tracking applications	Very long range
433 MHz	Not yet well standardized in Europe Few cycle time constraints at present… Rather crowded	Long range (>1km)
868 MHz	Fairly well standardized in Europe Strict rules on spectrum occupancy time	Medium range
2.4 GHz	Standardized worldwide Increasingly crowded (Wi-Fi, Bluetooth, etc.)	Short range but highthroughput
5.8 GHz	etc.	

Table 13.3. *Main bands used without a license*

ISM band: 863-870 MHz

In Europe, the ERC and ETSI regulation (reproduced in Table 13.4) sets aside the frequency band from 863 to 870 MHz for license-free operation, with the possibility to use analog modulation, FHSS, DSSS, with a transmission duty cycle of 0.1%, 1% or 10% per hour depending on the band, – i.e. a "Listen Before Talk" (LBT) system, with and/or without Adaptive Frequency Agility (AFA).

Frequency Band in MHz		Power / Magnetic Field	Spectrum access and mitigation requirements	Modulation / maximum occupied bandwidth	Notes
h1.1	863–870	25 mW e.r.p.	≤ 0.1% duty cycle or LBT (notes 1 and 5)	≤ 100 kHz for 47 or more channels (note 2)	FHSS
h1.2	863–870	25 mW e.r.p. Power density: 4.5 dBm/100 kHz (note 7)	≤ 0.1% duty cycle or LBT + AFA (notes 1, 5 and 6)	Not specified	DSSS and other wideband techniques other than FHSS
h1.3	863–870	25 mW e.r.p	≤ 0.1% duty cycle or LBT + AFA (notes 1 and 5)	≤ 100 kHz, for 1 or more channels modulation bandwidth ≤ 300 kHz (note 2)	Narrow/ wide-band modulation
h1.4	868–868.6	25 mW e.r.p.	≤ 1% duty cycle or LBT + AFA (note 1)	No spacing, for 1 or more channels (note 2)	Narrow / wide-band modulation. No channel spacing; however, the whole stated frequency band may be used
h1.5	868.7–869.2	25 mW e.r.p.	≤ 0.1% duty cycle or LBT + AFA (note 1)		
h1.6	869.4–869.65	500 mW e.r.p	≤ 10% duty cycle or LBT + AFA (note 1)	No spacing, for 1 or more channels	Narrow / wide-band modulation The whole stated frequency band may be used as 1 channel for high speed data transmission
h1.7	869.7–870	5 mW e.r.p.; 25 mW e.r.p.	No requirement for 5 mW e.r.p., ≤ 1% duty cycle or LBT + AFA (note 1) for 25 mW e.r.p.	No spacing for 1 or more channels	Narrow / wide-band modulation. No channel spacing, however the whole stated frequency band may be used

Note 1: When either duty cycle, Listen Before Talk (LBT) or equivalent technique applies then it shall not be user dependent/adjustable and shall be guaranteed by appropriate technical means.
For LBT devices without Adaptive Frequency Agility (AFA), or equivalent techniques, the duty cycle limit applies. For any type of frequency agile device the duty cycle limit applies to the total transmission unless LBT or equivalent technique is used.
Note 2: The preferred channel spacing is 100kHz allowing for a subdivision into 50 kHz or 25 kHz.
Note 5: Duty cycle may be increased to 1% if the band is limited to 865–868 MHz.
Note 6: For wide-band techniques, other than FHSS, operating with a bandwidth of 200 kHz to 3 MHz, the duty cycle can be increased to 1% if the band is limited to 865–868 MHz and power to = 10 mW e.r.p.

Table 13.4. *Reproduction of ERC 70 03 regulation*

ERC 70 03 - ANNEX 1: Non-specific Short Range Devices

NOTE.– From editions of ERC 7003, dated September 2015 – available from www.erodocdb.dk – the names of the bands changed, from a "g" label to an "h 1.x" label... with a few nuances.

Author's note.–

The most interesting possibilities for long distances in IoT in terms of power, bandwidth and duty cycle for our applications are highlighted in the table.

REMARK ON NOTE 1 in Table 13.4.–

The technique of Adaptive Frequency Agility (AFA) is used to prevent transmissions on channels that are already occupied. For this purpose, the radio transmitter wishing to transmit locally and periodically scans its radio environment and notes the channels which are occupied. On the basis of that observation, the transmitter chooses an operating frequency which is not yet in use, to prevent any collisions/interference.

This technique is very useful when a frequency band is shared, either by a large group of users (the case of IoT Things), or if the band is/must be shared with another service which has a higher priority, and thus must not be impeded. Very often, AFA (performed, for example, using Frequency Hopping Spread Spectrum – FHSS) is twinned earlier on with another complementary technique: Listen Before Talk (LBT), meaning that the transmitter listens to its radio environment before commencing transmission so as to be sure it is operating on a free channel.

The content of this table from ERC 70 03 and its standards of measurements associated with EN 300 220 and EN 300 422 can more explicitly be expressed as an image! See Figure 13.4.

Of course, when they use these bands, the "Long-Range" solutions which we shall examine later on must conform to these ERC/ETSI regulations pertaining to duty cycles.

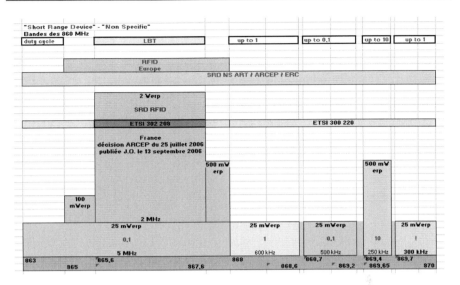

Figure 13.4. *Content of ERC 7003 – October 2016. For a color version of this figure, see www.iste.co.uk/paret/connectedobjects.zip*

13.3.2.3. *In the USA and Canada*

Just like the European band, the American/Canadian ISM band from 902 to 928 MHz (i.e. a 26 MHz band, whose central frequency is 915 MHz) is regulated by the FCC in accordance with the following standards:

– FCC Part 15.247

– FCC Part 15.249

– FCC Part 90 25 kHz

– FCC Part 90 12.5 kHz

– FCC Part 90 6.25 kHz

This band can be used in different ways and segmented into different channels in accordance with the envisaged techniques, and the numerous frequency plans desired.

Very often, users work by dividing the band on the basis either of the principle of frequency hopping modulation of several narrow-band channels, by the technique of FHSS, or sometimes by using a technique of DSSS, with additional use of the technique of bitcode oversampling (see Dominique Paret's book, *RFID en UHF et SHF*, published by Dunod, for example) and/or "chirps" (see later on in this chapter) to help improve transmission possibilities.

13.3.2.4. *In Asia, South America, Australia, New Zealand and China*

It is respectively the standards:

– ARIB STD T-67 (Asia – Japan);

– ANATEL 506, from 902 to 907.5 and 915 to 928 MHz (South America – Brazil);

– AS/NZS 4268 from 915 to 928 MHz (Australia and New Zealand),

which govern matters and, in China, it is possible to transmit in the ISM band from 779 to 787 MHz.

13.3.3. *RF bases*

In order to better understand the rest of this chapter and the technical ins and outs of radiofrequency in IoT, here is a reminder of some of the necessary technical fundaments.

13.3.3.1. *Power in W or dBm*

The RF power normally expressed in Watts is often expressed in decibels, dB milliwatts – dBm. "0dBm" then corresponds to a power reference of 1mW (see Table 13.5).

$$dBm = 10 \log \frac{P \text{ in mW}}{1mW}$$

power	
in W	**in dBm**
1 W	+ 30 dBm
25 mW	**+ 14 dBm**
100 mW	**+ 20 dBm**
10 mW	+ 10 dBm
1 mW	**0 dBm**
100 µW	– 10 dBm
10 µW	– 20 dBm
1 µW	– 30 dBm
...	
1 nW	– 60 dBm
100 pW	– 70 dBm
1 pW	– 90 dBm
100 fW	– 100 dBm
1 fW	– 120 dBm
0.1 fW	– 130 dBm
0.01 fW	– 140 dBm
0.001 fW	– 150 dBm

Table 13.5. *Power – correspondence of Watts to dBmW*

13.3.3.2. *Noise Floor*

Knowing that the value of the thermal noise is equal to the product k.T.Bw, where k is Boltzmann's constant, T the absolute temperature in Kelvin and Bw the bandwidth in Hertz, we can easily show that the value of the theoretical noise floor (denoted NF) in a 50 Ω resistor at ambient temperature (27°C = 300°K) is given by the expression:

NF in dBm = – 174 dBm + 10 log (Bw /1Hz)

so, for example, see Table 13.6 for different bandwidth values.

bandwidth Bw	noise floor thermal noise power
10 MHz	– 104 dBm
1 MHz	– 114 dBm
100 kHz	– 124 dBm
10 kHz	– 134 dBm
1 kHz	– 144 dBm
100 Hz	**– 154 dBm**
1 Hz	– 174 dBm

Table 13.6. *Level of theoretical noise floor as a function of the bandwidth*

In principle (but just in principle – see later on), this NF level corresponds to the smallest signal which a normal receiver is able to detect.

It is not uncommon for a receiver to have to detect power levels as low as 0.01 fW. In addition, it is common to allow safety margins so as to be absolutely sure of being able to operate.

13.3.3.3. *Link budget*

It is easy to estimate the value known as the link budget, which represents the difference in power values EIRP or ERP, measured in dB, between the transmitted and received signals.

EXAMPLE.–

For emitted frequencies within the ISM band from 868 MHz to 868.6 MHz, on transmission, the maximum authorized radiated power is 25 mW ERP, which is +14 dBm.

If the sensitivity of the receiver (for a given bandwidth and BER – see below) is –126 dBm, we have a maximum free-space link budget of +14 – (–126) = 140 dB.

13.3.3.4. *Possible operating distance*

The relation between the radiated power Pbs, the transmission antenna gain Gbs, the received power Pt, the receiving antenna gain Gt and the operating distance r is given by the Friis transmission equation.

$$P\_rec\_eirp = (P\_trans\_erp \times G\_ant\_trans) \times \left(\frac{\lambda}{4\,\pi\,r}\right)^2 \times G\_ant\_rec$$

where:

P_rec_eirp	= received Power in W_eirp
P_trans_erp	= transmitted Power in W_erp
G_ant_trans	= Antenna gain of transmitter in dBi
G_ant_rec	= Antenna gain of receiver in dBi
λ	= wavelength in meters
r	= distance in meters
note 1	(P_trans_erp $\times$ G_ant_trans) = P_trans_eirp in W_eirp
note 2	$1 / (\lambda / 4\pi r)^2$ = att. = attenuation
note 3	in dB: P_rec_eirp_dB = P_trans_eirp_dB – att._dB + G_ant_rec_dB

The attenuation $1 / (\lambda / 4\pi r)^2$ of a signal due solely to its propagation in air is equal to (beware of the units here!):

att (dB)   = 32.5 + 20 log f + 20 log r   with "f" in GHz and "r" in m

Thus, for example at 868 MHz:

att (dB)   – 32.5 + 20 log (0.868) + 20 log r

att (dB) @ 868 MHz = 31.27 + 20 log r   r, in meters

Consider a new example, where we want to calculate the value of "r", supposing that the attenuation in the propagation medium (air, presence of obstacles, etc.) is equal to, say, 131.14 dBm,

20 log r = 131.14 – 31.27

= 99.87

so   log r   = 4.99

so   r   = 98 km... in the ideal free space!

13.3.3.5. *Losses due to the environment*

For many reasons of the physical qualities of transmission, UHF waves (in the frequency band of 300–3000 MHz), and particularly those in the 800–900 MHz band, have been chosen for our example. Indeed, the frequencies of 868 in Europe and 915 MHz in the USA offer good conditions for local or regional propagation. Unfortunately, the reality of the situation is quite different, due to losses during propagation in air/the atmosphere, attenuation due to any number of other things (such as buildings, trees, etc. which are always present over such a distance – see below), interference with other signals, and so on, the signal which actually reaches the receiver may be very weak. In addition, it is usual to allow safety margins so as to be sure of being able to operate. Table 13.7 shows a few figures typical of these parameters.

Frequency	868 / 915 MHz
Burial losses	~30 dB
Average losses due to buildings	~20 dB
Losses due to weather-related fluctuations	5-8 dB max
Average losses due to tree impact	~10–20 dB
Average losses of a 20% impact of the Fresnel zone (effect of hilly ground)	~30 dB
Margins recommended for stability without channel coding	15 dB

Table 13.7. *Examples of losses due to the environment*

The total of these losses (around 115 dB) represents a corresponding reduction in the usable link budget, and obviously reduces the true distance over which communication can take place (…though not the commercial value!). Far from the wondrous hundred kilometers or so that are theoretically possible, the truly usable distance is generally ten or so, or even only a few, kilometers!

EXAMPLE.– link budget = 140 – 115 = 25 dB

Thus, we have a typical distance of between 4 and 15 km

When using ultra-narrow band, for normative powers of 25–500 mW, "regional" propagation (up to 40 km in a rural environment) is typical.

NOTE.–

A transceceiver operating in LBT mode, so constantly listening before it can talk, will practically always find a weak signal within the band, but one whose value is much higher than its fixed decision threshold (order of magnitude of –96 dBm), which often prevents it from working properly. Hence, this mode of operation is generally to be avoided.

13.3.3.6. *OFDM – Orthogonal frequency-division multiplexing*

OFDM (Orthogonal frequency-division multiplexing) is a process of encoding digital signals by dividing the signal in the form of multiple subcarriers of orthogonal frequencies. This technique helps combat the presence of frequency-selective channels by performing low-complexity spectrum equalization. These sensitive connection channels notably occur when multiple paths are taken by the signal, which is all the more detrimental when the transmission data rate is high. Therefore, this technique is often adopted in high-throughput IoT applications.

Note that there are multiple variants of OFDM – for instance:

– DMT (Discrete Multi Tone) is a baseband OFDM transmission system;

– COFDM (Coded Orthogonal Frequency Division Multiplexing) introduces an error correction code;

WCP OFDM (Weighted Cyclic Prefix Orthogonal Frequency-Division Multiplexing) adds a weighted cyclic prefix to the transmitter's output signal, to adapt to multi-path mobile channels.

In the case of a multi-path channel, receiving multiple echoes in phase opposition can cause the disappearance/weakening of the signal, due to substantial attenuations over a portion of the frequency band. In the context of an OFDM system, it is generally impossible to reconstruct the symbols transported by the subcarriers which are affected by these signal-loss phenomena. This is due to the fact that non-precoded OFDM does not introduce redundancy (or frequential diversity). It is possible to deal with this shortcoming by using COFDM, with the tradeoff being a decrease in spectral efficiency (number of bit/s per Hz).

As OFDM is a blockwise transmission system, it is usual to add a safety interval between each block. This helps eliminate possible interference between successive blocks in the presence of multi-path channels, and facilitates equalization, provided the safety interval is longer than the time taken for the last path to complete. Two types of buffers are commonly used:

– cylic prefixing, whereby the last samples in the block are copied onto the beginning of it;

– zero-filling, which consists of inserting a string of zeros at the start of the block.

These two techniques also lead, naturally, to a decrease in spectral efficiency.

Latest-generation mobile networks (LTE, 4G) use a multiple-access technique based on OFDM, called OFDMA: Orthogonal Frequency-Division Multiple Access.

13.4. LTN – Low-Throughput Network

Sooner or later, it is normal to think that we need to establish numerous mono- and/or bidirectional RF connections to communicate with Things in applications where the devices are generally (very) far apart (i.e. "long-range" applications); the devices speak little and infrequently (hence, we are dealing with low data-rate communications), and thus can use narrow band (NB) or ultra-narrow band (UNB) or other similar options, and should consume little energy (low power).

LTN technology – standing for Low-Throughput Network – describes a networking possibility that is adaptable to IoT bidirectional wireless communications which, in comparison to the existing networks, facilitates the transmission of data dedicated to low-throughput, long-range communications (distance in "free space" of around 40 km), and/or the establishing of communications with buried devices, capable of supporting elements whose energy consumption is minimal (a few milliwatts for transmission), meaning they can function for several years on standard batteries. This new technology also offers possibilities to create device-to-device (D2D) communication systems, fitting into the desired economic target of IoT.

This LTN technology has been standardized by ETSI (since 2014) in the form of three international specifications: GS LTN 003, 002 and 003, describing how to implement signal-processing using two different techniques – either in (ultra) narrow band, (U)NB, or with spectrum spreading, DSSS. Both techniques offer effective defense against interferences.

LTN is particularly well suited for the communication of a Thing delivering a limited volume of data, at a low data rate, where latency is not a high priority. Conventional examples of applications include tele-measuring (readings for the distribution of water, gas and electricity for smart cities), monitoring of air pollution or public lighting, etc. In addition, it should be noted that the complementarity of LTN for LTE-M cell networks means that they can cooperate to deal with use cases where redundancy, additional connectivity or an alternative are needed.

Figure 13.5, in 3D, clearly indicates the relations between the transmitted power, the data rate and the range, and also defines the footprint of the technical field catered for by LTN, which is currently covered by no other technical solution.

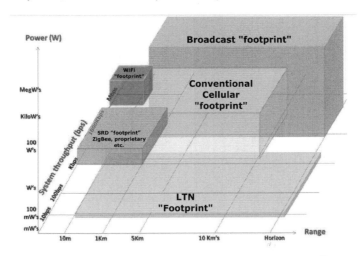

Figure 13.5. *Relations between emitted power, data rate and range. For a color version of this figure, see www.iste.co.uk/paret/connectedobjects.zip*

Let us now examine the numerous variants of LTN – particularly the LR (Long Range) option.

13.4.1. *Long Range LR - LTN*

Certain new needs of the Internet of Things – low throughput networks LTNs, long range LR, low power LP – are damaging to the performances of conventional mobile networks, and have led to the emergence of new mobile connectivity technologies. With these technologies, it is possible to achieve very low costs for the Things and very low levels of energy consumption. They are often spoken of collectively as LPWANs (Low-Power Wide Area Network).

Concerning the technical solutions dedicated to the demands of LR IoT, standardized LTNs, etc., on the market, the different technical roads which lead to Rome are, today, of two main types:

a) narrow-band or ultra-narrow-band communications, known as UNB LR LTNs; and

b) spread spectrum communication techniques known as DSSS LR LTNs.

Worldwide, there are numerous techno-commercial products available in these domains, and each of them, of course, has its own specific technical properties.

– the first, type a) solutions are represented by the concepts SIGFOX, Qowisio, etc.;

– the second, type b), are represented by the concepts LoRa, Ingenu (formerly On-Ramp), etc.

Note that there are many others also, including Weightless-N and Wireless M-BUS as just two examples.

NOTE.–

In fact, for new applications (IoT) and their specific constraints, as we shall see a little later on, to everybody's surprise, SIGFOX and LoRA successfully sought to exploit the hidden possibilities of certain frequency bands that are very little used.

Remembering that the permanent and ultimate aim of this book is to focus on the "design and concrete realization of a Thing", the numerous paragraphs below present the main technical characteristics of each of them, so that every reader can establish the content of his/her own solution in full awareness, and in particular, having taken care not to fall into the trap of making comparisons (...which are often tendentious, because they are all too often steeped in sales rhetoric!).

13.4.1.1. *LR LTR NB and UNB*

Here is a sensitive point in the story of IoT, which is worthy of lengthy discussion and a little technical examination to help understand all the subtle nuances involved in IoT designs and their concrete industrial production.

Before looking in detail at the protocols SIGFOX and LoRa, (...which everybody is talking about), let us first explain why we speak of NB and UNB – Ultra Narrow Band – and its applications in LTNs – Low-Throughput Networks – and LPWAN – Low Power WAN. What are these things, exactly?

What exactly are NB and UNB – Narrow Band and Ultra Narrow Band?

An NB or UNB is a portion, a band, of the radio spectrum – fairly narrow – often divided/divisible into channels over which we can communicate.

Are we dealing with an NB or UNB in terms of Hz? Of Data rate? Of spectrum?

This is an excellent question!

In fact, all these are more or less the same thing… barring a few significant nuances.

– by principle, the width of a frequency band can only be defined in Hertz. Case closed!

– the bit in the base signal emitted is encoded (bit coding, or **source coding** using NRZ, BSK, PSK, BPSK, etc.). Thus, it has a format, a duration, and a binary data rate (in bits/second). Depending on the type of **channel coding** used (type of modulation ASK, OOK, FSK, GFSK, QPSK, etc., error-correcting codes, etc.) and spectrum spreading FHSS or DSSS applied to the source coding via the resulting parameters of "spectral density and efficiency of the channel coding", the total bandwidth in Hertz necessary for the transmission can be estimated on the basis of the initial bitrates (bits/second);

– the overall shape of the emitted spectrum depends on the type of bit coding of the base signals and the type of channel coding (notably the type of modulation and/or spectrum spreading) and the channel correction systems (FEC – Forward Error Corrections) use.

Is the transmitted power expressed in W? In dBm? In W/Hz? In dBm/Hz?

Curiouser and curiouser!

Obviously, when we transmit, we emit a degree of power W, in Watts… which is radiated in accordance with Maxwell's laws, with a surface power density (in W/m^2) stemming from the associated Poynting vector, and recovered by the receiver in accordance with the Friis equation, mentioned above. In addition (often leading to confusion), there are various different ways of expressing power – in watts ERP, in watts EIRP (with a $\lambda/2$ dipole antenna whose gain is G = 1.64), in dBmW (abbreviated as dBm), or indeed in power watts EIRP expressed in dBm as a function of the bandwidth – i.e. in dBm/Hz.

In terms of duty cycle?

In addition to this, so there is not too great a degree of anarchy in the communications (collisions, etc.), generally, devices are only allowed to "talk" for specific lengths of time (usually short or very short), in the form of a value of the "duty cycle", generally defined per hour, and perhaps in addition use a "Listen Before Talk" mode of operation with "Adaptive Frequency Agility" (LBT AFA), as mentioned above.

To conclude, users are very fond of not having to pay a license fee to transmit – i.e. transmitting in the ISM bands.

Here, we have painted a broad picture of the situation. Now let us take a closer look at the details.

13.4.2. *LR LTN in (U)NB – SIGFOX*

Historically, the Toulouse-based company SIGFOX was the first in France to design and promote a completely proprietary LTN – LPWA (Low-Power Wide-Area) – (U)NB network devoted to IoT, which came out of nowhere; the conventional telecoms operators (Orange, Bouygues, SFR, etc.) were taken by surprise. In addition, the company has taken up position as a new operator – calling itself Local SNO (SIGFOX Network Operator) – and also as a technology supplier.

Figure 13.6. *SIGFOX logo*

13.4.2.1. *A few important points*

SIGFOX provides a so-called "vertically integrated" model, because the concept includes firstly the proprietary communication protocol, and secondly the network operator. For its part, the SIGFOX operator provides international coverage on its network, relying either on its own networks of antennas installed abroad, or on partnerships run with local SNO operators in the various countries. For example, we can cite the cases of SIGFOX antennas already installed by the partner networks

Abertis in Spain, Aerea in the Netherlands and Micronet in Russia, etc. Thus, a Thing equipped with SIGFOX "chips" can work equally well in France or anywhere else in Europe (indeed, anywhere the operator has a presence), and thus there is no problem of roaming from one operator to another; the operator simply has to comply with the local regulations.

As we shall see in detail in the coming paragraphs:

– *the Thing decides, of its own volition, when it wants to send and transmit its message*, simply selecting a pseudo-random transmission frequency in the available frequency band (+/- its own frequency shift).

– the transmitted signal is then detected by the nearest base stations, and decoded;

NOTE.– there is no signaling or negotiation between a Thing and a base station;

– it is then transmitted to the network server;

NOTE.– message duplications and other protocol operations are handled by the network itself;

– the messages are then transmitted to the user for his/her own applications, made accessible through the SIGFOX API.

Only the first and last points of the above list are accessible to the user. This is a positive for numerous companies, because it means that the user does not need to worry about the installation or maintenance operations, and can therefore focus on his/her own application project, completely forgetting about the communication side, because there is no need to configure the elements. SIGFOX is fundamentally designed, and plays the role of a "plug & play" technology. Users only need to create and launch a message, and it works!

In addition, technology to support the development of connective modules and integrated circuits is freely accessible on the market (Texas Instruments, Microchip, NXP, On Semi, Telit, etc.) but on the other hand, the Things and terminals must be certified, and it is mandatory to use only SIGFOX's proprietary Cloud.

In the understanding of the regulator ARCEP, SIGFOX is an "operated telecom network", because SIGFOX has enough of its own investment capital to roll out its technology all over the world. In addition, the LPWAN – (U)NB technology used is capable, for example, of covering over 90% of the territory of France with around 1000 antennas, and is also able to reach buried devices in places not accessible to GSM waves.

On the other hand, this solution offers only low throughput, because the bandwidth with a (U)NB technique is only able to send digital data through at a rate of a few kbit/s. We shall show, in the next few paragraphs, that a SIGFOX Think can send at most around 140-150 messages per day, each containing 12 bytes. This is doubtless one of the reasons why the SIGFOX network cannot, and would not attempt to, compete with high-throughput GSM networks. This technology is designed for a different purpose, and holds interest for numerous other connected Things and IoT solutions. Of course, solutions involving Things such as cameras, which involve high data throughput, are confined to wideband networks. Conversely, though, its high degree of penetration and low energy consumption by the Things mean that SIGFOX is an excellent addition. Therefore, the telecom operators GSM and SIGFOX, with mutually complementary technologies, have far more to gain by working together than by competing.

Figure 13.7 represents SIGFOX's footprint in the arena of range/power/bandwidth.

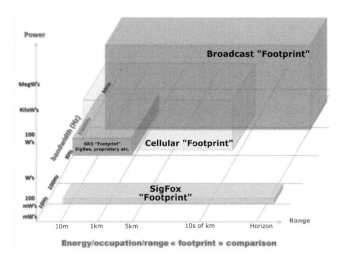

Figure 13.7. *SIGFOX footprint in terms of range/power/bandwidth. For a color version of this figure, see www.iste.co.uk/paret/connectedobjects.zip*

13.4.2.2. General overview of the solution

An overview of SIGFOX's proprietary product and service is shown in Figure 13.8. Its architecture is standard in the arena of IoT (for details on operation, look again at Chapter 10).

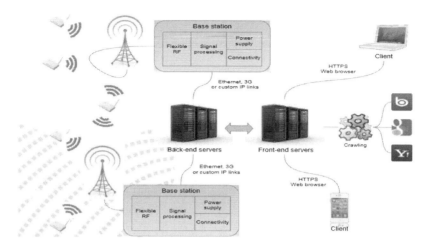

Figure 13.8. *Standard architecture of a SIGFOX structure*

13.4.2.3. *Technology – description*

Let us briefly describe the main technical features of SIGFOX technology.

General properties

The Thing always initiates communication, and may, if required, allow for bidirectional communication (Thing ↔ network). The network's structure is designed for short messages sent "every now and then". It is not a network designed/appropriate for the use of high-throughput signals that require wideband (e.g. multimedia, continuous broadcasting, etc.).

SIGFOX, in IoT, emphasizes its products' energy efficiency, meaning it can envisage building Things capable of running for years on a standard battery.

Technical properties of the network

The guidelines of the SIGFOX proprietary network must remain compatible with the following regulations:

– ETSI: maximum radiated power 25 mW e.r.p. = 14 dBm e.r.p.

Duty cycle $\delta = 1\%$ over 1 hour, i.e. 36 seconds/hour

– FCC: compatible with this standard.

Uplink – from the Thing to the network:

– unlicensed transmissions in the ISM bands, in accordance with the ETSI in Europe at 868 MHz and the FCC in the USA between 902 and 915 MHz;

NOTE 1.– in France, the SIGFOX network currently operates in the 868 MHz band, but it can also work very well at 68, 169, 433 MHz or 2.4 GHz;

NOTE 2.– at 868.00 and 868.60 MHz, in accordance with local legislation in Europe, the maximum transmitted power is limited to 25 mW e.r.p., with a maximum duty cycle of 1%;

NOTE 3.– LBT (Listen Before Talk) and/or AFA (Adaptive Frequency Agility) modes are not implemented in the (U)NB solution;

– use of a classic technique of carrier modulation: Differential Binary Phase Shift Keying (DBPSK);

NOTE 1.– Owing to UNB transmission, the use of DBPSK helps reduce the complexity of the modem's filter and of the base station architecture, using a simple quartz crystal as a clock reference, rather than a temperature-compensated oscillator (TCO);

NOTE 2.– The fact of using a (U)NB technique means that the noise density tends to be spread across the whole spectrum. Therefore, the SIGFOX signal, which is in a narrow portion of the spectrum, is more likely to be situated above the noise floor. The flip side of this is that the noise peaks located in narrow parts of the spectrum may interfere with the signal – see Figure 13.9;

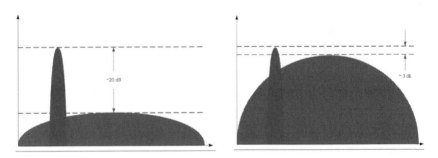

Figure 13.9. *Narrow Band signal as a function of interference in Wide Band. For a color version of this figure, see www.iste.co.uk/paret/connectedobjects.zip*

– baud rate is: 100 bauds in Europe,

                              600 bauds in the USA;

– very low communication throughput: 100 bits/sec;

– transmission bandwidth: 100 Hz;

– channelization mask: 100 Hz (600 Hz in the USA);

– precision of the central frequency: unimportant, because we suppose there is no significant frequency drift during the transmission of an uplink packet.

13.4.2.4. *Bidirectionality*

Usually, this technology is used in unidirectional operation, from the Thing to the network, but in certain conditions, it is capable of bidirectionality. This bidirectional communication is used for applications which need, from time to time, to send/transmit/push a configuration parameter to the Things. Even in this case, the Thing is in charge of initiating the communication, and may ask the central information system whether there are data to be downloaded; this function is implemented as "polling".

EXAMPLE.–

A thermostat reports the temperature every hour. Following one such transmission of data, it decides to actively listen for a few seconds longer (at most four times per day), to be able to receive an instruction to increase or decrease the temperature.

This way of working prevents the need for constant connection, and therefore means a two-directional communication can be established, whilst the system remains a low-energy one.

13.4.2.5. *Radiofrequency protocol*

Although it has not officially been divulged to the public (technical details available to professionals in the field, integrated circuit manufacturers, etc., on the signing of an NDA), this proprietary protocol designed for LR LTN UNB was put forward a few years ago for ETSI standardization and, in 2014, was freely published in ETSI LNT 001-003, and more recently (July 2016), by J-C. Zuniga and B. Ponsard, technical manager at SIGFOX and a member of the Network Working Group. In addition, it has been introduced many times, here and there, at numerous presentations by SIGFOX themselves.

Uplink – from the Thing to the network

With the SIGFOX uplink LR LTN UNB, the frame length of a Media Access Control (MAC) message is minimal, and it comprises (see Table 13.8a):

Uplink MAC Layer					
uplink frame					
Preamble	Frame Sync	Dev ID	Payload	Msg Auth Code	FCS
19 bits	29 bits	32 bits	0 – 96 bits	16 – 40 bits	16 bits
2 x 8 + 3	5 + 3 x 8	4 x 8	0 – 12 x8	2 x 8 to 5 x 8	2 x 8
2 bytes + (3 bits)	5 bits) + 3 bytes	4 bytes	0 – 12 bytes	2 – 5 bytes	2 bytes
total max		= 2 + 1 + 3 + 4 + 12 + 5 + 2 = 29 bytes max.			

Table 13.8a. *MAC frame on uplink*

a 4 byte identifier + payload + CRC + Frame scrambling and channel coding.

Let us discuss the fields in this frame in a little more detail:

– preamble	2 bytes + (3 bits)
– frame synchronization	5 bits + (2 bytes)
– unique identifier (ID) of the Thing	4 bytes
– payload	0–12 bytes
– authentication	variable length – 2-5 bytes
– frame check sequence (FCS):	2 bytes

Thus, we have a maximum total of around 26–28 bytes per frame to be transmitted.

a) For reasons of avoiding collisions with interfering transmissions, backend processing, coverage redundancy etc., the protocol absolutely requires that the message frame be repeated three times, altering the transmission frequency to three different pseudo-random frequencies in FHSS mode in the 868–868.6 MHz band; thus: one transmitted message = a burst of three frames.

b) Unique Identifiers – IDs.

This field, with a capacity of 4 bytes (32 bits), represents the possibility of identifying a little over 4 billion "unique elements".

Authors' note: having both experienced the saga of MiFace contactless chip cards from their creation, we feel this value is a little low, because fairly quickly, IDs had to grow to 64 or 96 bits, and in time, we foresee the need to change the size of this field if the IoT grows as expected!

c) The true maximum payload per message is 12 bytes, but messages can also be shortened to eight, six or even four bytes.

12 bytes is ample to cater for the needs of Things which transmit data for numerous applications, such as the placement of a device, an energy consumption reading, an alarm or any other type of sensor-based information.

There are no constraints on the way in which the payload is to be structured, and SIGFOX can neither interpret nor transform the payload. Only the user knows how it is structured.

d) Given that:

i) firstly, networks of this type operate at a very low data rate – typically 100 bits/s, and therefore a period of 10ms will be needed per bit, and the maximum authorized payload of a SIGFOX message is 12 bytes, with bytes of 8 bits ($12 \times 8 = 96$ bits), the duration for transmission of a payload will therefore be 0.960s – i.e. around 1 second;

ii) secondly, in the 868 MHz band in Europe, European regulation ERC 70 03/ETSI allows for a transmission duty cycle of only 1% per hour, i.e. at most 36 seconds of transmission/hour (3600s in an hour), and given that in SIGFOX, everything is predefined and non-configurable, the transmission of a single SIGFOX frame (4 byte identifier + payload + CRC + Frame scrambling and channel coding), with a payload of 12 bytes, so a total of around 26 bytes, which is $26 \times 8 = 208$ bits, may take around 2s, and for the sake of the surety of transmission (see below), it is compulsory to repeat it three times, so we have a message of up to $\sim 3 \times 2 = 6$ seconds, so a maximum of six messages per hour (one every ten minutes), or $6 \times 24 = 144$ messages per day.

iii) Roughly speaking, then, if we transmit messages of only a 4-byte payload, we should be able to transmit 250-300 messages per day, … but then we find that it is not authorized by SIGFOX! Perhaps the day will come when it will be…

The network was designed to handle Things which send one message each week or each month, up to a limit of one message every ten minutes. Thus, it must be borne in mind that if your system can cope with transmitting a maximum of six messages per hour (i.e. 140 messages per day), SIGFOX would be perfect, but if not, you need to investigate other solutions.

Downlink – from the network to the Thing

The format of the downlink frame is the following (see Table 13.8b):

Downlink MAC Layer					
downlink frame					
Preamble	Frame Sync	ECC	Payload	Msg Auth Code	FCS
91 bits	13 bits	32 bits	0 – 64 bits	16 bits	8 bits
11 x 8 + 3	5 + 1 x 8	4 x 8	0 – 8 x 8	2 x 8	1 x 8
11 bytes + (3 bits	5 bits) + 1 bytes	4 bytes	0 – 8 bytes	2 bytes	1 byte
total max.		= 11 + 1 + 1 + 4 + 8 + 2 + 1 = 28 bytes max.			

Table 13.8b. *MAC frame on downlink*

In Europe, in the (U)NB range of frequencies chosen for downlink (from the network to the Thing), between 869.40 and 869.65 MHz, the authorized power is 500 mW e.r.p., with a 10% duty cycle;

– GFSK is used for carrier modulation;

– baud rate: 600 bauds;

– dynamic selection of channelization mask;

– in receiver mode, it is recommended that the Thing have a sensitivity greater than -135 dBm. This value leads to a connection budget greater than $(14 + 135) =$ ~150 dBm. Higher values (around 162 dB) are generally achieved, and can be used to deliver long-range communications, much better than with GSM.

Note that with, say, a data rate of 100bit/s and a receiver sensitivity of -142/-143 dBm, we can obtain a BLER of around 10%.

To recap:

A BLER – block error ratio – is defined as the ratio between the number of erroneous blocks received and the total number of blocks sent. A block is considered erroneous if its cyclic redundancy check (CRC) is false.

Following specific events or at precise moments, in order for the Thing to be able to receive messages, we can also transmit to each device, a maximum of four messages per day, with a payload of eight bytes. The Thing must be programmed to request and then receive data from the server. The eight bytes sent to the Things can be used to send configuration data as and when required, but of course, we can optimize the battery life by using only unidirectional communications if the application does not need bidirectional communications.

Remarks on SIGFOX in the USA

In the USA, too, SIGFOX allows for 140 messages/day for uplink and four messages/day for downlink.

The most notable difference pertains to the throughput of the modulation used by the Thing, which, for the USA, is 600 bps (compared to 100 bps in Europe), and the maximum permissible transmitted power, which is 14 dBm e.r.p (in Europe) and 22 dBm e.r.p (i.e. 158 mWatts) in the USA.

Integrity of messages

It is the responsibility of the network to detect incoming messages, and validate and copy them. The message is then available in the SIGFOX cloud, and can then be transmitted to any third-party cloud chosen by the user.

Authentication of "non-replay" system

In addition to the mechanisms and CRC, frame obfuscation, coding of the channels via the Frequency Hopping (FHSS) algorithm mentioned above, and a sequence number to avoid the presence and need for a third-party element to transmit with an original identity (unique ID of the element), SIGFOX is based on network authentication.

Indeed, each message is signed with information specific to the element (including a unique key specific to the element) and to the message itself. Each message is authenticated by a hashing mechanism. This provides protection against "replay" attacks (when an attacker tries to replay the message), and prevents the alteration of authentic messages and identity theft. SIGFOX uses an encryption mechanism to authenticate the Thing. For its part, the content of the communication itself is not encrypted. Encryption and obfuscation of the payload data are not supported by SIGFOX itself, leaving it up to the end user to make the most appropriate choice based on his/her own applications.

Security, protection and data redundancy

Narrowband (NB) radio protocols also offer great structural strength and security against interference (difficulty in finding the transmitted frequencies) and obfuscation (look again at Figure 13.9). In addition, these problems can be detected by network notifications.

Data protection

– scrambling of the Thing's transmission is only possible when the scrambler is very close to the Thing;

– the Meta Data protocol includes a timestamp and a unique ID for each Thing. The data carried over the air contain time/date data identifiable for the client;

– the IDs and Payloads of the things are very short in terms of time, and in terms of data transmission, there is an optimal ratio between payload, device ID, timestamp, etc. (1.6-second message, 1-1.8-second frame, 3-frame burst duration of up to 6 seconds);

– the radiated RF signal is of low power (initial value at most 25 mW), and almost always hidden in the ambient noise.

Transmission redundancy

Using a narrowband communication model, to prevent potential obfuscations, the systematic repetition of the same messages on the same frequency or the same channel, the Things implement systems with frequency agility or frequency hopping (FHSS). These devices are also used to combat difficulties due to the properties of multi-path propagation and, applied to each message, to each transmission frame, the consequence of this is major difficulty in finding and scrambling the signal.

However, despite the pseudo-random nature of the frequency-hopping sequence (as is generally required by the regulation), a packet/message may be lost, and/or subsequently, we may see a loss of synchronization of hops between transmission and reception channels, thus hopping into a channel that is already occupied and/or transmitting on that frequency during a transmission the device is awaiting. In addition, any loss of synchronization between the transmitter and the receiver requires Thing/base station couples to observe a period of rediscovery and recovery of synchronization. In SIGFOX, with the exception of a few bytes of bit synchronization, no synchronization is needed, regardless of the Thing's static frequency error (low frequency precision).

The obligation to use frequency hops also leads to an increase/redundancy of packets/messages, which is the case here, threefold. Although narrowband receivers generally require only a short preamble to synchronize, we have to retransmit a message header so that the receiver can be sure that the transmission received is actually addressed to it. In addition, for the purpose of security, most frequency-hopping systems remain active for a further few milliseconds on the last channel on which they have just transmitted, to minimize the likelihood of this channel being blocked by another, undesired transmission. Thus, in the case of a low-data-rate narrowband transmission, this significantly increases the overload.

13.4.2.6. *Conclusions*

We have now described the main features and operation of layers I (physical) and II (MAC – Medium Access Control) of the OSI model as applied to SIGFOX.

Now, as all the rest of the network structure is proprietary, there is nothing else to explain, and we now only need to send the "payloads" of 12 bytes of data to a "SIGFOX UHF antenna (+ base)", deported to a long range, which, in turn, acts as an Internet bridge via a new connection – once again, a totally proprietary SIGFOX connection (xDSL, backed up by a 3G or GSM, etc., connection), a satellite connection to a SIGFOX cloud, in which your millions of precious data of 12 bytes from the Things belonging to you will be carefully arranged instantaneously (…and those of many others as well, for the same price!). Next, using Cloud Computing tools (for example, see Chapter 17, AWS from Amazon, Azure by Microsoft, etc.), you can work on your own collected data, to present (and sell or use) applications to your end clients.

Having completed our examination of NB LR LTN IoT, let us move on to DSSS LR LTN IoT! Goodness – this looks like Double Dutch!

13.4.3. *LR LTN in DSSS (spectrum spreading) – LoRa, from Semtech*

LoRa, which is the abbreviated form of "Long Range" is a wireless technology for a LPWAN (also French) and was designed by the Grenoble startup Cycléo SAS France, bought up in 2012 by the American Semtech Corporation.

Figure 13.10. *LoRA logo*

13.4.3.1. *LoRa, LoRaWAN and LoRaWAN Alliance*

Before going any further, it is important to immediately point out that the term LoRa, taken in isolation, describes the proprietary protocol of the physical layer (PHY – layer 1 in the OSI model), and absolutely does not describe the functions of the upper layers, dubbed LoRaWAN which, for their part, in certain conditions, are open to the public through the "LoRaWAN Alliance" and, precisely because of this openness, LoRa requires far more explanation in this book than its predecessor did, SIGFOX !

NOTE 1.– LoRa, LoRaWAN and Semtech are Semtech registered trademarks.

NOTE 2.– LoRa is an open alliance, in the sense that any organization can buy LoRa hardware and build its own networks without going through any centralized authority or having to pay fees.

13.4.3.2. *LoRa – physical layer*

To avoid any confusion and remedy any ambiguity, LoRa is the particular implementation of a proprietary physical PHY layer which is fundamentally agnostic to the possible implementations of the upper layers. This means, for example, that if we so desire, LoRa can coexist and be interoperable with different pre-existing network architectures.

In the LoRa physical layer, we can design modems (in the true physical sense of the word: "modulator–demodulator"), to achieve long-range RF communications with a high degree of immunity from interference, and to minimize the Things' energy consumption.

In order to do this (…and to make things easy ☺!), LoRa technology uses:

– a carrier modulation technique: classic (G)BPSK (Gaussian Binary Phase Shift Keying);

– this is embellished with a conventional technique: Direct Sequence Spread Spectrum, which increases the transmitted bandwidth and makes the transmitted signal appear similar to noise (see numerous technical details on DSSS and its peculiarities in Dominique Paret's *RFID en UHF et SHF*, from Dunod);

– using a special additional technique of "chip" bit coding, known as "chirp spread spectrum" (CSS), patented by Semtech and described as a "frequency modulated (FM) chirp", with which it is possible to negotiate between elements as to the bit rates depending on the desired sensitivity in a channel of a given bandwidth;

– this technique, "DSSS – CSS", uses a variable data rate and orthogonal spreading factors (Orthogonal Sequence Spread Spectrum – OSSS), which enables the system designer to negotiate a data rate on the basis of the distance or power emitted by the Thing, so as to optimize the network performances with a constant bandwidth;

– with this modulation technique, it is possible to transmit data with a signal at a level much lower than the noise floor;

– owing to the technique "DSSS–CSS" and the level of the signal, a channel-coding correction, known as FEC, for forward error correction, is built in, with a view to significantly increasing the resistance to interference;

– at the time of writing, there are many component manufacturers offering integrated circuits. Examples include Semtech, STMicroelectronics and Microchip.

This proprietary technique, "DSSS + CSS", which is very precise, very advanced and complex to implement both in terms of transmission and reception (hence the numerous Semtech patents!), lends a system the following general technical properties and abilities:

– high receiver sensitivity of around –148 dBm;

– demodulating a signal at around –20 dB below the noise floor;

– delivering long-range connectivity (>15 km);

– reducing the Things' energy consumption (the devices can thus operate on batteries for 8-10 years, depending on the applications);

– supporting a high capacity of nodes (up to 1 million nodes);

– a reduced synchronization overhead;

– avoiding or reducing hops when using mesh networks;

– establishing robust, secure and efficient communications;

– additionally, facilitating localization applications;

– and finally, lending significant advantages over conventional modulation techniques by providing answers to the traditional design compromise between distance, immunity from interference and energy consumption.

13.4.4. *A discussion of spectrum spreading – SS*

To help you in the reading of this part of the chapter, here are some (lengthy) technical discussions necessary for proper understanding and assimilation of what follows.

13.4.4.1. *SS – Spread Spectrum*

Before going into detail on these techniques, in SS and similar systems, it is necessary to define a few new generic terms.

13.4.4.2. *DSSS – "Direct Sequence Spread Spectrum"*

The technique of DSSS is a specific method whereby the spectrum of RF signals radiated is spread during the final modulation of the carrier by the presence of a "spreading sequence" included in the modulating signal.

Briefly put, generally, in the traditional DSSS technique, the signal modulating the radiated RF carrier (often by phase modulation) is typically obtained by "multiplying" the initial information signal (the data/useful data to be transmitted) by a pseudo-random digital signal (known as a "spreading code" or "chip sequence" – see later on) whose frequency/chip rate is equal to several times that of the bit rate. The result of this technique is that (quite unlike what happens with FHSS), the spectrum of the radiated signal on a carrier whose value is constant has a much wider spectrum than the spectrum representing the initial data signal – see Figure 13.11.

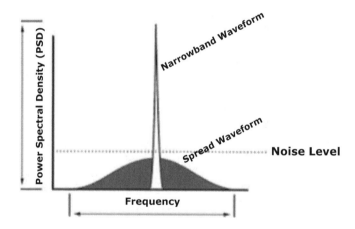

Figure 13.11. *Comparison between an NB-modulated signal and a signal having undergone spectrum spreading with DSSS*

NOTE.–

When we speak of "phase modulation", it implies, somewhere, PSK, BPSK, QPSK, xQAM, etc., so numerous states, and hence, the ideas of symbols and relations between bit rates, symbol rates, and randomization of the energy with an energy spreading sequence, using a particular pseudo-random sequence.

Let us present a few explanations of certain terms specific to these modulation techniques.

Chip (in terms of digital radio communication)

The DSSS technique uses a preparatory device for spectrum spreading of the radiated signal, one of the main elements in which is the so-called "chip".

The term "chip" is used to represent the smallest possible coding data element for spectrum spreading of the data to be transmitted, in relation to the longest bit of non-coded information.

Figure 13.12 illustrates the concept of a "chip".

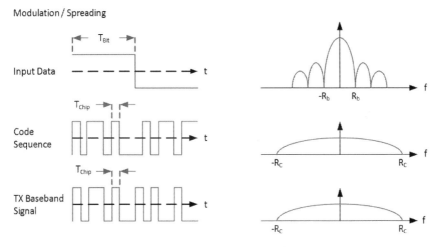

Figure 13.12. *Representation of a "chip"*

The chip is defined by its value, its length/duration and its data rate.

– its value

- a chip may take one of two values: -1/+1 in polar notation, or 0/1 in binary notation;

– its length/duration: t_chip

- the chip signal obviously has its own specific duration – t_chip (generally expressed in µs). Although in principle, it is not obligatory, in practice, it is generally a whole sub-multiple of the duration of the data bit;

– its "chip rate": Rc

- when we speak of duration we must speak of data rate as well. By definition, the value of that data rate "Rc", expressed in chips/s, is called the "chip rate", and of course, corresponds to the inverse value of t_chip.

Processing gain

The "processing gain – PG" is one of the main parameters of SS systems. It is also often defined in the literature as being the "spreading ratio" or "spreading factor – SF" of the spectrum.

$$PG = SF = \frac{\text{Value of the "spread" bandwidth}}{\text{Value of the bandwidth of the baseband signal}}$$

Whichever the SS technique employed, the larger this ratio is, the greater the bandwidth of the communication channel will be, the more the spectrum is spread, and the better the overall spreading performances will be. Consequently, this parameter helps to determine numerous qualities such as the maximum number of users the system can support, the quality of the multi-path reduction effect, resistance to obfuscation, quality of signal detection, etc. Thus, it is important indeed!

In DSSS, the spectrum spreading value PG or SF above is also expressed by the ratio between the "chips per bit" to the sequence of chips for the desired data rate. Thus, we can rewrite the above equation as the ratio:

Processing Gain of DSSS = SF = rate_chip/rate_bit = t_bit/t_chip

or, expressed in dB.

$Gp = 10 \times \log (Rc / Rb)$ in dB

or Rc = chip rate (in chips/second)

Rb = bit rate (in bits/second)

Once again, the higher this ratio is, the greater the bandwidth of the communication channel will be, the greater the spectrum spreading, and the better the overall performances.

For information:

– the American regulatory body, the FCC, allows no values under 10;

– for example, IEEE 802.11 (Wi-Fi) imposes a processing gain of 11;

– the majority of commercial systems work with a value of around 20 and for LoRa, the SF value sits at between 7 and 12.

All things being equal, in comparison to FHSS, DSSS is capable of achieving much higher digital data rates in Mbit/s.

Spreading sequence

The "spreading sequence" is the pseudo-random sequence (based on a "Pseudo-Random Noise Code" – see next section) of data coding elements (chips), used to code each bit of the logic data. In order to properly understand how it works, let us examine how its content is made up.

Length of the sequence or number of chips "n"

In principle, the number "n" may take any value. In fact, all other things being equal, the longer the sequence, the greater the desired spectrum spreading effect will be.

Duration of the sequence

The duration of the spreading sequence is, obviously, linked firstly to the number of chips "n" present in the sequence, and to the duration t_chip of each of them. Thus, duration = "n" × (t_chip).

REMARK.– the data rate of the sequence is equal to that of the chip rate.

The hitch – there is indeed a hitch – stems simply from the fact that generally, we want that duration to be equal to the duration of the data bit, but on the other hand, we want the value of "n" to be as high as possible. At high data rates (high bit rates), this sets the bar pretty high in terms of the duration of t_chip!

Its value

The value of this spreading sequence is not in any way insignificant. Indeed, it must be such that the result obtained when the signal is processed results in a spread spectrum of the signal... but not spread in any which way!

To do it right – i.e. to create a system that is resistant to obfuscation, to espionage-type detection, etc. – the spectrum obtained must be as close as possible to that of white noise, so that all the components of the spectrum are represented and the spreading is as close to perfect as possible. With this in mind, we need to look at the way in which its structure is set up.

Structure of its value

To ensure that the "spreading sequence", made up of chips with the values −1 or +1 (in polar values) or 0 or 1 (in binary values) has properties similar to that of noise (preferably white noise), there must be a very weak correlation between the codes of the sequence, which must be "Pseudo-Random Noise codes" – abbreviated as "PNcodes".

Pseudo-Random Noise Codes, or "PNcodes"

To be usable for DSSS applications, a PNcode must satisfy the following requirements:

– the sequence must be constructed on two levels (which is, thankfully, the case... phew!);

– the codes must have a low cross-correlation value. The lower that value, the more potential users will be able to use the same band. This must be true for all or parts of the PNcode. This remark stems from the fact that in most applications, the Things randomly pass into the electromagnetic field, at unforeseen times, and two or more PNcodes may overlap at any time and in any way, which may cause problems for dynamic management of the collisions engendered;

– the PNcodes must be "balanced", meaning that the ratio between the number of "1s" and "0s" is equal to 1, in order to ensure a uniform spread of the spectral density over the whole extent of the frequency band;

– the PNcodes must have precise auto-correlation (of the width of a chip) to validate the synchronization of the code.

In practice, for DSSS applications, the PNcodes stem from "Walsh-Hadamard" codes, "M-sequences", "Gold-codes" or "Kasami-codes". From a mathematical point of view... and a very distant vantage point as well... these sets of codes may be divided into two categories: orthogonal and non-orthogonal codes. (Orthogonal codes are codes such that there is no interaction between the results obtained).

Walsh sequences belong to the first category, whilst the others are part of the sequences obtained with well-known shift registers. PNcode sequences, therefore, are easy to create.

In DSSS systems, when the length of the shift register is "n", we can say that the period of the groups of codes cited above is such that the length of the code is the same as that of the spreading factor. This being the case, if we combine each "data symbol" with a complete PNcode, the "DS processing gain" is equal to the length of the code and, for all the reasons mentioned above, it is easy to obtain high levels of DS processing gain.

Chirp

In its general form, the term "chirp" conveys a good idea of the content of birdsong, and the vocalizations of cetaceans, dolphins and bats. To conclude this zoological documentary paragraph, note that certain fish emit chirps to communicate with one another.

After this brief detour into the animal kingdom, to return to the realm of the technical, in our profession, a chirp is, by definition, a pseudoperiodic signal C modulated firstly in frequency, around a sinusoidal carrier frequency and, secondly, simultaneously, in amplitude by an envelope signal a whose variations are slow in relation to the frequency of oscillations of the phase ϕ. The real part of the signal, therefore, is written thus:

$$c(t) = a(t) \cos \phi(t)$$

The simplest chirp, the most common, called a linear chirp, has a linear frequency ramp and a constant envelope. Figure 13.13 shows the example of a chirp with linear frequency modulation and constant amplitude.

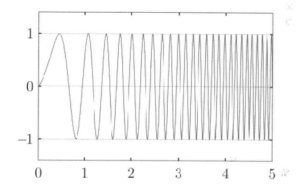

Figure 13.13. *Representation of a "linear chirp"*

Thus, its equation is:

$$c(t) = Ae^{i(a.t + b).t + c}$$

As the basic pulse of the chirp is of finite duration, the equation of its amplitude is a gate function.

If the signal has a duration of T and begins at t = 0, the frequency band Δf swept is centered on fo, that signal is written:

$$c(t) = \begin{cases} Ae^{i2\pi(f_0 + \frac{\Delta f}{2T}.t - \frac{\Delta f}{2})t} & \text{if } 0 \le t < T \\ 0 & \text{else} \end{cases}$$

We can show that if the product Δf.T >> 1, the amplitude of the linear chirp spectrum can be approximated by the following function:

$$G(f) = A\sqrt{\frac{T}{4\Delta f}} \text{ if } |f - f_0| \le \frac{\Delta f}{2}$$

and its value is almost null everywhere else.

Chirp spread spectrum – CSS

CSS has been in use in radar applications since WWII (so, strictly speaking, our exposé on it is hardly a scoop!). The concept of chirp spread spectrum (CSS) is a well-known spectrum spreading technique using frequency-modulated chirp pulses to over-encode the basic binary information. (See Dominique Paret's *RFID en UHF et SHF*, from Dunod.) In recent years, this modulation technique has seen the field of its applications broaden, because of new possibilities for operating at relatively low transmission powers, and the high intrinsic robustness of channel degradation mechanisms such as multipath, fading, the Doppler effect and the presence of scramblers in the band.

A physical layer, "PHY CSS", has also been adopted for applications requiring long operating range and mobility performances better than those obtained with the physical layers O-QPSK DSSS PHY of the IEEE standard 802.15.4 for Low-Rate Wireless Personal Area Networks (LR-WPANs)

To return to our subject and to IoT applications, the technique of CSS exhibits interesting specific advantages:

– as is the case with other spectrum spreading methods, CSS uses the whole of the allocated bandwidth to broadcast a signal, rendering it robust against channel noise;

– because the chirp uses a broad spectrum, CSS offers very good resistance to multi-path fading, even in cases of very low received power levels;

– in addition, chirp spread spectrum is resistant against the Doppler effect, which typically plagues mobile radio applications.

13.4.4.3. *LoRa and the Chirp Spread Spectrum – CSS*

Following these theoretical (...but necessary) diversions, let us finally come back to LoRa!

Although the LoRa physical layer is proprietary and not open to the public, we find a very great deal of information detailing its operation, either in the patents published by François Sforza (head of Cycléo, now taken over by Semtech) – primarily the documents EP2278724 A1 (2009) and WO2011000936 A1 (2010) – or in numerous application notes from Semtech Corporation that are available on the Web: particularly note *AN1200.22 LoRa™ Modulation Basics* from May 2015, or ETSI's LTN 003, published in 2014.

Spectrum spreading with LoRa modulation is achieved by generating a chirp whose frequency constantly varies. One of the advantages of this method is that the temporal and frequential shifts between the transmitter and receiver are equivalent, which considerably reduces the design complexity of the receiver. In addition, the bandwidth of that chirp is equivalent to the spectral bandwidth of the signal. The sought data signal is chipped at a higher data rate, modulated on the chirp signal.

Orthogonal Sequence Spread Spectrum - OSSS implementation

The so-called Orthogonal Sequence Spread Spectrum – OSSS – technique which we mentioned earlier is known for its effectiveness in:

– obtaining good spectral efficiency, mainly in cases of high density;

– increasing the reception sensitivity and thus extending the transmission range, even in cases of limited transmission power.

Implementation of OSSS transmission

The main radio specifications of the OSSS link are described in ETSI LTN 003:

– chip rate: 8 kbits/s – 500 kbits/s;

– data rate: 30 bit/s – 50 kbit/s;

– channelization mask: 8 kHz – 500 kHz (depending on spreading factor);

– modulation scheme: equivalent to DSSS with orthogonal signaling;

– recommended receiver sensitivity: better than –135 dBm;

– center frequency accuracy: one quarter of the chip rate (e.g. 868 MHz and 125 kbit/s gives 35 ppm);

– intra-packet frequency drift: not relevant, provided the crystal quart of the oscillator is properly defined.

Structure of OSSS PHY frame

The OSSS physical frame is made up of (see Figure 13.14):

– a preamble of 12 symbols (eight of which are for detection of the signal and four are for synchronization);

– a header field, containing the packet size, fragmentation flag, coding rate and CRC flag;

– a header CRC that verifies the physical header integrity;

– a payload field that carries the OSSS MAC frame.

Field Size	12 symbols	20 bits		variable
Field Name	Preamble	Physical Header	Header CRC	Physical Payload

Note: The sizes of the fields in the OSSS PHY frame are given in symbols or in bits, because their true sizes depend on the OSSS spreading factor

Figure 13.14. *OSSS physical frame*

Structure of the OSSS MAC frame

The OSSS MAC frame is represented in Figure 13.15. Its format is in keeping with the recommendations of IEEE standard 802.15.4.

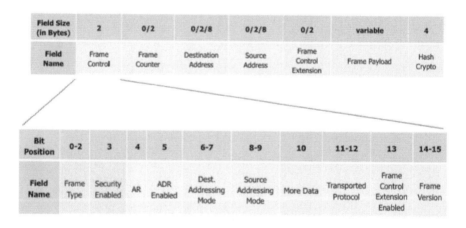

Figure 13.15. *Format of the OSSS frame*

A few calculations

To begin with, remember that the packet is divided into a number of different elements, as Figure 13.16 shows.

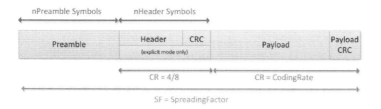

Figure 13.16. *Format of the LoRa packet*

Knowing that the LoRa specification defines chirp rates as being called SFs ("spreading factors"), and if we set:

SF = spreading factor (7..12),

BW = bandwidth of the modulation (Hz),

for LoRa modulations, the relations between the bitrate of the data sought, the data rate/symbol rate can be expressed as follows:

Remembering that the bandwidth BW defines the chip rate, the time/duration of the symbol Ts is defined as the time taken to send 2^{SF} chips at the data rate of the chip rate, i.e.:

$$Ts = \frac{2^{SF}}{BW} \; secs$$

The symbol rate Rs is therefore equal to the inverse of this value – i.e.:

$$Rs = \frac{1}{Ts} = \frac{BW}{2^{SF}} \; symbols/sec$$

Thus, let us define the bit rate Rb of the modulation:

$$R_b = SF * \frac{1}{\left\lceil \dfrac{2^{SF}}{BW} \right\rceil} \; bits/sec$$

In addition, the chip rate Rc is:

$$Rc = Rs * 2^{SF} \ chips/sec$$

As, by definition, the LoRa specification states that: "…one chip is sent per second per Hz of bandwidth…":

$$Rc = \frac{BW}{2^{SF}} * 2^{SF} \ chips/sec$$

In order to improve the robustness of the transmitted signal and avoid redundancy (e.g. absence of message retransmission), LoRa modulation also includes FEC (Forward Error Corrections). This leads us to redefine and rewrite the equation of the nominal bit rate of the data signal in the form:

$$R_b = SF * \frac{Code\ Rate}{\left[\dfrac{2^{SF}}{BW} \right]} \ bits/sec$$

where the "code rate" is:

$$Code\ Rate = \frac{4}{4 + CR}$$

In these equations:

CR = code rate (1..4)

SF = spreading factor (7..12);

BW = modulation bandwidth (Hz).

We can immediately see the new value of Rb:

$$R_b = SF * \frac{\left[\dfrac{4}{4 + CR} \right]}{\left[\dfrac{2^{SF}}{BW} \right]}$$

NOTE.–

To easily evaluate the data rate for different configuration options, Semtech offers a "LoRa Modem Calculator", downloadable from its website: semtech.com/ apps/filedown/down.php?file=SX1272LoRaCalculatorSetup1%271.zip

In concrete terms, as the LoRa physical layer is based on the general principle of DSSS, it is still possible to obtain greater sensitivity of Processing Gain thanks to a modem that can filter the message signal content while the constant ramp signal of the chirp is present. To this effect, a long "constant chirp" preamble (the eight symbols mentioned above) is transmitted in order to lock the LoRa signal (see Figure 13.17). Hence, we can obtain a very high receiver sensitivity by using integrated circuits and inexpensive quartz chips in spite of the very low level of power transmitted, and therefore received at the other end.

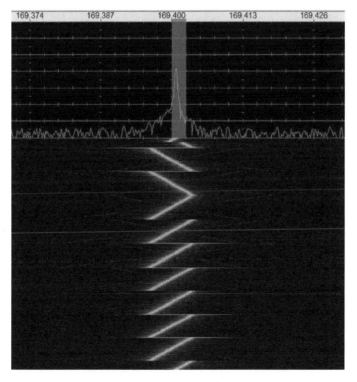

Figure 13.17. *Demodulation of the LoRa Semtech preamble. For a color version of this figure, see www.iste.co.uk/paret/connectedobjects.zip*

This preamble can be defined as a variable number of "symbols", which are simply the number of chirps. As one might imagine, there is no difference in selectivity between a preamble generated by one LoRa transmitter and one generated by another. If there is a constant chirp, at the correct frequency and the right chirp rate, a LoRa demodulator will listen to it, whether or not it comes from an expected system. The management of a LoRa reception system must therefore be able to deal with not only normal power interference, but LoRa interference as well.

Once the LoRA modem is locked onto the signal of the preamble, the end of the preamble is indicated by a "reverse chirp" – see Figure 13.18. Then begins the data transmission, which comprises a series of "symbols" that function much like M-ary FSK symbols, but occurs rather like chirps. See Figure 13.18 and https://www.link-labs.com/what-is-lora/

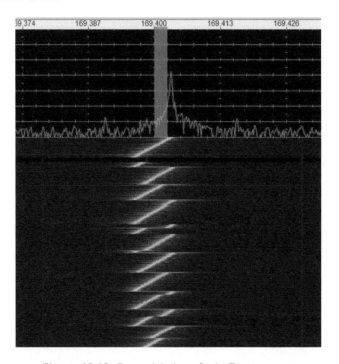

Figure 13.18. *Demodulation of a LoRa message*

LoRa is also able to demodulate several "orthogonal" or simultaneous signals transmitted on the same frequency, as long as they have different chirp rates, meaning that all gateways are able to decode various "tones" of chirps and build very broad networks.

Whilst respecting the regulation on the 1% maximum duty cycle, LoRa offers greater resources and standard transmission data rate possibilities (from 300bit/s to 6kbit/s), and is therefore capable of transmitting more messages per hour;

– on the other hand, the data rate influences the possible transmission distance that the message is able to travel. That distance is linked to the type of network to which we are connected, and also to whether or not the element is mobile and/or the quest for better communication conditions. Ultimately, though, for radio quality similar to that of the SIGFOX-style network (300 bit/s), we can expect to double the number of messages;

– based on the fact that LoRa transmission does not require a message-repeat procedure, we can also expect to transmit three times more messages than with a LTN NB-style network;

– the protocol also enables us to define, as desired, the size of the messages to be transferred and, if we reduce the messages to six bytes, this enables us again to approximately double the number of messages;

– by combining all the points described in the last few paragraphs, we can hope to transfer over twelve times more messages per day in comparison to a LTN NB-style network. In addition, if we operate with 6 kbit/s communication, we can increase this to over 240 times more! Instead of having an LTN NB limit of one message per 10 minutes, this means that with LTN in DSSS, we can send around one message per 50s, or up to one every three seconds!

LoRA in the USA

American Things, instead of operating in DSSS mode, must be capable of operating in the UHF band from 902 to 928 MHz, in FHSS mode (in this band, according to the FCC, the maximum permissible power is 20 dBm, and the transmission time on a frequency must not exceed 400 ms), and the devices must have a data channel structure to store the parameters of 72 channels. (Note: a data channel structure corresponds to a frequency and a series of data throughput rates which can be used on that frequency).

If we wish to use the procedure of activation of a Thing "*over-the-air*", the terminal must, at random, broadcast the JoinReq message, alternately on one 125 kHz channel out of the 64 channels defined with the DR0 parameter (DR stands for data rate), and one random 500 kHz channel out of the eight channels defined with DR4 (see Figure 13.19). The terminal must change the channel for each transmission.

Upstream						
Channels			linearly incremented by	BWkHz	P_max dBm	
n b	n°	from ... to				
6 4	0–63	902.3 MHz 914.99 MHz	200 kHz	125	+ 30	DR0 to DR3
8	64–71	903.0 MHz 914.2 MHz	1.6 MHz	500	+ 26	DR4
Downstream						
8	0–7	923.3 MHz to 927.5 MHz	600 kHz	500	+ 26	DR10 to DR13

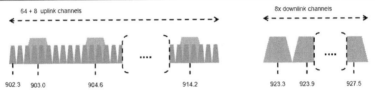

Figure 13.19. *Specifications of LoRa for the USA. For a color version of this figure, see www.iste.co.uk/paret/connectedobjects.zip*

LoRA in China

In the same spirit as in Europe and the USA, the Chinese ISM band is defined as being between 779 and 787 MHz, to be used only with a power EIRP less than 10 mW (i.e. 10 dBm) and duty cycle less than 1%.

In this band, we should see a data channel structure to store the parameters of at least 16 channels. (A data channel structure corresponds to a frequency and a set of 16 data rates that can be used on that frequency.)

The first three channels correspond to the frequencies 779.5, 779.7 and 779.9 MHz, with DR0 to DR5, and must be implemented in each Thing. These default channels are non-modifiable, and provide a minimal common channel between the Things and the gateways of all networks. The other channels can be freely distributed across the whole range of authorized frequencies on a network-by-network basis.

13.4.4.4. LoRa™ Alliance and LoRaWAN

LoRa Alliance

The "LoRa Alliance" (in France, notable members are Bouygues Telecom, Orange, Actility, Qowisio, etc. – see Figure 13.20) was set up in early 2015 by Semtech to demonstrate and promote, to public and private operators, the capacities of the LoRa platform and network which, unlike the closed solution SIGFOX, are open. The standardized specification of its communication protocol is known as "LoRaWAN".

Figure 13.20. *Logo and members of the LoRa Alliance*

It should also be noted that, at the start, the "LoRa Alliance" was created to standardize, and make public, the properties of the MAC layer 2 and above in the OSI model of the LoRa concept, with spectrum spreading technology, from 290 bps to 50 kbps, >50 bytes/frame and oriented for the ITU regions operating in the ISM bands at 868 and 915 MHz.

NOTE.–

LoRa is an open alliance, in the sense that any organization can buy LoRa hardware and build its own networks without going through any centralized authority and having to pay fees.

This technical openness means, in terms of commerce, that we can construct three main families of network development:

– a totally private, proprietary solution, using only the LoRa physical layer and the components managing this bottom layer;

– use of LoRaWAN product(s) connected to a private LoRaWAN network;

– or finally, the use of LoRaWAN product(s) connected to a LoRaWAN network, operated by a conventional operator.

LoRaWAN™

LoRaWAN is the acronym for "Long Range Wide-Area Network".

LoRaWAN is a communication protocol developed in cooperation with numerous actors in the LoRa Alliance. This model, which is open to the coexistence of multiple operators belonging to the alliance in the same geographic area, naturally led to the development of an interoperable standard, meaning terminals using LoRa technology can operate on the various networks employed internationally – both in the private and public domain.

Structure of a LoRaWAN

A wide-area network based on the LoRaWAN protocol, facilitating low-data-rate RF communication between Things using LoRa technology, uses a standard structure comprising the four main entities of an IoT network described in Chapter 10, and is connected to the Internet via gateways, as in the very typical setup illustrated by Figure 13.21. Thus, it is possible to design global applications for the Internet of Things, machine-to-machine (M2M) networks, and smart cities.

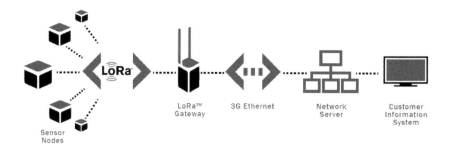

Figure 13.21. *Standard architecture of a LoRA and LoRAWAN system*

Gateway

In view of the fact that the majority of LoRa operators are also GSM/cell operators, the infrastructures already in place on the ground can often be reused – in particular the high points and infrastructure capabilities which are unused by the main harvesting network.

Server

The LoRa network server manages the network. Its role is to take measures to eliminate duplicate packets, organize acknowledgements, adapt data rates, etc.

Content of the layers of LoRAWAN

The layers in the LoRaWAN™ standard contain numerous points, affecting varied domains, of very different levels. The standard comprises parts pertaining to all the upper layers of the OSI and TCP/IP models. Simply in keeping with the flow of the concept of LoRA, it is presented here (see Figure 13.22), but this presentation could also belong in Chapter 16.

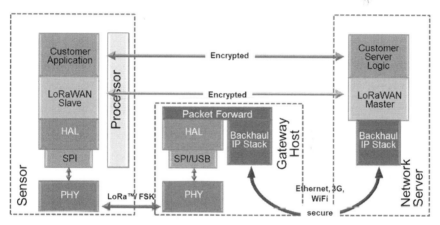

Figure 13.22. *Content of the layers of the LoRaWAN™ standard*

Its many qualities are listed below:

– it is a specification for a Low Power Wide Area Network (LPWAN), designed for wireless Things, powered by batteries and used in a regional, national or global network;

– it corresponds to layer 2 and numerous functions of the upper layers (3, 4, 5 and 6) of the OSI model, such as gateways, boosters, addressing, adaptive data rate, message repetition, message receipt confirmation and high capacity OFDM of downloaded signals;

– it is perfectly well suited for applications in ITU region 1, where the restrictions of duty cycles by the ETSI considerably limit the role that the base station can play in the network (duty cycle $\delta = 1\%$ and 10% in the bands around 868 MHz);

– it was originally designed for applications greatly orientated toward uplink connections, where a great many devices are present, or for applications where only a few downlink messages are required (limited either by the applications at hand or by the number of Things involved);

– it caters for the main requirements of the Internet of Things, and possible location services, mobility and secure bidirectional communications;

– it offers interoperability between smart Things without the need for complex local installations, giving businesses a measure of freedom back;

– it generally involves a star network topology, where the gateways are transparent bridges relaying messages between the Things and a central network server at the backend;

– the gateways are connected to the network server via standard IP connections, although the Things use simple wireless communications with one or more gateways;

– all the Thing's communications are generally bidirectional, but also support operations such as multi-casting, allowing for "over the air" software updates or other mass distribution messages in order to reduce communication time on the air;

– it defines a bit rate of 300 bit/s to 50 kbit/s.

– the selection of the data exchange rate is a compromise between the desired/necessary range and the duration of the communication message;

– the communications between the Things and gateways are spread over channels of different frequencies, which may have different bit rate values;

– owing to the spectrum spreading technology used, communications with different data rates do not interfere with one another, and create a set of "virtual" channels, increasing the gateway's capacity;

– in order to maximize both the battery life of the Things and the overall capacity of the network, the LoRaWAN network server is able to individually manage the data rate and RF output power of each Thing, using an Adaptive Data Rate (ADR) setup, which is generally updated every 24 hours;

– it provides easier interoperability between Smart "Things" without the need for complex local installations, further facilitating the Internet of Things;

– it is a server-side implementation of a multi-access protocol designed to minimize collisions with a large number of Things. This requires an application server to execute the MAC functions on a network connection;

– the client logic is integrated into the network server;

– gateways situated in the same network need a synchronization device;

– it requires several antenna devices, because all the Gateways are listening to the same uplink channels.

Security of the LoRaWAN protocol

To begin with, the national/international networks aimed at applications for secure connected Things, such as critical/essential infrastructures, confidential/personal data or essential functions for the companies in which they are implemented, have specific needs to secure the communications.

Encryption and encryption keys

Beyond the encryption and authentication carried out in AES CCM (128-bit) and in many other systems as well, in LoRaWAN, this has been solved by multiple layers of encryption, implementing three different levels of encryption to ensure security for the infrastructures;

– unique Network session key (EUI 64), ensuring security at the level of the server/network;

– unique Application session key (EUI 64), ensuring security for the Application server/Application;

– Device/Application-specific keys (EUI 128) for the Thing/terminal.

This means that, in the presence of multiple networks, public and private, operating on the same frequencies, we can be sure, firstly, of not handling the data from another network, and secondly, that a third party cannot eavesdrop on the data from our own device.

Attacks/Obfuscations in RF

A second important aspect of security lies in being able to deal with scenarios where an attacker seemingly tries to cut off / switch off / prevent you from receiving communications from your Thing. As in the LR LTN NB or DSSS networks (such as SIGFOX or LoRa), we cannot stop a remote Thing from transmitting, because by its very function, it is capable of transmitting without authorization, whenever, and wherever it is. To carry out such attacks, the easiest course of action is to prevent/interfere with the reception of its signal. In addition, by general principle, whether the Thing is SIGFOX or LoRa, its reception can only be disturbed when a high-powered transmitter is situated nearby to the transmitting device itself, and therefore, the only way to completely cut off communication would be to generate a high level of power or noise as close as possible to the antenna of each of the Things in the network... which is physically impossible to do!

LoRaWAN requires the Thing to receive the configuration from the network channel during the connection sequence, once it has received that information, it can begin to communicate independently. The connection sequence is initiated at the first communication and, when the Thing is not mobile, we can suppose that it has already been done before the attacker commences his/her attack. When a Thing is mobile, we can assume that it will need to reconnect whenever it passes from one cell to another; in this scenario, we can discontinue all subsequent communication from the Thing.

Configurations of the Things

The third facet to be taken into consideration is that of the configuration of the Things, which is connected to security.

On LoRa, as indicated previously, we have to define all the encryption keys. As one of them is linked to the network, we need to change the key as a function of the network operator we choose. In certain cases, this is not a problem, but in most cases, we must devise a method to configure the Thing on the site where it is to be installed and operate. That strategy would resemble connectivity in the style of BLE or Wi-Fi or USB, enabling the end user to perform this final configuration. This is a complexity of hardware that must be examined and resolved, and we also need to study its effect on the industrial process. In case of a private network, it is possible to simplify this step.

These last two configuration sequences, then, are involved in the security of the communication.

Network architectures

A fourth aspect also needs to be taken into account. The world of IoT is truly different from conventional modes. Indeed, in order to limit the quantity of data needing to be transmitted, and to simplify the communication protocol, the data received must pass through a network operator interface. The operator stores the data in its cloud, and offers a solution to transfer them at the appropriate moment, to reach the actual backend user.

– In the case of SIGFOX, the connectivity or subscription is worldwide today. Regardless of the country in which the Thing is situated, the communication channels over which the data travel are shared;

– the case of LoRaWAN is very different:

- in the case of management of a completely private network, built on the concept of LoRa, you need to construct your own backend structure, or else allow an external company to run it for you,

- in the opposite case, where you do not manage your own network, you must rely on the different backend structures of your various network providers and manage the different contracts. Each of them will have their own API to manage the peripheral devices and harvest data. Eventually, you will have to implement all this complexity in your own backend structure or pay third parties to manage this complexity on your behalf. In addition, thereafter, you will need to keep up with enhancements made to the backends of the different operators in order to maintain compatibility.

Modes/Classes of operation for LoRaWAN

To conclude our discussion on the subject, LoRaWAN defines three modes of operation or classes of protocol of Things, able to serve the needs of a very wide range of applications of "bi-directional Things":

Class A

The first mode of operation, known as "class A", enables a Thing to establish bidirectional communication by, sending information to a base during the uplink, and then receiving information from the server during the downlink immediately after sending, during two short downlink reception windows. The timeslot for transmission on demand allowed by the Thing is based on its needs for communication with a small variation, on a random timebase (ALOHA-type protocol).

This class-A way of operating is the lowest level for applications which, shortly after the Thing has sent an uplink, only require a downlink communication from the server.

NOTE.– If the server wants to send data to the Thing, it is obliged to wait for the Thing's next transmit/send cycle. This way of working is less energy-hungry.

Class B

In addition to opening up random reception windows in class A, the mode of operation called "class B" also enables a Thing to establish bidirectional communication and to receive data at regular intervals by opening additional reception windows at planned times. In order for the Thing to open its reception window at the planned moment, the gateway sends it a synchronization signal/tag. This lets the server know when the Thing is listening.

Class C

Class C lets a Thing also establish bidirectional communication, and means it has the maximum number of reception slots available. During communication, the Things' transmitters are practically closed, and therefore, their receivers practically continually have open reception windows, and receive data continuously.

Of course, because of its mode of operation, class C proves far more energy-hungry than classes A and B.

We have now finished the technical presentations of LR LTN NB and DSSS. Let us now move on to LR WB!

13.4.5. *LR WB*

LR (Long Range) devices also exist in WB (Wide Band). We typically find two types: non-operated and operated networks. We shall begin with an example of a "non-operated" LR WB network.

13.4.5.1. *LR WB in RPMA – Ingenu (formerly On-Ramp Wireless)*

The American company On-Ramp Wireless, founded in 2005, has long been an active player in the professional market of networked communicating Things. Its main business model was to sell – primarily in the Americas – to companies, and to build and control their own networks founded on digital RF applications, useful in oil prospecting and natural gas extraction. In 2008, it became Ingenu, and extended its field of applications to the construction of public-sector networks, mainly in the USA, for which it sells radio modules and rolling data plans. It should be noted that many of Ingenu's customers are suppliers of M2M and IoT solutions, including in urban environments (smart meters), agricultural domains and oil fields.

Note that Ingenu's LPWAN design is a proprietary solution in the sense that Ingenu is/seems, at present, to be the only developer and manufacturer of the hardware.

This solution operates in the worldwide free ISM band of 2.4 GHz, which, for the same amount of emitted power, gives it a poorer theoretical range than systems operating at 900 MHz (Friis equation – see earlier on in this chapter), and also greater propagation losses due to obstacles such as water or ground. This loss of range is compensated by a regulation which allows for greater transmission power. It is also worth noting that in Europe, at 2.4 GHz, the final device requires certification, and certain countries may require licenses for use of this frequency outdoors, which is very often the case in IoT.

RPMA

This solution is based on the use of the technical concept known as RPMA – Random Phase Multiple Access. This technology is also a variant of DSSS communication, but with multiple access:

– the bandwidth is 1MHz, with a high spectrum spreading factor;

– the uplink data rate is 624 kbit/s, which is higher than SIGFOX and LoRa, though of course, at the cost of greater energy consumption;

– the downlink data rate is 156 kbit/s;

NOTE.– when the Things are in motion, the data rates of RPMA drop to 2 kbit/s, as is typically the case for wireless connections. These data rates are sufficient for the majority of IoT applications, being faster than 2G and SIGFOX.

– this technology facilitates efficient bidirectional transmission, and requires the device to have a reception sensitivity of –142dBm, with a total link budget of 172 dB (thus, 30 dBm = 1W for transmission, and so an extensive range in spite of using the 2.45 GHz frequency).

A few additional points on protocol

In contrast to a cellular network which is designed to deliver a high bit rate but require a great deal of power, RPMA is optimized to have maximum coverage whilst minimizing the Thing's battery consumption. Indeed, to save battery life, a particular connection protocol has been developed whereby, during access to the Thing, the parent system verifies the device's status, and whether it is indeed receiving all the data.

The protocol Ingenu is also able to carry out geolocation and precise tracking of the Thing, whilst LR LTN NB and DSSS systems do not offer the same levels of precision for tracking, and even at the time of writing, often have need of a separate global navigation satellite system (GNSS) module for geolocation applications.

13.4.5.2. *Other LPWAN protocols*

To conclude, although the three protocols mentioned above – SIGFOX, LoRaWAN and Ingenu – are currently the most fashionable and the best established, with numerous wide-range rollouts in various domains, it must be noted that the market also includes other, overlapping LPWAN solutions, which target different specifications. Let us quickly cite three of them:

– Weightless standard, developed and maintained by the Weightless Specialty Interest Group (SIG), of which there are a number of implementations (Weightless-W, -N and -P);

– Dash7, supported initially by the American company SAVI Technology and now maintained by the Dash7 Alliance;

– ThingPark Wireless, based on LoRaWAN and marketed by Actility.

13.4.5.3. *Conclusions on non-operated LR NB and WB networks*

We stated at the start of this book that we would not present a table comparing protocols, etc. on the basis of sales trends. The table shown in Figure 13.23 is purely technically factual.

Solution	Model	Frequency	Range	Data transfer rate	Packet Size
Sigfox	Proprietary	868 / 902 MHz	rural: 30-50 km urban: 3-10 km	upload: <300 bps download: 8 bits per day	12 bits
LoRaWAN	Alliance	433 / 868 / 780 / 915 MHz	rural: 15 km urban: 2-5 km	upload: 300 bps – 50 kbps download: 300 bps – 50 kbps	user-defined
Ingenu	Proprietary	2.4 GHz	rural: 5-10 km urban: 1-3 km	upload: 624 kbps download: 156kbps	6 bits – 10 kbits
Weightless-W	Alliance	400-800 MHz	5 km	upload: 1 kbps – 10 Mbps download: 1 kbps – 10 Mbps	>10 bits
Weightless-N	Alliance	<1 GHz	3 km	upload: 100 bps download: 100 bps	<20 bits
Weightless-P	Alliance	<1 GHz	2 km	upload: 200 bps – 100 kbps download: 200 bps – 100 kbps	>10 bits
Dash7	Alliance	433 / 868 / 915 MHz	<5 km	upload: 10, 56, or 167 kbps download: 10, 56, or 167 kbps	<256 bits

Figure 13.23. *Overview of non-operated LR NB and LR WB networks (Source: Isaac Brown, from Lux Research)*

In the coming paragraphs, in simple but factual fashion, by way of a mini-conclusion on non-operated LR networks, we shall present a brief technical statement, from which everyone can draw their own conclusions.

We have shown that:

SIGFOX

– is a rather "closed" system, in that all the data traffic must be sent through the proprietary SIGFOX cloud platform, forcing users to sign a contract and continue to pay the company to help and continue its rollout;

– is "open" in the sense that users can freely buy SIGFOX hardware and components from numerous suppliers;

– is well suited to the rollout of numerous applications consisting of the sending of simple messages from the Thing to the Cloud.

LoRa

– allows users to deploy their own networks, and manage those networks privately;

– is an "open" system because users can obtain LoRa modules and gateways from their material suppliers;

– yet seems somewhat "closed", because Semtech seeks to keep control over the manufacture of certain radio chips but, further downstream in the process, there are many suppliers who sell the necessary communication material.

LoRa and SIGFOX

Both

– have achieved a significant degree of penetration in Europe, and are extending their systems to cover North America;

– have experienced delays in international rollout, because of having to adjust their settings to the local regulatory requirements (respecting spectrums of different frequencies, etc.)

– are experiencing difficulties when trying to expand into new regions of the globe, with terrains that have frequency bands under license and different spectrums.

Ingenu

– Users can buy the hardware directly from Ingenu, and then use it to roll out their own, self-managed communication solutions;

– Ingenu also sells data plans for public networks which the company itself manages.

SIGFOX and Ingenu

Both:

– have enjoyed sustained growth;

– have the potential to become Global IoT MNOs offering regional and worldwide IoT data plans;

– are prime targets for acquisition by conventional MNOs, who are seeking to become the main facilitators of M2M.

13.4.6. *Operated LR WB networks*

Of the wireless technologies employed over Long Range (LR), in Wide Band (WB), we can state mainly that certain MAN-type or WAN-type networks are operated on frequencies with exclusive authorizations. In France's ANFR, in this situation, they speak of extended rollout as operated networks:

– classic cell networks, most of which belong to the set of historical cell networks, almost exclusively used with 2G, 3G, 4G etc. technologies… (and 5G who knows when?)

– LPWAN-type solutions via cell networks are at the very end of the process of standardization by the group 3GPP at ETSI: EC-GSM, LTE M and NB-IoT, but at the time of writing, they are in the full throes of being rolled out widely.

Sometimes, LPWANs (Low-Power Wide-Area Networks) such as LoRa, Qowisio, etc., make use of a classical operator to handle the large-scale implementation and operation of their networks.

13.4.6.1. *LTE and LTE-M*

LTE (Long Term Evolution), which is more commonly called "4G", is a very high data-rate technology for mobile communications.

Under the auspices of the ETSI, in the 3GPP, the working group on radio access networks (RAN) is in charge of the specifications of mobile network technologies (GSM, UMTS, LTE), and since late 2014, has been working on a version called LTE-M (LTE – Machine to Machine), which is now in the final stages of its overall definition. These efforts have laid the groundwork for the next generation of mobile networks – 5G – which is predicted to come into force in 2020, and in which the IoT, and notably LPWANs, should be crucially important.

The challenges of LTE-M in IoT

Viewed in perspective, in relation to the solutions LR LTN NB and DSSS (e.g. SigFox and LoRa) presented in the previous paragraphs, LTE needs to have its own (technical and) commercial M2M solution, to ensure it is able to compete with these two new standards on the market. Let us here briefly examine the numerous requirements for M2M and IoT LTE applications to be viable.

Satisfying a broad range of Things

Any LTE M2M system must be capable of supporting a hugely diverse range of Things, ranging from smart meters to drinks machines, vehicle fleet management tools and the safety of medical devices, etc., which is a vast field of application! All these different devices have very different requirements, and any LTE-M system must be capable of demonstrating very great flexibility of use.

Offering low-cost Things

The majority of M2M Things will be small in size, and their prices will be very closely studied. LTE-M needs to offer the advantages of a cellular system… but at a low cost!

Having Things with extremely long battery lives / lifespans

In numerous applications, the M2M devices will be left without supervision for long periods of time, in areas where there may be no power supply available. Maintenance and battery replacement on site are costly, and therefore all the Things must have a battery life of up to ten years. This means that an LTE-M system must be capable of consuming very little energy.

Having improved RF coverage

LTE-M applications will need to operate in various locations – not just in places where RF reception is good! They will have to work inside buildings, and often in difficult-to-access places where reception may be poor. Consequently, LTE-M must be capable of operating in all these conditions.

Furthermore, besides the licensed bands, the question of the use of non-licensed ISM bands and transmission powers also arises.

Tolerating a large volume of Things and low bit rates

As, in time, the volumes of products on the market for remote Things are expected to be huge, the structure of LTE-M must be such that the networks are able to cater for a large number of connected Things, supplying only small quantities of data, at low data rates, but often with peaks for short periods.

It should be borne in mind that, in cases contrary to the scenarios outlined above, an LTE solution cannot serve for the realization of these Things!

13.4.6.2. *The response to the challenges – LTE-M: version 13*

To serve these needs of M2M and IoT applications, during 2016, the 3GPP group issued release 13 of the specifications for LTE-M technology, including two new M2M-oriented categories:

– LTE Cat 1.4 MHz, with data rates of approximately 1 Mbit/s, a reduced transmission power of 20dBm max., and a spectral occupation of 1.4MHz, which is much lower than that of LTE technology;

– LTE Cat 200 kHz, often called LTE-M NB IoT (Narrow Band-IoT), whose PHY (RAN1) and MAC (RAN2) specifications began with Q3-15, and which allows for NB (Narrow Band) IoT, with a reduced bandwidth of 200 kHz and an uplink and downlink data rate of around 150 kbit/s (see Figure 13.24).

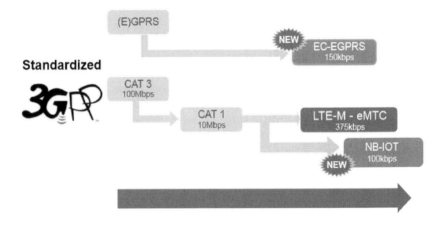

Figure 13.24. *Presentation of the different LTEs*

This means that today, the overall LTE-M provision can be summarized in terms of the UE categories shown in Table 13.14.

Comparison of LTE-M versions				
		Rel. 8	Rel. 12	Rel. 13	
		CAT 4	CAT 0	CAT 1.4 MHz	CAT 200 kHz LTE-M NB IoT
Uplink Peak Rate	Mb/s	50	1	1	0.250 (multi-tone) Single-tone: 2 configurable transmissions are supported: 3.75 and 15 kHz □ A prefix cyclic is inserted □ Sincpulse shaping–Multi-tone 0.200 kHz transmissions are based on SC-FDMA - The UE shall indicate the support of Single-tone and/or Multi-tone
Downlink peak rate	Mb/s	150	1	1	channel transmission with 15 kHz subcarrier spacing for all the scenarios: in-band standalone, guardband,
Number of antennas		2	1	1	1
Duplex mode		Full	Half	Half	Half
Receiver bandwidth	MHz	20	20	1.4	0.2
Transmit power	dBm	23	23	20	23
Modem Complexity	%	100	40	20	<15

Table 13.14. *Comparison of versions of LTE-M*

Figure 13.25 is a spider graph comparing the performances of these technologies.

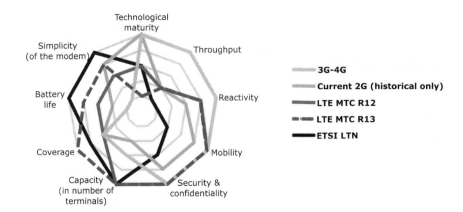

Figure 13.25. *Brief comparison of the performances of the different technologies (source: ARCEP)*

13.4.6.3. *Applicational and structural similarities, known as network edge*

Faced with the emergence of IoT services or optimized content distribution for local broadcast such as analysis of video feeds (surveillance cameras, etc.), geolocation, augmented reality, etc., with a view to expanding the applications of IoT and heralding the arrival of 5G (see all previous sections), the big mobile network operators are now seeking to add functions of analysis of large volumes of unstructured data, as close to the users as possible so as not to overburden the networks. With this goal in mind, they are beginning to install increased computing power at the so-called "edges" of the networks so as not to send enormous data streams to the datacenters untreated, at the risk of overloading the backbones of their communication infrastructures. These deported processing nodes are known as Mobile Edge Computing – MEC. Their main functions are characterized by ultra-low latency, high bandwidth and real-time access to the features of the radio network.

This new "brick", situated on the borderline between telecommunication, IoT and cloud computing resources, is in the process of being standardized by the ETSI in the ISG (Industry Specification Group) – MEC working group. The first three specifications devoted to Mobile Edge Computing are.

– GS MEC 001 – terminology pertaining to the conceptual, architectural and functional elements of an MEC device;

– GS MEC 002 – specifications of the technical requirements for the rollout and interoperability of mobile computing nodes at network edges, and descriptions of example use cases;

– GS MEC 003 – framework and reference architecture, enabling MEC applications to be run effectively and transparently in a mobile network.

Thus, Mobile Edge Computing becomes a key element in the evolution of wide-band mobile networks toward 5G, and now we are only waiting for true mass rollout of LPWAN solutions to judge the reception of all these solutions on the ground, and their fields of applications in comparisons to LTNs such as NB SIGFOX and/or DSSS LoRA. The future most likely holds a number of norms/standards which will be published simultaneously, each one pertaining specifically to an applicational niche, and there will continue to be competition between these disciplines at the boundaries of their optimal performance parameters.

To summarize and conclude this extremely long chapter, Figure 13.26 offers a technical table. Some of the points below are still being debated or are in the process of evolving.

Feature	LoRaWAN	Narrow-Band	LTE Cat-1 2016 (Rel12)	LTE Cat-M 2018 (Rel13)	NB-LTE 2019(Rel13+)
Modulation	SS Chirp	UNB / GFSK/BPSK	OFDMA	OFDMA	OFDMA
Rx bandwidth	500 - 125 KHz	100 Hz	20 MHz	20 - 1.4 MHz	200 KHz
Data Rate	290bps - 50Kbps	100 bit/sec 12 / 8 bytes Max	10 Mbit/sec	200kbps – 1Mbps	~20K bit/sec
Max. # Msgs/day	Unlimited	UL: 140 msgs/day	Unlimited	Unlimited	Unlimited
Max Output Power	20 dBm	20 dBm	23 - 46 dBm	23/30 dBm	20 dBm
Link Budget	154 dB	151 dB	130 dB+	146 dB	150 dB
Batery lifetime - 2000mAh	105 months	90 months		18 months	
Power Efficiency	Very High	Very High	Low	Medium	Med high
Interference immunity	Very high	Low	Medium	Medium	Low
Coexistence	Yes	No	Yes	Yes	No
Security	Yes	No	Yes	Yes	Yes
Mobility / localization	Yes	Limited mobility, No loc	Mobility	Mobility	Limited Mobility No Loc

Figure 13.26. *Brief chapter summary*

From the Base Station to the Server

This new sub-part is given over to the links and protocols existing between base station and server, and in servers themselves.

The base station, or gateway, receives messages from the Things, and is primary purpose is serve as a relay, a link, and then transfer the data to the collection network and its server, generally via a system of terrestrial links.

The following is an important philosophical question: is it the base station which steers the exchanges and feeds information back to the server (in which case, the "server" is more "served", and is inaptly named)… or is it the server which makes requests and asks the base station to feed it information (in which case, again, the name is inappropriate)!

The answer is: a little of both. That is what we shall show over the course of the coming chapter!

Network Access Layer – IP

Let us now go further down the stack of layers, and examine the premises of the "IP" layer.

14.1. IPv4

Version 4 of IP – more commonly called IPv4 – (layer 3 of the OSI model) is the main network protocol for packet transport and routing used today on the Internet and in most private networks. It uses addresses encoded on 32 bits (in theory, yielding 4,294,967,296 possible addresses), meaning every user can have a unique IP address which identifies him/her on the Internet.

A few details about the header of an IPv4 message are given in Figure 14.1, where the first field of an IP packet is composed of four bits, indicating the version of the protocol being used.

IPv4 header																															
0	1	2	3	4	5	6	7	8	9	10	11	12	13	14	15	16	17	18	19	20	21	22	23	24	25	26	27	28	29	30	31
IP version		Header length		Type of service												Total length															
Identification																Indicator			Fragment offset												
Life span								Protocol								Header checksum															
Source address																															
Destination address																															
Option(s) + filling																															

Figure 14.1. *Details of an IPv4 message header. For a color version of this figure, see www.iste.co.uk/paret/connectedobjects.zip*

14.1.1. *Operation*

When two terminals communicate with each other via that protocol, if no specific path for the data transfer is pre-defined, we say that the protocol is a "non-oriented connection". By contrast, for a system such as the public switched telephone network (PTSN), the path to be taken by the voice (or data) is established at the moment the connection begins. This protocol is known as an "oriented connection".

14.1.2. *Services provided*

In terms of service quality, IP protocols offer "best-effort delivery" of the packets. They are not concerned with the packets' contents, but simply provide a method to transport those packets to their destination.

14.1.3. *Reliability*

However, the IP protocols are considered to be "non-reliable"! This does not mean that they do not correctly send the data over the network, but rather that they offer no guarantee for the sent packets in regard to the following points:

– the order of the packets' arrival (a packet A may be sent before a packet B, but packet B might arrive before packet A);

– loss or destruction of packets;

– duplications of packets;

– corruption of data.

In terms of reliability, the only service offered by an IP protocol is to ensure that the packet headers transmitted contain no errors, by use of a checksum – CRC. If the header of a packet contains an error, its checksum CRC will be invalid, and the packet will be destroyed without being transmitted. In case of the destruction of a packet, no notification is made to the sender (although an ICMP packet may be sent).

The guarantees not offered by an IP protocol are delegated to the protocols of the higher layers. The main reason for this lack of management of reliability is the desire to reduce the level of complexity of the routers and thus make them quicker. The intelligence (smartness) is then deported to the endpoints of the network.

14.2. IPv6

The IPv6 (Internet Protocol version 6) specifications were finalized in the document RFC 2460... a long time ago... in December 1998. Thus, IPv6 is a false new version of the IP protocol base layer of the Internet, because in the early 1990s, the profession became aware that IPv4 was approaching its limits in terms of addressing capacity, due to a maximum field of 32 bits (i.e. ~4 billion addresses) and there would no longer be enough available addresses to connect new machines. In addition, a large portion of IPv4 addresses had, historically, been attributed to large groups (in slices of 16.8 million addresses, known as Class A addresses).

14.2.1. *Differences between IPv6 and IPv4*

The main specifications of IPv6 were published in 1995, by the IETF, and thus far, only a small proportion has been used. Among the main differences from IPv4, we can point out that the length of IPv6 addresses has been extended to 128 bits (i.e. 16 bytes), as compared to an IPv4 address, of 32 bits, allowing for a larger number of addresses. With IPv6, then, we have around 3.4×10^{38} addresses, meaning that in order to exhaust all this available stock of addresses, we would have to place ~667 million billion connected devices on every square millimeter of Earth's surface! This makes possible new applications, which had hitherto been ruled out by certain limitations of IPv4, and means that everyone (and everything – we do mean both people and Things, here) can have an address on the Internet (or several, even!), which is far from the case at the time of writing.

The IP packet was simplified by the new version, and the option was introduced of adding extensions to perform new functions. This speeds up routing, and introduces, amongst other things, the concepts of quality of service, security and mobility in IP, thereby remedying the major shortcomings of IPv4.

The header of the IPv6 packet (see Figure 14.2) is a fixed length of 40 bytes (in IPv4, the minimum size is 20 bytes), with options meaning it can be extended up to 60 bytes, though in practice, these options are rarely used.

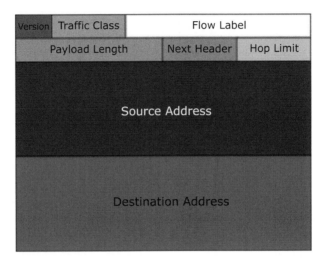

Figure 14.2. *Details of the header of an IPv6 packet. For a color version of this figure, see www.iste.co.uk/paret/connectedobjects.zip*

The meaning of the fields in this IPv6 header framework is as follows (Table 14.1):

Version	(4 bits)	fixed at the value of the number of the Internet Protocol version – 6
Traffic Class	(8 bits)	used in quality of service.
Flow Label	(20 bits)	used for marking (labeling) a flow for differential treatment as it passes through the network.
Payload length	(16 bits)	size of the usable payload in bytes.
Next Header	(8 bits)	identifies the type of header immediately following, using the same convention as IPv4.
Hop Limit	(8 bits)	decreased by 1 by each router. The packet is destroyed if this field reaches 0 during transit.
Source Address	(128 bits)	source address.
Destination Address	(128 bits)	destination address.

Table 14.1. *Meaning of the fields in an IPv6 header*

With IPv6, users enjoy the latest advances in networking, giving a greater guarantee of Internet security, because, for instance, one or more extension headers may follow the IPv6 header. The routing header, for example, means that the sender can specify an exact path for the connection to follow.

14.2.2. *Problems of privacy and/or anonymity?*

Given that every living person on the planet may have one, or multiple, IPv6 addresses, it is perfectly reasonable to consider the issue of privacy (see Chapter 7) – this situation poses a potential threat to privacy, facilitating the surveillance of individuals and intrusion into their private lives, and would be a sort of identity card we could never get rid of, which would prevent anonymity where it is desired.

Readers may point out that millions of people already use an IPv4 address to connect to the Internet, and that address could be used to find the connected individual. This is a perfectly valid point. As, with IPv6, a greater number of addresses are available for the same person for each connection, it is possible to use different addresses for different needs on the IoE (which is definitely not possible with IPv4). This by no mean guarantees anonymity, but may help to muddy the waters somewhat.

Finally, note that from its very inception, IPv6 has included security support, facilitating the authentication and encryption of the data packets.

14.3. 6LoWPAN

6LoWPAN is the acronym for "IPv6 Low Power Wireless Personal Area Networks" or "IPv6 LoW Power wireless Area Networks".

To recap: Generally speaking, a LoWPAN is made up of a set of Things possessing little in terms of resources (CPU, memory, battery), connected through a limited-throughput network (up to ~250kbit/s). Furthermore, in general, such networks are made up of a large number of Things.

The basic specification developed by the 6LoWPAN group is published in the form of two main RFC documents:

– the main document pertaining to this issue is RFC 4919;

– the specification in itself is the object of RFC 4944.

However, IPv4 and IPv6, which are known for their efficiency in delivering data over local area networks (LANs), metropolitan-area networks (MANs) and wide-area networks (WANs) such as the Internet, are difficult to implement in sensor networks and other systems and wireless RF hardware, which are constrained notably by the size of their headers. With this in mind, the 6LoWPAN group defined mechanisms for encapsulation and header compression, thereby enabling IPv6 packets to be sent or received via the RF communication protocol IEEE 802.15.4.

14.3.1. *Description of the technology*

In IEEE 802.15.4, the maximum size of the PSDU (Physical layer Service Data Unit) is 127 bytes. In view of the 25 bytes of the MAC (Media Access Control) sublayer, having no security, we are left with 102 bytes for the rest of the data link layer. When we add the bytes necessary for the security of the data link layer (AES-CCM-128), only 81 bytes are available for IP. We also need to take account of the increased load due to IPv6 headers (40 bytes), any extension headers, UDP headers (8 bytes) or TCP headers (20 bytes). Ultimately, the usable data account for little of the size of the packet (33 bytes on UDP and 21 on TCP – see Figure 14.3), and it is therefore impossible to comply with the specifications of IPv6, which impose a minimum MTU of 1280 bytes.

Figure 14.3. *Breakdown of an IEEE 802.15.4 frame*

14.3.2. *Integration of an IPv6 packet into an IEEE 802.15.4 frame*

Let us examine the problems inherent to LoWPANs following the integration of an IPv6 packet into an IEEE 802.15.4 frame.

14.3.2.1. *Problems inherent to LoWPANs*

To adapt to the IEEE 802.15.4 framework, the device (Thing) often needs to fragment an IPv6 packet into several frames, and the device on the other end of the connection must reassemble all the received frames to recreate the original IPv6 packet. These tasks consume a great deal of resources (memory and CPU power), and give rise to latency (notably buffering, time taken to generate/check the headers) and increased energy consumption.

Fragmentation and reassembling of the messages

The constraints on packet size imposed by IPv6 and 802.15.4 pose problems of excessive fragmentation and reassembly.

Compression of the IPv6 header

In light of the current size of the IPv6 header (40 bytes), the usable payload is reduced. Therefore, it is necessary to compress the IPv6 header in order to optimize data transfer on a 6LoWPAN network.

Routing

In IoT, LoWPAN networks are made up of a multitude of nodes and Things. They are generally organized into "mesh/multi-hop" or star topologies. A routing protocol capable of supporting such networks needs to be put in place. In addition, that protocol must conform to the constraints of the Things themselves (small CPUs and small memories), and to those of 802.15.4 (low throughput and small packets). Given their size, IEEE 802.15.4 devices tend to be easily transportable. Therefore, mobility also has to be taken into account.

14.3.3. *Autoconfiguration of an IP address*

Stateless address autoconfiguration (SLAAC, RFC 4862) in IPv6 is advisable, because it reduces the workload the devices have to perform. This necessitates the generating of an EUI-64 interface ID or a 16-bit short ID on the devices.

14.3.4. *Network supervision and management*

The supervision/management of a 6LoWPAN network is a crucial element. SNMP – Simple Network Management Protocol – (RFC 3410) is already widely used in IP networks, and exhibits the advantage of having a multitude of pre-existing tools. Owing to the constraints imposed by IEEE 802.15.4 and to the characteristic of the equipment, the adaptation of SNMPv3 for use with 6LoWPAN is still under study.

14.3.5. *Constraints on "upper-layer" applications*

Because of the characteristics of LoWPANs, applications requiring a great deal of resources are not really appropriate. Thus, it may be necessary to adapt applications to the constraints of LoWPANs (reduced device resources, data rate and packet size on 802.15.4).

14.3.6. *Security*

In order to ensure the integrity of the data transmitted over a 6LoWPAN network, the security of the data transfer must be implemented at the IP level, in addition to the security offered by IEEE 802.15.4 (via AES).

14.3.7. *Routing*

The routing in 6LoWPAN can be done in either of two different modes: "mesh-under" and "route-over" (see Figure 14.4).

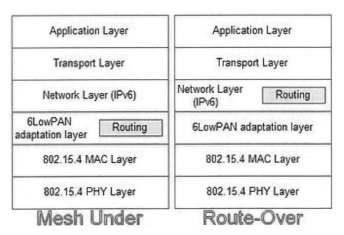

Figure 14.4. *"Mesh-under" and "route-over" routing*

14.3.7.1. *Mesh-under*

"Mesh under" consists of implementing routing at the level of the adaptation layer (which occurs between the data link and network layers of the OSI model). In a mesh-under setup, the routing decision is made at the 6LoWPAN level, and therefore only with the fragments of the IPv6 packet. The IPv6 packet is only reconstructed when it reaches the destination device.

14.3.7.2. *Route-over*

"Route over" implements the decision at the level of the network layer (see diagram of routing in 6LoWPAN). In route-over, the IPv6 packet is reconstructed on every one of the intermediary devices to make the decision on routing.

Consequently:

– mesh-under offers a shorter transmission time;

– route-over is more effective in degraded conditions (with loss of packets).

We have now come to the end of this brief overview of the main protocols of the network access layers used in IoT.

15

The Server

Although the subject under discussion is truly vast, here is a brief transitional chapter; for further details on structures, and on the server function in general, readers should refer to more specialized works.

For the mere mortal, the term "Server" suggests too many things. Figure 15.1 offers an illustration of the usual idea of a room containing numerous servers, and the software- and hardware problems they bring (anti-hacking, earthquake-resistant buildings, bomb-resistance, attack-resistance, etc.), management of their power supply and consumption, evacuation of the heat that they produce when they are enclosed in sealed spaces (the need for air-conditioning units... which themselves heat up and need to be cooled... and so on!), etc.

Figure 15.1. *Example of a room of servers*

In this photo, all those servers can sometimes form a single, enormous server, or else each unit is (or can be) a private, dedicated server.

15.1. Conventional functions of a server in IoT

Let us now briefly describe the function of a server in the context of IoT applications.

In IoT, the network Server – in every conceivable guise – depending on the languages and control software (see the next, lengthy chapter) preloaded on it, has the following main roles:

– to manage the IoT network and ensure that it works properly – for example:

- using the most appropriate protocols for the exchanges,

- organizing acknowledgements of messages,

- taking measures to eliminate duplicate packets,

- adapting data rates to the different existing peripheral devices,

- etc.

– to manage the end-to-end security of the transported data;

– to refine the data if necessary;

– to store the data;

– to distribute the data to the various users/subscribers, via a broker;

– etc.

Today, the management of an IoT server is no longer handled solely by the end user, as was the case a few years ago. Nowadays, the owners of immense banks of servers (e.g. OVH, AWS, etc.) sell/rent out services and become suppliers of higher-level computer services which (for a fee) relieves end users of handling the hardware and software maintenance of the servers, optimization of the hard and soft resources needed for their applications, security and duplication of data on other remote servers arranged and distributed in the form of a "server farm" or what is known as a "Cloud" (of servers). In such cases, there is no way of knowing where, geographically, the data are being manipulated and acted upon… which can sometimes be a major issue in the signing of certain contracts specific to sensitive data!

After this brief taster, let us now examine, in detail, the extent of transport- and messaging protocols which may/must be loaded onto the server depending on the types of IoT applications to carry out these tasks of secure, reliable communication.

16

Transport and Messaging Protocols

This long chapter describes numerous transport and messaging protocols considered to be the most widely used in the world of IoT. As we shall soon see, many of these protocols are very similar, and are often considered to be in competition with one another, to a greater or lesser extent. In fact, this is not entirely true, because all of them have subtle nuances making them apt and optimal applications for use in certain applicative branches of IoT.

16.1. Transport

To recap, TCP (Transmission Control Protocol) is, in connected mode, a reliable transport protocol, documented in the IETF's RFC 793. For information, TCP was developed in 1973 (nearly 45 years ago!), and then adopted by Arpanet in 1983.

In the Internet model, TCP is located in the layer above IP, and in the OSI model. It corresponds to the transport layer, between the network layer and session layer. Put briefly:

– applications transmit data flows over a network connection;

– TCP breaks up the bitstream into segments whose sizes depend on the maximum size of a packet that can be transmitted at once without fragmentation (the MTU – maximum transmission unit) underlying network (data link layer).

16.1.1. *Operation*

A TCP session works in three phases:

– establishment of the connection;

– data transfer;

– termination of the connection.

During the establishment phase, the connection is made by "handshaking" – successive alternate exchanges in three steps – during which parameters such as the sequence number are initialized to ensure reliable transmission of the data (in the correct order, with no losses).

At the breaking of the connection, a handshake is also used – this time in four stages.

16.1.2. *Structure of a TCP segment*

The TCP frame organized over 32 bits width is arranged as laid out in Table 16.1. Readers can refer to networking publications for the decryption and meanings of the fields of the bits' values, which go beyond the scope of this book.

0	1	2	3	4	5	6	7	8	9	1 0	1 1	1 2	1 3	1 4	1 5	1 6	1 7	1 8	1 9	2 0	2 1	2 2	2 3	2 4	2 5	2 6	2 7	2 8	2 9	3 0	3 1
Source Port: 2 bytes																	Destination port: 2 bytes														
Sequence number																																
Acknowledgement number																																
Header size || Rese rved || EC N/ NS	C W R	E C E	U R G	A C K	P S H	R S T	S Y N	F I N	Window																					
Checksum																	Urgent pointer														
Options																									Filling							
Data																																

Table 16.1. *Structure of a TCP frame*

What must be noted from this is that the architecture and the binary content of the different fields in that frame lend transport reliability to the message transported.

16.2. "IoT messaging" technologies

Before diving into the depths of each protocol, we shall now present a brief, non-exhaustive examination of the main general parameters which each of them must support.

16.2.1. *Main protocol parameters*

16.2.1.1. *Data-centric and message-centric communication models*

Let us begin by examining the two main communication models and technologies which focus on user data and what they represent.

Data-centric Model

The "Data-centric" model focuses, as the name indicates, on the proper routing of the data/messages independently of their meaning.

The Things interact with a data model, but not with one another (e.g. by making requests of a base). This allows for:

– major abstraction (Thing orientation);

– greater interoperability.

However, it is difficult to add new models ("profiles"), because a standardization process must be observed.

Message-centric Model

In the "Message-centric" model, the message content is defined by each user, and it is not transparent for other addressees. This leads to:

– lesser abstraction ("transport layer" for the messages).

Independently of the transfer between two points, the routers must be able to exchange routing information. An IGP (Interior Gateway Protocol) and an EGP (Exterior Gateway Protocol), as well as the BGP (Border Gateway Protocol), serve that need.

16.2.1.2. *Messaging structure*

As we continue, let us take a closer look at the messaging structure.

Publish/Subscribe

One of the most common messaging structures is the well-known "publish/subscribe" (abbreviated as "pub/sub – P/S"). As is suggested by the name, with this model, it is the Thing which supplies data at its own pace, and which tends to send them (or "push" them), rather than the Thing requesting information. In other words, therefore, "publish/subscribe" is an abstraction layer between the things which supply data and the services which consume those data.

This model preserves the termination points, with a broker (see later on for the definition of the term and its function), keeping a record of who publishes what and who wishes to consult the data. Depending on the standard used, the publisher may or may not know who has subscribed to his/her data. This is one of the crucial points of this concept, as it constitutes the basis of a subscription, but sometimes, the question also arises of whether or not we can directly communicate with another peripheral device.

Request/Response

Another model commonly employed in IoT, stemming from HTTP, is "*request/respond*" (often abbreviated as "req/rep", or "R/R"). This model is very different from the "pub/sub" model in numerous points, because as its name suggests, one side issues a request, and the other responds. In other words, "request/respond" tends to extract data – figuratively speaking, to "pull" them.

Peer-to-Peer

There are many other models which are less frequently used in IoT: for instance, Point to Point, or Peer to Peer, equally well-known, abbreviated as "P2P" for "Peer-to-Peer".

16.2.1.3. *Quality of Service (QoS)*

Quality of service – QoS – also called message reliability, is a vast subject, with a very wide range of functions. Amongst them, we could cite, for example:

– ensuring delivery;

– obtaining confirmation of receipt;

– management of wait time or of queuing, where a subscriber is momentarily or permanently disconnected, perhaps with a "time-to-live" setting, such that one would never expect that subscriber to return (and what might happen when a message is not delivered);

– etc.

Note that several of the protocol layers above TCP and the TCP layer itself have a certain level of delivery guarantee. If a protocol has to redouble the effort to offer better QoS, it suggests that there are shortcomings in it, and with TCP, there may be delays in realizing that there is a network problem, and there are certainly more elaborate protocols than TCP.

16.2.1.4. Security

Let's start at the very beginning; that's a very good place to start! Does the protocol define its own security? If so, then how? Good question! If not, then how is security actually implemented? Numerous protocols depend on the security offered by the SSL and TLS protocols; with others, it is shifted further upstream, in the application layers; some use DTLS.

16.2.1.5. Addressing

Addressing someone is all very well, but we still need to know whether the addressee exists! In the principles which can answer this existentialist question, there are two philosophies often in coexistence:

– no discovery mode, where everyone involved is known from the start;

– discovery mode, where we have to go on the hunt to discover who the participants are.

For example, in the context of no discovery, when we wish to activate a particular Thing or obtain an exact measurement from one, the general publish/subscribe mode is not helpful, unless we want to have a distinct subject for each Thing. In addition, in that context, when we do not know the IDs of the Things, if we want to implement code in a device with limited memory resources, it is better to choose the CoAP and MQTT protocols.

16.2.1.6. RESTful or RESTless

The term REST means "REpresentational State Transfer", and RESTful means operation which satisfies the conditions of REST... and by contrast, RESTless is "any system that is *not RESTful*" – we must have the courage to think in that manner!

This topic really covers two issues which are connected to the programming style used in creating the systems... but which are distinct problems:

– with the first, in general, users view the RESTful APIs used for HTTP requests as being familiar and pleasant for Web- and server programmers, who must then discuss amongst themselves, how to balance the workload on networks and unreliable connections;

– the second lies in the fact that the programming style is more familiar to the programmers of embedded systems using "real" programming languages such as C/C++ and Java. The difference is that, with REST, everything can fairly well be done using only four commands: PUT, GET, POST and DELETE.

Knowledge of a language, though, is merely a superficial difference. The difference is more marked in the way in which the application's "status" is managed.

RESTless

In RESTless approaches, we have specific APIs which depend on the protocol used or on its implementation, and we deem that a connection is in the process of being established, or that there is at least one predictable destination to which to send messages.

The transfer status is implicit in RESTless messages.

EXAMPLE.–

If we send a message saying "stop the fan", followed by another saying "shut off the power", this implicitly introduces the idea of communication in which the concept of time is present, where first of all, the fan has been stopped, and then it has been powered down. The final hypothesis, implicitly, is that the fan has, indeed, been successfully shut off (simply because the message has reached its intended destination… but this does not actually mean that the action has successfully been carried out!).

RESTful

The REST architecture makes none of these hypotheses. It does not contain such concepts as long-term connection or conversation. You ask something, you obtain a response, and you have completed your task.

EXAMPLE.–

When you have just finished sending an instruction such as "stop the fan", the system has no memory of it after having passed along the message to be carried out. Each new message sent is as fresh as the first one ever sent. For example, when a load distributor/balancer sends two messages to two different servers, we cannot count on one of those servers to remember what has just happened. You need to program your system differently.

With RESTless systems, it is possible to envisage also having a sort of confirmation of receipt at the level of the application.

On the other hand, in a RESTful configuration, we must first test the fan to ensure that it is not switched off accidentally. There is an explicit concept in the transfer of information.

Another classic example is that of altering a parameter/setting – say, for example, the reference temperature on a thermostat. If we say "reduce the temperature by 2 degrees", we cannot be sure that this command will actually be carried out on an unreliable installation. On the other hand, if we say "set the reference temperature to 36 degrees", the Thing can check its own current settings, and either increase or decrease its reference value.

16.2.1.7. Constrained resources

Certain protocols are specially designed for Things having scant resources (memory space, etc.); some are not; and some may facilitate implementations to deal with these constraints. Exactly what constitutes a "constraint" varies on the basis of a great many parameters. Some think in terms of a few thousand bytes of code. According to the RTI, the limited version of DDS (Data Distribution Service is a norm specified by the OMG – Object Management Group) is nearly 500K bytes.

This concludes the discussion of the main general parameters which the protocols presented below must satisfy.

16.3. Protocols

To begin with, Table 16.2 shows the main issues of specifications for "IoT messaging" protocols on the market.

Issuer	Norm/Standard	Definition
ITU	ITU-T Y.2060	Concept IoT
	ITU-T Y.2060	Interface machine-application
IEEE	IEEE 802.15.4	Data link layer
	6LoWPAN	IPv6 Low Power Wireless Personal Area Networks
	CoAP	Constrained Application Protocol
IETF	RPL	IPv6 Routing Protocol for Low-Power and Lossy Networks
GS1	ONS	Object Naming Service
	EPC	Electronic Product Code
OASIS	MQTT	Message Queue Telemetry Transport
	AMQP	Advanced Message Queuing Protocol
	DDS	Data Diffusion Service

Table 16.2. *Main issuers of "IoT messaging" protocols*

According to a survey carried out in 2016, the two messaging protocols most widely used on the ground are the classic HTTP and MQTT, with CoAP in third place (see Figure 16.1).

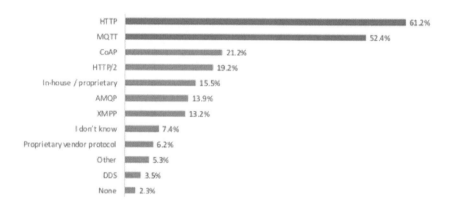

Figure 16.1. *Distribution of messaging protocols on the ground*

Now, in the context of the enormous diversity of IoT applications, we shall briefly (as briefly as possible, at least...) recap the main distinguishing features and performances of the main protocols used in IoT.

NOTE.– This is not intended to be an inventory like Jacques Prévert's! Simply put, each protocol has specific performances rendering it more appropriate for certain applications than for others. As, in IoT, they are extremely numerous and very different from one another, there are a very great number of protocols to be examined!

16.4. HTTP – HyperText Transfer Protocol

HTTP – HyperText Transfer Protocol – is a well-known client/server communication protocol, mainly developed and implemented for loading pages on the World Wide Web. It uses the platform of TCP as the transport layer, and can work on any reliable connection.

Thus, by default, an HTTP server uses port 80 (443 in the case of HTTPS).

The best-known HTTP clients are Web browsers, enabling a user to access a server containing the data. These clients connect to HTTP servers such as Apache HTTP Server or Internet Information Services.

HTTPS (where S stands for "secure") is the variant of HTTP for secure browsing, using the secure transaction protocols SSL or TLS, notably used for secure payment.

16.5. HTTP/2

HTTP/2 is a revised version of HTTP. It is not, in itself, a messaging protocol, but in the specification, there are suggestions indicating that the past limitations of performances could be partly resolved by this revision, which could make it appropriate for IoT and communications with the Cloud. It handles flows, and a "push" server. Whereas a server cannot always initiate a connection (only the clients can do that, which is important for security), this protocol can initiate data flows within an open connection. The headers have been one of the greatest problems with HTTP. For small Things which have limited resources, a Huffman code is used to compress them. HPACK is an example of an implementation of this function.

16.6. MQTT – Message Queuing Telemetry Transport

IBM was partly responsible for the development of the messaging protocol MQTT – "Message Queue Telemetry Transport" – which also operates above the TCP layer of the TCP/IP protocol, with the latter providing a simple and reliable data flow. It was created in 1999 in "publish/subscribe" mode, and made available to the Open Source community. Its open specification, therefore, was published, and is free of copyright. The version of the protocol MQTT v3.1.1 has become an OASIS standard whose specification is available in HTML and PDF formats.

As the name indicates, its original purpose was to be oriented toward telemetry or telesurveillance applications. Its aim is to harvest data from numerous devices, transport those data and make them available to the IT infrastructure. All the elements connect to a server/data concentrator.

MQTT is an extremely simple, lightweight messaging protocol, designed for systems and networks in which it is necessary to minimize the need for bandwidth resources and which have significant latency, whilst trying to ensure reliability, a certain degree of assurance and quality of delivery, and also to manage the battery performances of the deported elements. Thus, it does not need to be particularly quick and, in that context, its "real-time" aspect is generally measured in seconds… which is often ample for many IoT applications.

MQTT needs a bidirectional, ordered, lossless connection. Fundamentally, it offers some aspects of QoS, which are:

– the sending of the message at most one time (…but it is possible for that message never to arrive);

– the delivery of the message at least once (perhaps to obtain a duplicate);

– the delivery of the message exactly once.

Generally, MQTT clients initialize the connections, and servers act as brokers.

Additionally, to our knowledge, this protocol does not support any discovery process, and for this reason, specific/direct addressing of a Thing is difficult to achieve. That is why SMQ was created (see later on in this chapter), whose main aim was to make it easy for one Thing to directly address another. In addition, this latter protocol has specific stipulations, and management for abnormal events and the lifespan of the messages. Thus, security is better because of better practices.

Hence, MQTT is very well suited to extensive networks of small Things and to systems needing to harvest data from numerous sources which need to be monitored or controlled (e.g. "machine-to-machine" (M2M) applications, most industrial IoT solutions or the world of connected and mobile devices), and it has a few control options operable from the Cloud, because numerous software platforms installed in the Cloud support MQTT (Bluemix from IBM, AWS IoT from Amazon, Azure IoT from Microsoft, etc.).

Furthermore:

– on the software side, communications take place with five types of packets: connect, publish, subscribe, unsubscribe and ping, and numerous libraries are available, most using the languages C, C++, Java, JavaScript, PHP, Python, etc. and on the majority of platforms (Linux, Windows, iOS, Android, Arduino, etc.);

– on the hardware side, Arduino cards support MQTT to communicate with the Cloud.

Whilst the broker projects of Eclipse/Paho and Mosquitto from the Eclipse company are based on MQTT and offer open-source implementations of open messaging protocols and standards designed for new and emerging applications of M2M (Machine-to-Machine) and the Internet of Things (IoT), numerous projects implement MQTT.

16.6.1. *Security in MQTT*

With version V3.1 of the MQTT protocol, it is possible to transmit a username and password with a packet. Furthermore, independently of the MQTT protocol itself, the encryption of the network can be done with SSL (it should be noted that SSL is not the lightest of security protocols, and therefore adds significantly to the network's workload).

One final point: further security measures may be added by an application to encrypt the transmitted and received data, but this is not easy to integrate if we want to keep the protocol simple and lightweight.

16.7. CoAP – Constrained Application Protocol

As the successor to SOAP, CoAP – Constrained Application Protocol – is part of the protocols in the "application" layer of the TCP/IP model.

CoAP largely derives from HTTP, including a few modifications stemming from the REST (Representational State Transfer) model mentioned above. Thus, it is somewhat similar to HTTP (but with smaller packets) and, to some degree, is in competition with MQTP.

It is a transfer/Web messaging protocol aimed at facilitating interactive communication between very simple, small Things over the Internet, on which the nodes present also have restricted, limited resources (for example, in terms of data rate, energy consumption, etc.). Hence, this protocol is particularly well suited to small sensors with scant resources, switches, valves and components which have to be controlled or kept under remote supervision through standard Internet networks, and where great efficiency is needed.

CoAP offers a client/server model and question/response interactions between Things, and supports an integrated system of discovery of services and resources, and also integrates key concepts of the Web such as media type management, the structure of URI and Internet data. It is designed to easily interface with HTTP for integration on the Web, but still respects the specialized requirements such as supporting multicast IP, a very low overload and great simplicity for constrained environments. These are points which are extremely important in IoT and Machine-to-Machine (M2M) devices. Unlike with traditional Internet elements, these nodes whose architecture is deeply anchored in the "embedded" (everything on the silicon chip) are often equipped with 8-bit microcontrollers having only small ROM and RAM memories, and consuming little energy, whereas networks such as IPv6 over Low-Power Wireless Personal Area Networks (6LoWPANs) often have high error rates for the packets, and a typical data rate of around 10 kbit/s.

To render the protocol appropriate for IoT and M2M applications, the Internet Engineering Task Force (IETF) working group "Constrained RESTful Environments (CoRE)" worked on the normalization of this protocol, adding various new functions. The basis of the protocol is specified in RFC 7252.

CoAP works above UDP... which has no guarantee of delivery, but in particular uses four REST commands whose meanings are slightly different to those of HTTP. It is here that the REST nature may be useful. Indeed, if we want to obtain confirmation of receipt (with time-out, and an exponential resending model), there are options with which the messages can be tagged as "confirmable", which may be important, depending on the IoT application. In addition, the messages may be mono-cast or multi-cast. Furthermore, CoAP can operate on most elements handling UDP or a solution similar to UDP.

Promoted by Cisco, supported by the community of developers Eclipse, chosen by ARM M9 and Amazon AWS, CoAP has had real successes in the domains of M2M networks and energy management in applications for Smart Cities, building automation and IoT platforms.

16.8. XMPP

XMPP, meaning "Extensible Messaging and Presence Protocol", is designed essentially to carry out instantaneous person-to-person or point-to-point messaging (via a server) in the form of textual messages. Note that there is an extension to implement a "pub/sub" model.

XMPP is a protocol based on XML, and its default format is text, rendering communication between people very easy. In the same way as HTTP and MQTT, it works above the TCP layer. In the context of IoT, the main advantage to it is having an addressing pattern as name@domain.com, which offers an easy way of addressing a Thing, meaning we can easily find the needle it represents in the enormous haystack that is the Internet! This is particularly practical if the data are exchanged between Things that are far apart, usually with no relation between the devices. Furthermore, it is possible to confirm the presence or availability of a specific Thing. In this case, the Things must take care of managing the discovery mode. Additionally, a protocol called BOSH (Bidirectional stream Over Synchronous HTTP) can be used to fragment the push messages into several pieces.

XMPP was not designed to be quick. In fact, most implementations use it to communicate a method of polling or update only on demand. The "real-time" aspect of XMPP is generally measured in seconds, and it offers an excellent method, for example, to connect the thermostat of a house to a Web server so as to access the information from a mobile telephone. Its strengths in terms of addressing, security and evolutivity make it ideal for IoT hinging on mainstream applications.

16.9. DDS – Data Distribution Service

DDS – "Data Distribution Service" – at the level of the application layer in the OSI Model, is a middleware protocol having arisen from the defense sector. It is oriented around standard data, and favors interactions between industrial and embedded applications, using highly efficient "real-time" systems.

Unlike "message-centric" messaging services, DDS is a "data-centric" messaging service; it and others are based on an operating principle stemming from a "publish and subscribe"-type mechanism, whereby an application is able to:

– modify shared data and consequently notify other applications by publishing;

– subscribe to certain shared data, and thus receive the relative modifications made by remote applications.

Put briefly, DDS:

– can be easily deployed on a large scale;

– is independent of the language and the OS;

– its data are described in appropriate languages, such as the Interface Definition Language (IDL) rooted in the CORBA standard, whose analysis enables DDS services to provide appropriate accessors and modifiers;

– the applications have an application programming API, so they are able to use numerous services;

– can effectively simultaneously deliver millions of messages per second to numerous receivers;

– introduces the concepts of domains, which cover a set of machines distributed throughout the network and share common data;

– unlike MQTT and XMPP, the Data Distribution Service (DDS) is targeted at devices directly using the data from the Thing, and serves mainly to connect Things with others and distribute the data to other Things;

– does not intrinsically have a broker. It works with an interconnection "bus", but can be implemented with or without a broker.

Keep in mind that IoT elements require very different data than those required by IT infrastructures. To begin with, certain Things are rapid, "real-time" systems (often measured in microseconds), and must communicate with a large number of other Things in a complex manner, so the simple and reliable point-to-point topologies of TCP are far too restrictive. Instead, DDS offers extensive possibilities for QoS, multicasting, configurable reliability and omnipresent redundancy. In addition, the system's "fanning out" is one of its major selling points. Furthermore, DDS offers powerful filtering capabilities, enabling a source to select exactly where the particular data go to, and that "where" may represent thousands of destinations simultaneously. Therefore, the Hub-and-Spoke architecture is completely inappropriate for data use. On the other hand, DDS implements direct "device-to-device" communication (a bus) with a relational model of the data.

Note that there are light versions of DDS which are run in the restricted environments of small Things.

Owing to the performances mentioned above, the field of application of DDS lies mainly in high-performance IoT systems, and the system is aimed mainly at industries subject to stringent constraints of reliability and performance, such as aeronautics, defense, military systems, telecommunications, windfarms, hospital integration, medical imaging, asset management systems, automobile testing and safety tests, etc., where the data being handled may be complex and sensitive in nature. It is the only technology which offers the flexibility, reliability and speed necessary to create complex applications, in real time, which can be used to connect distributed applications working at rates directly linked to physical phenomena.

16.10. AMQP – Advanced Message Queuing Protocol

AMQP (Advanced Message Queuing Protocol) is a middleware protocol in the OASIS family. Based on the "message-centric" model, it was developed in the banking industry and the financial sector, and is capable of quickly and reliably handling thousands of queued exchanges and transactions.

True to its origins in the banking sector, AMQP mainly focuses on the quality of the routing of the messages, avoiding losing any messages *en route*, and on QoS, carefully monitoring messages and ensuring that each one reaches its intended addressee, whatever breakdowns or restarts occur on the network. This requires a completely reliable transport layer and point-to-point connection. With this in mind, the communications operate above the TCP layer and send transaction messages between servers, where the Things involved have to acknowledge receipt of each message. In addition, the standard also sets out an optional transaction mode, with a formal multi-phase validation sequence.

AMQP is used primarily in server-to-server business messaging. Typically, the "elements" of the network are mobile/portable handsets, to communicate with back-office datacenters. In the context of the IoT, this protocol, which also necessitates the inclusion of an authentication and encryption cell (SASL/TLS) and a broker, is more appropriate for control plans or analysis functions based on the server.

16.11. SMQ

SMQ is a protocol proprietary to the company "Real Time Logic", which addresses certain perceived weaknesses in MQTT and CoAP for applications using small Things. Its main distinctive feature is the use of an "ephemeral" ID, attributed and broadcast in a message by the broker, so that responses can be addressed to a specific Thing, the reason being that it is much easier to control or communicate with a specific node in this way.

Generally, communications are begun by "enhanced" HTTP using a Websocket connection (basically TCP, with the concept of a higher level of packets) and the software implementation is written in the scripting language Lua.

16.12. JMS – Java Messaging Service

JMS, which stands for Java Messaging Service, is an API developed by Sun to quickly, reliably and asynchronously send and receive message between applications or Java components. Thus, it is used only by Things capable of running Java, enabling them to use messaging services in Java applications, as the API JDBC does for databases.

JMS is "Message Centric", and like its predecessors, is based on a distributed-software-style architecture, using the same principles, design rules and properties as HTTP. It also operates above the TCP/IP transport layer, using a restricted set of verbs for all use cases, referred to as CRUD: CREATE, READ, UPDATE and DELETE, in the REST – Representational State Transfer – mode, explained earlier.

Although the Client/Server (request/reply) style uses specific interfaces, it can operate in "Publish/subscribe" and "Point-to-point" modes, with good QoS in terms of the supply of the Message.

16.13. Other protocols

To recap, there are a great many more protocols (listed below in alphabetical order), linked to data transfer, which may also be helpful to use, depending on the application:

– DNS (Domain Name System): match seeking between names and IP addresses IP – a system for resolving Internet names;

– FTP (File Transfer Protocol): a protocol used for transferring files over the Internet;

– FTPS (File Transfer Protocol Secure): subdivision of FTP for secure file transfer;

– ICMP (Internet Control Message Protocol);

– IMAP (Internet Message Access Protocol): mode of e-mail exchange;

– IRC (Internet Relay Chat): instant chat protocol;

– NNTP (Network News Transfer Protocol): message transfer protocol used by Usenet discussion forums;

– POP3 (Post Office Protocol version 3): e-mail exchange protocol used for receiving;

– SMTP (Simple Mail Transfer Protocol): e-mail exchange protocol used for sending;

– SSH (Secure Shell – secure remote connection);

– …and BGP; DHCP; IMAP; LDAP; MGCP; NNTP; NTP; ONC/RPC; RTP; RTSP; RIP; SIP; SNMP; Telnet; TLS/SSL;… and many more, right down to XYZ!

Let us now examine a new entity that is present in the IoT chain: the "broker".

16.14. The broker

The term "broker" is mainly used in the finance sphere, meaning someone who "serves as an intermediary between two parties for an operation". This exactly describes the function of the broker in the IoT architecture!

The broker function, used and absolutely necessary for an IoT structure, is designed to, firstly, handle a huge quantity of "uploaded" data, from numerous small messages sent by the Things, and secondly to serve as an intermediary – a "broker" – to disentangle and route all these data/inputs to specific outputs for action. The primary function of a broker, therefore, is to redistribute the information "published" by "sensors" to all "subscribers" to that data (see Figure 16.2).

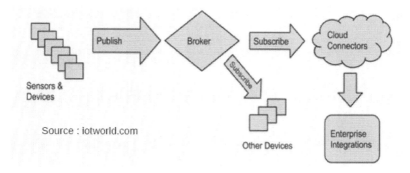

Figure 16.2. *Architecture of a broker*

Amongst the best-known names, we can cite the main suppliers of open-source software, the majority of which work with the MQTT protocol, and are known as "MQTT brokers":

– Active MQ;

– Mosquitto;

– Rabbit MQ;

– Apollo;

– Joram MQ, OW2 JORAM,

– etc.

They serve various functions, and some of them include additional functionality, implemented on physical machines (PCs, etc.) or virtual machines (OVH, AWS machine), or as infrastructure, known as "platform as a service" – PAAS (AWS service), acting as brokers. This is specific to their MQTT implementation, and many servers have far more wide-ranging possibilities going beyond simple MQTT.

16.14.1. *Examples of possibilities*

The table in Figure 16.3 offers some examples of possibilities served by certain broker programs.

Server	QoS 0	QoS 1	QoS 2	authentication	bridge	$SYS	SSL	dynamic topics	cluster	Web sockets	plugin system
Mosquitto	✔	✔	✔	✔	✔	✔	✔	✔	✘	✔	✔
RSMB	✔	✔	✔	✔	✔	✔	✘	✔	✘	✘	?
WebSphere MQ											

Figure 16.3. *Examples of possibilities of certain broker programs*

16.15. Programming languages

Unsurprisingly, also, in the Cloud, Java is the most widely used of the programming languages used by the protocols listed above. Note, however, that in the object-oriented open-source language Python, under license, is becoming increasingly popular with developers, and is amongst the three flagship languages of the IoT, the other two being Java and C.

In the area of embedded systems, note that the C language is on top, and is increasingly popular with developers, and on more evolved platforms, we find Python and Java.

16.16. Operating systems

The survey referenced above also showed that 70% of users of IoT applications have implemented the Linux OS operating system, which is therefore streets ahead of the rest of the park in evolved hardware platforms and systems which are not battery powered. Furthermore, 23% of them prefer to use no operating system at all, preferring to create their own setups which can be directly run using the silicon chip. Such is the case of platforms more specifically designed with battery power in mind.

To conclude this chapter, note that the rise in power of operating systems specifically devoted to IoT, such as mbed from ARM, Contiki, RIOT, Zephyr, etc. seems to be relatively limited as of yet.

From the Cloud Server to the Various Users

With this final sub-part, we are gradually coming to the end of our overview of the IoT chain. This final technical stage is one of the most important, because it is at this stage that the applicative frameworks of your software applications are enacted, and you create the commercial applications you will offer your clients, for sacks full of jingling cash, and with which we hope you will be able to earn a living!

Indeed, having managed to gather up your relevant data and sent them to the Cloud as described in the previous chapters, you still need to do the following:

– firstly, all the organizing, sorting, selection, etc. of data stored very temporarily in the Cloud using software running on operating systems (OS) from the general market, such as Linux, for example;

– secondly, organizing how usable information will be returned to the users, and then organizing the dispatching/venting of those data on various communication channels (GSM, Internet, etc.), to the people duly authorized to receive them on computers, tablets, mobile phones/ smartphones, etc. – in short, on any conceivable "Man–Machine Interface" – MMI (e.g. a screen, a PC, etc.). Of course, this also includes people authorized by clients, various service providers, various IoT network managers, end users and initial users, who will have signed contracts with you to send them that information, thus providing the life-blood of your business.

Therefore, for a typical user, it may appear that with a remote computer, it is possible to control and/or monitor the activities of the Things or harvest their data, with the whole of the network described in the previous chapters being nearly transparent.

17

Cloud and Fog Computing

The term Cloud, often also referred to as Cloud Computing, covers all remote data storage solutions. Where, you ask? In the clouds! To be clear, your IoT data, instead of being stored on your hard disks or local memories, are available on remote servers, accessible via the Internet. For this purpose, the various players involved in Cloud computing have enormous banks of storage servers, commonly referred to as Datacenters.

17.1. Cloud computing?

According to the definition given by the National Institute of Standards and Technology (NIST), Cloud computing is "a model for enabling ubiquitous, convenient, on-demand network access to a shared pool of configurable computing resources (e.g., networks, servers, storage, applications and services) that can be rapidly provisioned and released with minimal management effort or service provider interaction", with charges potentially being levied for its use. Thus, it is quite simply the delocalization of computing infrastructure.

Cloud computing, then, is the operation of computing power or storage on remote servers by means of a network (generally the Internet). Very frequently, these servers are rented on demand by users, usually per time slice and per use based on technical criteria (power, bandwidth, server time occupied, etc.), but also for a flat fee. (Example: some Cloud computing services including "AWS" – Amazon Web Services).

17.1.1. *What is its mode of operation?*

Cloud computing is characterized by great flexibility in its use.

Indeed, depending on the user's (client's) level of competence, he/she may be able to manage his/her own server, or content him/herself with using remote applications in SaaS – Software as a Service mode. SaaS is a model of commercial software operations where the software is installed on remote servers rather than on the user's machine(s). Clients do not pay for a usage license for a version, instead using the service online for free, or, more generally, paying a subscription. The main applications of this model are, for example, customer relationship management (CRM) or, in IoT, the sending of information to the clients and/or end users.

17.1.2. *Advantages and benefits in IoT applications*

Cloud computing offers an easy way to access powerful servers, to have large storage space and to access databases, along with a broad range of application services on the Internet without having to make huge initial investments in hardware or software. In addition, it means users do not have to waste precious time on managing the hardware/tools, and needlessly spending money to ensure the operation and maintenance of Datacenters, as Cloud computing providers own and maintain the network-connected hardware needed for these application services.

Thus, the "Cloud" offers essential operations to a company, and rapid access to flexible computing resources at a low cost. This new tool enables companies to:

– set themselves apart from their competitors by focusing solely on customer projects, rather than on necessary infrastructures, rack cable management, software stacking and power supply to the servers;

– allocate precisely the type and size of resources necessary for the computations to create new applications or manage the appropriate computer service, and thus only use the resources needed, through a Web application;

– replace a large part of the functional and capital expenditure (abbreviated as CAPEX) with variable operating expenditure (OPEX);

– gain near-instantaneous access to all the resources that are needed;

– pay only on the basis of the computing resources their operations have consumed;

– no longer pay for datacenters and servers before actually knowing how they are going to use those resources;

– make investments in other domains;

– benefit from great savings in terms of scale, as the usage of hundreds of thousands of customers is all concentrated in the Cloud, by Web service providers;

– have lower usage prices;

– obtain a lower variable cost than the company on its own would have had to bear;

– no longer guess at what the necessary computing resources will be in terms of infrastructural capabilities;

– no longer find themselves short on computing power, or, on the other hand, find themselves with resources not being used, which costs dearly;

– access all the resources they want, be they little or great, and increase or reduce them as required in the space of just a few minutes, because it only takes a few clicks to obtain extra computing resources;

– greatly reduce and optimize the time needed (which shrinks from several weeks to only a few minutes) to make those resources available to developers;

– considerably increase the flexibility of the organization, because the cost and time needed to experiment and develop applications are greatly reduced;

– easily roll out applications in only a few clicks. Thus, the companies can offer reduced latency and a more pleasant experience for customers, very simply and for a low cost.

17.1.3. *Types of Cloud computing*

Cloud computing is divided into three main types, generally known as:

– IaaS – Infrastructure as a service;

– PaaS – Platform as a service;

– SaaS – Software as a service.

By selecting which one(s) of these three Cloud computing solutions is/are most appropriate for their own needs, it is possible for a company to gain an optimum level of control and also avoid the need for a complete overhaul of their computing structure.

17.1.4. *Cloud products and services*

Without wishing to unduly advertise one service or another, certain companies such as Amazon Web Services (AWS) and many others such as Microsoft's Azure, etc., offer a wide range of services for computing, storage, databases, analysis and rollout, as well as application services. These services are designed to help Clients/Organizations evolve more quickly, reduce their computing costs, manage their infrastructure without giving ground on extensibility, security or reliability, and scale up their applications to suit the market.

Thus, it is in this direction that the field of future IoT applications is expanding, and it is in this arena that technology developers will examine all the ramifications of the range of applications which will be the specific selling point of new products. After the design of the Thing itself, therefore, it is the second major step in an IoT project. We then simply need to produce a detailed breakdown of its true cost (see Chapter 19), and finally, as the last step, find and construct a strategy as to how to sell the IoT system in order to make money!

The platforms most widely used in the Cloud are, in order: Amazon's AWS, followed by proprietary solutions, followed by Microsoft's Azure IoT platform (see Figure 17.1).

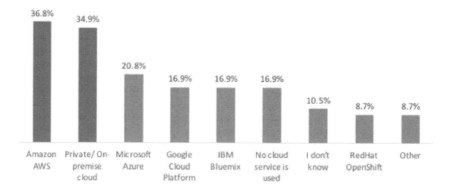

Figure 17.1. *Histogram of platforms used in the Cloud. For a color version of this figure, see www.iste.co.uk/paret/connectedobjects.zip*

17.2. Example: the PaaS platform AWS IoT

As a non-exhaustive example, Amazon Web Services, AWS, began life providing IaaS – i.e. virtual machines (Elastic Compute Cloud, known as EC2) and on-demand storage (Simple Storage Service, known as S3), and later, its provision expanded, adding in increasingly varied PaaS services, including:

– identity management;

– messaging;

– monitoring;

– machine learning

– etc.

Figure 17.2 gives an overview of the AWS IoT solution:

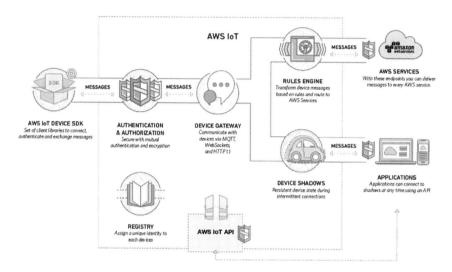

Figure 17.2. *AWS IoT solution. For a color version of this figure, see www.iste.co.uk/paret/connectedobjects.zip*

AWS IoT is based on:

– the integration of the MQTT protocol and its Publish/Subscribe logic. It should be noted that the WebSockets and HTTP protocols are also handled;

– security, because it is impossible to use AWS IoT without using cryptographic certificates and encrypted communications;

– a Shadow system, enabling the Cloud part to continue to operate and conduct a dialog with the Things, even if those Things are temporarily disconnected. The information (sensor data, orders to actuators) are synchronized anew when connectivity is restored.

All of these functions are based on other AWS modules (databases, identification, and so on).

17.3. How security is managed

Authentication and authorization is at the heart of the exchanges. Indeed, each Thing wishing to connect to AWS IoT (or more specifically to its MQTT broker) must have its communications authenticated and encoded in TLS (Transport Layer Security). For this purpose, a long list of encryption algorithms is available:

– ECDHE-ECDSA-AES128-GCM-SHA256 (recommended);

– ECDHE-RSA-AES128-GCM-SHA256 (recommended);

– ECDHE-ECDSA-AES128-SHA256;

– ECDHE-RSA-AES128-SHA256;

– ECDHE-ECDSA-AES128-SHA;

– ECDHE-RSA-AES128-SHA;

– ECDHE-ECDSA-AES256-GCM-SHA384;

– ECDHE-RSA-AES256-GCM-SHA384;

– ECDHE-ECDSA-AES256-SHA384;

– ECDHE-RSA-AES256-SHA384;

– ECDHE-RSA-AES256-SHA;

– ECDHE-ECDSA-AES256-SHA;

– AES128-GCM-SHA256;

– AES128-SHA256;

– AES128-SHA;

– AES256-GCM-SHA384;

– AES256-SHA256;

– AES256-SHA.

This means that the Thing must be able to securely save the authentication elements and ensure that no data exchange occurs between the Things and AWS IoT without identities having been verified. The authentication is based on the X.509 certificate.

HTTP connections can use different methods, whereas MQTT connections must use certificate-based authentication.

To simplify the operations, with AWS IoT, we can directly generate the certificates or use any certification authority. These certificates are able to manage the various authorizations, and may be rescinded at any time.

It is also possible to generate restricted or temporary certificates.

The corollary to all of this is that it is impossible to connect Things non-securely to another Thing (which is authorized on other platforms such as Azure). This requirement sometimes leads to certain difficulties, because the hardware must have at least a certain degree of encryption capability (certificate management), meaning that certain SDKs were slower to be integrated than on other platforms. Security, though, of course, comes at a price!

Figure 17.3 is a diagram of all the services than can be mobilized to ensure the security of the Things and storage of the data, but also the authentication of the users. The whole setup is based on the identity and access management (IAM) module.

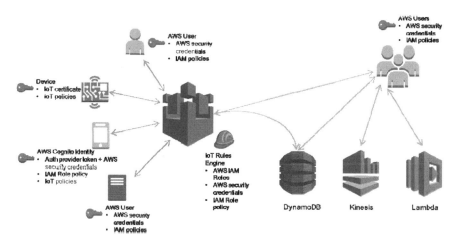

Figure 17.3. *Overview of services providing security for connected Things*

17.4. Fog computing?

In its principle, Fog computing offers hosted services similar to Cloud computing, such as processing resources, storage spaces or even applications which, instead of being a very long way away geographically from the Things (via LR (Long-Range) networks), are actually in their vicinity, not in immediate proximity but almost (MR and SR for Medium and Short Range). In addition, while Cloud computing is designed to handle a great many Things and huge amounts of data with immense computing capability, Fog computing is made up of a very great number of nearby mini-Clouds designed for more restricted applications, to prevent the management and processing of such a quantity of data by a single entity... which could be risky!

As tasks are carried out locally, the Fog has no need to use the Cloud or a Datacenter, which helps reduce the data management time and improve the quality of service provided. In addition, as these local data are not fed back into the Cloud network, its workload is greatly lessened. Fog computing, in fact, constitutes the layer below Cloud computing in connected Things.

Because the data processed are stored in a local "mini cloud" dedicated to those data, structurally, they have greater confidentiality and security.

To conclude, in the market of connected Things, Fog computing is growing rapidly. For local applications requiring greater fluidity, stability and rapidity, also benefiting from enhanced security, it offers users greater ease of use – for example, in the domain of connected vehicles, medical monitoring, connection between buildings or the different infrastructures which make up our environment, the availability of spaces in parking lots, or the energy consumption of a particular building.

17.5. Big data

Before they can work with "Big Data", companies have to undertake "Big rollouts". In this case, the IoT is characterized by the generation of a considerable mass of data (when it truly is rolled out *en masse*, as opposed to ten Things for Proof of Concept). Then, we still need to process the uploaded data, and in particular, extract any pertinent information. At this point, we find ourselves faced with three problems:

– how to eliminate the incoherent data;

– how to identify which data are useful;

– how to properly exploit those useful data.

Mass data harvesting makes it very difficult to identify weak signals. However, very often, businesses' information systems are not capable of handling these masses of hieratic data, and absolutely must be fed with synthetic, qualified data. It is in that area that platforms specializing in IoT can offer solutions.

First of all, it is helpful to specify how these continuous flows of information are to be processed. Unlike with traditional "Big data" approaches, which handle "cold" data (consumer behavioral history, frequenting of a certain store, etc.), the IoT works with "hot" data – "red hot", we could even say! Indeed, these data need to be processed almost in real time, and a response must be provided in a fraction of a second, or a few seconds. Consider the example of a customer passing in front of a store. We can quite easily see the importance of reacting in an instant, rather than waiting until the customer has gone home!

However, this type of processing generally uses the databases NoSQL and Hadoop, which require clusters running the data-processing software. This type of processing draws on the network and the data cache functions.

Another point relates to "Machine Learning", where we look for learning models in raw data. The process of designing learning models includes analysing the data, followed by the training of testing models.

Once we have defined these learning models, they can be reintegrated into the Things, to make the devices smarter and more autonomous.

17.6. Natural interfaces

With the Cloud, we can envisage very high-level services requiring considerable computation power, such as voice recognition in natural language.

Products such as "Amazon Echo", "Amazon Tap" and "Echo Dot" or "Google Home" operate recognition engines, which have the peculiarity of constantly listening for users' commands. The interactions then become extremely natural and effective, because they exploit all the power of the Cloud. These products enable you, for example, to order a pizza directly (when you are in the mood for pizza!) or add things to your shopping list.

PART 5

Concrete Realization of an IoT Solution
Examples and Costs

We come now to the fifth and final part of this book on secure connected Things in IoT/IoE! The ordeal is almost over!

We are unaccustomed to leaving readers unsatisfied, and from the very beginning of this book, the discussion has been orientated towards concrete realization of IoT solutions. The time has come!

Having lived it a great many times during our respective careers, we have extensive experience in the fields of Research, Applications and Industrialization of products, and we are keen to include this fifth part. This sort of practical application is fairly rare in technical (particularly when the discussion actually cites the true costs of solutions, rather than stopping short and giving only vague examples).

Of course, the cases discussed here are merely examples, and everyone must adapt the principles discussed to their own application, and must update the prices to reflect the situation at the precise moment when the calculations are being done, but the examples herein set out some essential orders of magnitude, so that readers can avoid various pitfalls from the very start of a project!

We wish you a pleasant reading of these last two chapters... and beware of a big surprise.

18

Examples of the Concrete Realization of Connected Things

Over the course of the coming sections, we will present a detailed example of a big-picture examination which any designer of a connected Thing – using a simple connection or an Internet connection – should/must carry out in analyzing his/her technical specifications, the design of the product, the need to produce a prototype, the proposed budget for the development of a project and its manufacture on a production line.

Obviously, to construct such an example of a project and remain reasonably close to a real-world, concrete situation, we have made a certain number of hypotheses on estimated timescale, development costs, scheduling for the production and estimation of the cost of manufacturing prototypes and the end product, which are set out in detail and at length in Chapter 19. Obviously, readers will have to refine the scenario to suit their own situation, in terms of costs and schedules, any updates and/or evaluate other scenarios if need be, depending on their own particular needs.

18.1. Subject/application taken as an example

We have chosen a characteristic example of a simple "connected Thing", with options (see Chapter 3) and connected to the Internet – a true communicating Thing with technologies of the Internet of Things.

The chosen application is that of certain home help services for the elderly or dependent people. In principle, it is simple, easy, and very widespread, but reality is a long way removed from the principle! This system must enable us to create a communication and a community of users (hence the name IoE, rather than just IoT!) linking the aid receivers (dependent people), specialized helpers (nurses, kinesiotherapists, etc.), the families, the various service providers coming to the home (offering hygiene, cleaning, meals, etc.), traders, neighbors, etc. In short, it is actually far less simple! We then come to understand that the physical Thing itself (mainly the hardware part) represents only the very small visible tip of the iceberg which is the system, and that its cost, which is certainly not insignificant (see details in Chapter 19), is generally swallowed up in a crowd of other parameters, and that we must watch every penny in order to make the complete solution not just sellable, but actually "buyable"!

Figure 18.1 illustrates the commercialized finished product.

Figure 18.1. *Concrete example of an IoT Thing*

Figure 18.2 shows the overall hardware architecture of the Thing chosen for this particular concrete case.

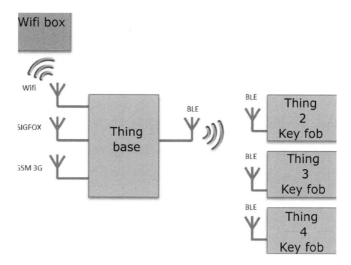

Figure 18.2. *Overall hardware architecture of the Thing*

18.1.1. *Architecture of the product: a communicating physical Thing*

The type of communicating Thing envisaged here is made up, functionally, of two main elements: firstly a *BASE*, and secondly one or more *TAGS* associated with that *BASE*:

– the "*BASE*" is the part located in the users' homes;

– one or more "TAGs", or key fobs, or other form factors of small Things, serve as tokens with access rights, enabling the various contributors to carry out different identifying functions, notably with the *BASE*;

and of course,

– these two elements of the overall product come in the form of ergonomic plastic boxes, each containing electronic chips.

In spite of the almost primitive appearance described above, the system's detailed (interwoven) characteristics are as described in the following section.

18.1.1.1. *The BASE*

In addition to a local radiofrequency connection using BLE (Bluetooth Low-Energy), which is necessary to ensure communication between the *BASE* and the *TAGs*, in order to communicate with the outside world and provide the "I" aspect (Internet) of IoT, various versions/options for RF connections with the *BASE* mentioned above must be possible depending on the degrees of the final applications, agreed upon with the customers:

– a Wi-Fi connection to communicate with the user's ISP box;

– an LPWAN, SIGFOX and/or LoRa connection to communicate with the gateway over a long distance (several kms);

– or a GPRS/3G connection, optional, on a 3G modem.

In addition, the *BASE* also functionally includes:

– a motion detector, button or LED, etc.;

– a power supply:

As the system installed in people's homes is permanent and immobile, it draws its power from the 220V mains supply using an external AC/DC adapter;

Depending on the final balance of consumption and the need for the product to run on batteries, only with a SIGFOX version of a device, the *BASE* may operate solely on batteries.

A slightly more detailed illustration of the *BASE* is given in Figure 18.3.

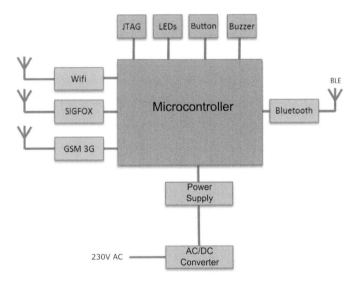

Figure 18.3. *More detailed illustration of the BASE*

The TAG

The *TAG* contains a:

– BLE link;

– a button cell, an LED;

– its power supply is drawn from the button cell.

The diagram of the *TAG* is given in Figure 18.4.

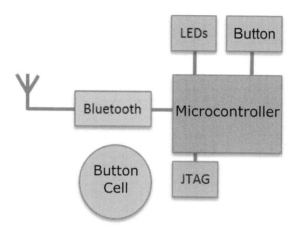

Figure 18.4. *Illustration of the TAG*

18.1.2. *Mandatory steps in creating the Thing*

Be careful: we are now playing in the big leagues, and amateurs may be seriously put off by the numerous zeros in front of the numbers stated when we mention the quantities and costs (see Chapter 19).

In this book, we have set out to demonstrate the industrial and commercial concrete production of IoT Things, as the press are fond of saying, with thousands of Things produced each year (for example, a quantity of 300,000 units a year!). Thus, in concrete industrial production of this product, for example, there are two main paths to be followed:

– the path of the development phases, including:

- designing the electronic cards with a view to industrialization and production on a major scale. – YES, the "*Reference Designs*" from component manufacturers and proponents of solutions, and the reports on POCs (Proof of concept), convey certain ideas and are helpful to gain knowledge, but NO, NO and NO AGAIN, they are not sufficient to carry out industrial development!

- integrating the firmware of the application and onboard software, and adaptations depending on the design of the cards,

- designing mechanical boxes with a view to produce working prototypes.

– the path of the industrial phase of the project, including:

- certification tests, conformance tests… (EMC, "EC", etc.),

- industrialization,

- serial production of the product in the intended quantities,

Rome was not built in a day… Nor are IoT devices, as some may believe or imply. In fact, a market launch often takes many months (just in terms of supply of materials, industrial action here and there, etc.), and problems are frequently encountered. In addition, in the case of VSEs, SMEs, it is common to have to deal with momentary holes in the budget, and numerous visits to and from your bank! (Note, we shall talk specifically about money in great detail in the hardware part in Chapter 19!)

As promised, we are talking in terms of concrete realization here!

We can consider two examples of overviews of options for architectures in the *BASE*:

– the first is a simple device (Figure 18.5), secured by using a (real) external Secure Element:

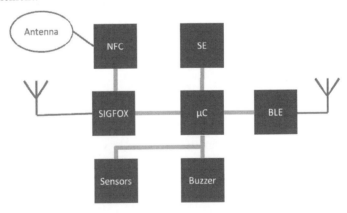

Figure 18.5. *Simple architecture, secured with an external Secure Element*

or else, in a more integral form, using a mono-chip (Figure 18.6):

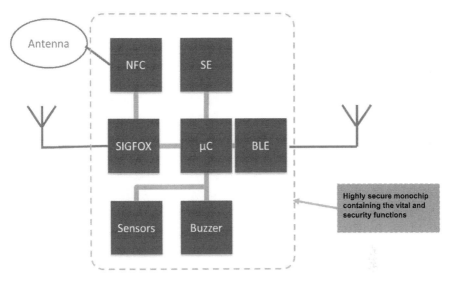

Figure 18.6. *Simple architecture, secured with an internal Secure Element*

– a second solution (Figure 18.7): it too is secured by a (true) Secure Element, but is also equipped with a micro-SD card so it can satisfy the specific securing of personal data in respect of users' privacy, in full accordance with the GDPR and the CNIL discussed in Chapter 7.

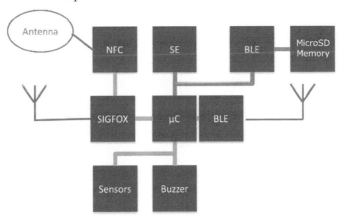

Figure 18.7. *Architecture secured by a Secure Element and equipped with a further microSD card*

Figure 18.8 illustrates the final produced versions (the antenna, as it should be, is inside the chamber of the BASE casing).

Figures 18.8. *Examples of products (with integrated antenna)*

Figures 18.9a and b show screenshots of a management terminal and of a user's mobile telephone.

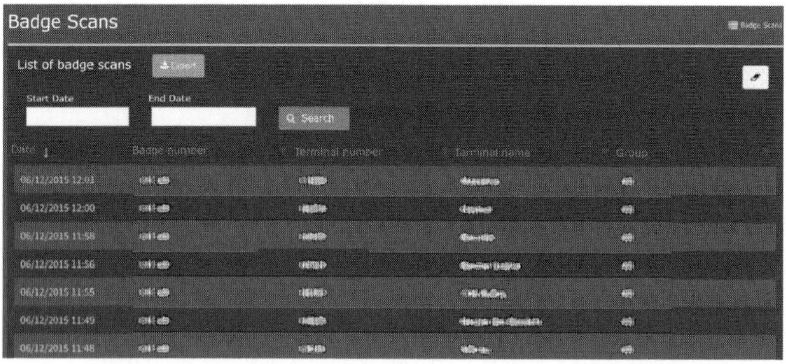

Figure 18.9a. *Screenshot of a management terminal*

Figure 18.9b. *Screenshot from a user's mobile phone*

Having had this technical overview, let us now move on to the costs of these solutions.

19

Cost Aspects

In the wake of all the previous chapters, discussing the points of solution architectures, technical principles, components, etc., to nicely round off this book, the present chapter goes into great detail about a point which is generally rather problematic: the costs of a solution comprising a secure connected Thing and IoT!

In every project, this issue must sooner or later be addressed, and it is best to know what to expect.

Knowing, in general, that numerous economical and financial points have already been examined in previous chapters – notably the viability of the project, meaning the financial and marketing aspects, i.e. the establishment of the provisional budget to be allocated to the study phase of the project (see Chapters 1-19) – let us now turn our attention to a whole host of new, highly concrete Things.

First of all, let us divide the costs we are going to talk about into two categories: CAPEX and OPEX!

19.1. CAPEX and OPEX are in the same boat...

"*CAPEX*" (*capital expenditure*) refers to immobilizations – i.e. to expenditure having a positive value in the long term.

EXAMPLE.– the purchase of a photocopier (non-consumable)

"*OPEX*" (*operational expenditure*) refers to the usual expenses incurred in running a product, a company or a system.

EXAMPLE.– the annual cost of paper and toner cartridges consumed.

These two concepts are fundamentally important in the way in which we industrialize and commercialize a project involving an IoT-connected Thing.

19.1.1. *CAPEX*

In IoT, CAPEX is divided largely into two domains:

– the cost of the hardware architecture, the price of the components – the BOM: Bill Of Material) and software specific to the Thing, included in the Thing itself (communication protocol management, etc.);

– the cost of the software architecture included in the Cloud, so that the application software has a spine.

Let us begin with the BOM.

19.1.1.1. *BOM - Bill of Material for the Thing*

Sooner or later, we need to produce the BOM – Bill of Material (material cost) of the Thing itself… which is only the very beginning of the story, but marks the endpoint for far too many people!

Important note:

In order to give readers a concrete idea, the prices and figures indicated exclusive of tax, based on typical figures in the business world, presented in Table 19.1, have been deliberately rounded, and are shown 1) at a given date (beginning of 2017); 2) are merely for illustrative purposes, and 3) it would always be a good idea to update these figures over the course of future studies… in the knowledge that these prices will only decrease over the coming months!

Below is an example of a BOM (Table 19.1), based on the example given in Figure 18.3 in the previous chapter.

BASE	Price excl. tax
Microprocessor	€3
Bluetooth BLE	€4
Buzzer / LED	€3
PCB – 6 layers	€3
Various components	€3
Long-range modem	€15
5V power supply	€6
Plastic shell	€9
TOTAL for components	**€46**

Table 19.1. *Order of magnitude of pre-tax prices typically used in business*

Readers can no longer claim that they do not have a concrete idea of the costs involved in a project!… and all of that is merely the BOM for the BASE, to which you must add your desired profit margin and VAT at 20%!… and then you must do the same thing for the TAG!

19.1.1.2. *Development of electronic cards and their environments*

The BOM is estimated, but for each of the parts – i.e. for the BASE and the TAG – it is necessary to spend time and money on the design, development and testing of the electronic cards they contain. The "treasure hunt" of these various industrial phases is described below.

– first of all, we need to draft a document giving a detailed description of the product's intended specifications. These include the hardware specifications of the electronic card, those of the onboard software, the mechanical specifications of the box, and describe the project's acceptance log;

– next comes the phase of physical development of the electronic card, which includes the research, drawing of the electronic diagrams of the card, the nomenclature, the constraints of positioning and routing, the layout of the card and prototype production logs;

– then we have the manufacture of the printed circuit boards, and the supply of components (beware: the component supplies may have an MOQ – Minimum Order Quantity!)

– and finally, we have the cabling of the earliest prototypes.

In parallel, a number of different phases take place:

– development of embedded software including the low-level software layers for resource management (for the functions Bluetooth, Wi-Fi, SIGFOX, 3G, button, LEDs, buzzer, etc.), the embedded application itself and the creation of the testing and validation environment, which will also be used during production;

– lengthy external application software development, comprising software applications on external servers (operators such as Orange, Bouygues, SIGFOX, etc., hosts, sites (OVH, AWS, brokers, etc.), on Smartphones, Tablets, etc.;

– development of the mechanical packaging of the Thing, including defining its "look", the choice of material, color(s) in the material, painted of silkscreened, marking, logos, text, etc.), the CAD mechanical study of the different parts (battery compartment, button, light guide, clip closing, screw closing, etc.) and molds, so we can design the mechanical aspects of the parts for the few (two or three) prototypes (3D printers are not enough when it comes to production! We need to think about plastic injection molds, which are very expensive and must be paid for very early on in the process, and be correctly sized for the desired quantity, and in terms of the quality of the metal, cooling, ejection systems to remove the parts from the molds, number of prints, and so on. The price of injection molds generally varies widely depending on the quantities needed!);

– integration of the embedded software and the electronic components into the prototype mechanical casing;

– testing of the prototype product's electronic cards and functional components;

– acceptance testing of the first prototypes.

Even after all of this, you only have a couple of initial working prototypes, almost finalized, upon which, following EMC testing and any necessary corrections (you can be sure that some corrections will, indeed, be necessary), you can make certain alterations to the position/routing of the cards, before updating the plans and files to launch the final prototypes, their industrialization (serial production tools, manufacture of the bare PCBs, wiring of the cards, programs for automatic implementation of CMSs, testing of equipped cards, serial production of the injection molds for the cases and the different parts, the functional test array, and the integration of the card into the plastic packaging with the different necessary components (including a battery for the tag)).

Finally, it will be necessary to create a test environment containing a BASE and a TAG to check that everything works correctly, before carrying out acceptance testing on the prototypes and finally green-lighting the production process and, after your precise and refined industrial hypotheses as to the annual quantities, quantities per batch, production site, delivery, definition of packaging, costs of guarantees, after-sales services, etc., you will finally know your stock price! Wow!

NOTE.–

Of course, thanks to the prototype phase, you can obtain an overall view of the likely cost for your project, cost ranges, necessary planning to develop the product, etc., so you can estimate the serial production price and make a projection for the large-scale production price.

19.1.1.3. *Scheduling*

In the wake of this lengthy discussion which was basically and concretely industrial, let us now look at the time parameter. This often takes the form of a schedule, with a provisional PERT diagram (*program evaluation and review technique*) for phases 1 and 2 of the project's development, and an estimation of the pre-serial production phase.

The time of the actual launch of the project ("t0") is often quite difficult to determine, because it varies as a function of numerous parameters. Once it has been established, all the players involved need to confirm that PERT, which often takes some time!

An example of a schedule covering all the necessary points mentioned above is given in Table 19.2 and, in spite of the numerous phases carried out in parallel, shows a period of around 7-8 months. Only extremely expert companies are able to contractually agree to, and properly stick to, this very tight schedule. Often, these periods run closer to ten months than eight!

	month	month	month	month	month	month	month
RESEARCH	1	2	3	4	5	6	7
Specifications							
Electronics develop.							
Software develop.							
Mechanical develop.							
Testing/Integration/ Approval							
Revision and second prototype							
Industrialization							
PRODUCTION							

Table 19.2. *Example of a schedule. Presented here solely for illustrative purposes in this book*

19.1.1.4. *Development costs*

To carry out all the little segments of the above schedule – first prototyping phase, review and second prototyping, industrialization (electronics and mechanical tools), for both the BASE and the TAG – takes time, which, multiplied by an hourly rate, costs money! In addition, the development costs are dependent on budget hypotheses that are hotly debated and set in stone by the company's Marketing and Sales departments (e.g. for manufacturing a quantity of products of several hundred thousand units a year, with the same mechanical tools).

In this book, unlike many others, we wish to give concrete and realistic industrial examples, and we are not afraid to cite figures, multiplying all these hours of work by a normal industrial market rate. For example, with rounded figures, this gives us the table shown in Table 19.3.

	Costs excl. Tax
BASE	
project management and specifications	€10k
hardware research and prototyping	€10k
embedded software research	€20k
mechanics research and prototyping	€15k
tests and integration of the first prototypes	€15k
Subtotal for research and initial prototyping	**€70k**
TAG	
project management and specifications	€10k
hardware research and prototyping	€5k
embedded software research	€10k
mechanics research and prototyping	€10k
tests and integration of the first prototypes	€5k
Subtotal for research and initial prototyping	**€40k**
REVIEW	
review of base and tag cards	€10k
EMC testing	€30k
Subtotal for review and renewed research	**€40k**
industrialization	
electronics of cards in base and tag	€30k
mechanics of base case	€60k
mechanics of tag case	€40k
Subtotal for industrialization	**€130k**
GENERAL TOTAL	**€280k**

Table 19.3. *Example of development costs*

...of course excluding warranty, after-sales service and transport, depending on the production sites (Europe, the Far East) and delivery, the size of the production batches (several batches or "single shot" production) and shipping.

In short, entry to the metaphorical club, including the BOM + research + industrialization, is enormously expensive, with the price tag set at around €300k excluding tax.

19.1.1.5. *Standardizations and certifications*

To this BOM, we must add the costs of standardization and certification of the products, but beware! Here, too, there are numerous snares and pitfalls along the way!

Indeed, before starting, it is essential to reach absolute agreement with the customer as regards the levels and depths of certification needed and/or wanted! In addition to this, we need to take into account (quite often) the industrial protection measures in certain countries (a random example might be the USA), with extremely complicated standardizations and certifications which practically force companies to produce and source their components locally.

Costs of standardizations, certifications etc.

Systems/Things are becoming increasingly complex, and increasingly, are able to support a great many protocols. Before we get to that stage, though, in order to have the right to legally commercialize the product, obviously we need to standardize and certify all this huge mass of protocols (Bluetooth, NFC, SIGFOX, LoRa, etc.), which requires knowledge, energy, time... and therefore money, which must be added to the CAPEX.

Again, these costs can be divided into two categories:

– those in the "run-up", corresponding to the passing of a host of "unofficial", less expensive pre-certifications, in laboratories which are highly technically advanced but do not hold official accreditation;

– those of so-called "D-Day" when, on pain of having to go right back to the drawing board, everything must be perfect when the product undergoes the real qualifications, certifications, approvals, etc. of all types in independent, state-accredited laboratories, such as COFRAC in France (examples also include FIME, EMITECH, etc.) or similar ones in other countries (examples: CETECOM, UL, etc.).

A few examples

Below are a few examples of requirements to which the product must conform.

CE pre-certifications and certifications

CE labeling is self-declarative, and the prices/costs levied by independent laboratories for CE pre-certifications or certifications are around €2k per day × 10 days = €20k.

Conformity with IEC safety regulations

We also need to think about running the electrical safety tests prescribed by European Norm IEC/EN 62061, pertaining to the requirements relating to the design of the machines' electrical safety control systems and subsystems, and non-complex devices. Similarly, in the case of sales in the USA, it is necessary to carry out the well-known tests UL94 V0, V1 and V2 regarding flammability and fire safety of the plastic materials used in various pieces of equipment and applications.

Conformity/certification for the ETSI and FCC RF regulations

The same is true when carrying out the ETSI European preliminary radiofrequency conformity tests and conformity tests, followed by the FCC tests if we want to export our wonderful Thing to the USA.

ANSSI security certification

In an additional (but welcome) fashion, in the IoT market, the certificates and standardizations of the security of products/Things are awarded – for example, in France, by the *Agence nationale de la sécurité des systèmes d'information* – ANSSI.

– CSPN – *Certification de Sécurité de Premier Niveau* (First-Level Security Certification)

Order of magnitude of costs is of €15k within 15 days.

– CC – *Critères communs* – Common criteria

Order of magnitude of costs is of €60-120k.

Conformity of operation/standard

In addition, if we want to be able to print wonderful logos on the Thing and not be prosecuted by the DGCCRF – *Direction générale de la concurrence, de la consommation et de la répression des fraudes* (General Directorate for Competitiveness, Consumption and Fraud Prevention) – for disloyal competition and misleading advertising, here again there are a number of hoops we must jump through:

NFC

When a so-called "NFC" certification is required (more specifically, NFC Forum), the product must be subjected to the NFC Forum test, carried out in testing labs accredited by the NFC Forum. It is mandatory to be a member of the NFC Forum, and membership is expensive!).

SIGFOX

The electronic components are certified by SIGFOX but, at the end of the process, the finished product must also be SIGFOX certified, with a handsome "SIGFOX Ready" label, in two different modes:

P1 module   (example: Telecom design 1208, etc.)

P2 the whole thing with casing, power supply, antenna, etc.

This certification can only be obtained through the SIGFOX laboratory.

LoRa

The LoRa Alliance has issued its certification program, which will be mandatory. The aim of this certification is to ensure that the connected Thing has successfully passed the tests of the "End Device Certification Requirements" published by the Alliance, that it is certified and it obeys the functional constraints of the LoRaWAN standard (see Figure 19.1).

Figure 19.1. *Example of a LoRA Alliance compliance certificate*

This certification can be obtained through LoRa Alliance-accredited testing laboratories, such as

– IMST, Espotel, etc.

– Bluetooth, others, etc.

Put briefly, it is a long path to be followed for each and every new Thing, for which, unlike what is commonly believed, the cost is not insignificant.

19.1.1.6. Cost price of the industrial product

We now have enough information to carry out an initial estimation of the cost of the industrial manufacture of the product, with, for example:

Adopting the hypothesis of a production run of only 100,000 Things

The price for NRE – Non-recurring engineering – (a "one-time" cost for research, development, designing and testing, averaged per Thing), would therefore be around 280,000 / 100,000 = €2.80, which can be rounded up to €3, added to the costs of the components, which gives us, roughly, the following table (Table 19.4):

BASE	Price excl. tax
Subtotal for components, BOM	€46
Assembly (30%)	€14
NRE*	€3
TOTAL for components	**€63**

Table 19.4. *Initial estimation of industrial production price*

With these hypotheses, we can estimate the cost of manufacture of the product, per installed product:

BASE   ~ €63 PU excl. tax

TAG (not detailed above)   ~ €5 PU excl. tax

Base delivered with three tags = 63 + (3 × 5) =   ~ €78 excl. tax

In addition, it is usual, on the market, that the couple "sales price excl. tax" - "factory cost price excl. tax" obeys a ratio of around 2, meaning a sales price of around €160 excl. tax.

This price difference generally includes:

– a part devoted to pursuing research for future product development;

– the cost of after-sales service;

– the cost of communication and advertising;

– a profit for the shareholders;

– and in particular, the payment made to the distribution network.

Thus, we have a sales price for the final customer of around €190 inc. tax.

19.1.1.7. *Software development for IoT applications via the Internet*

Once the hardware part of the product is established (see the previous section), we have reached the middle of the ford, because now we need to focus on the developments and costs of the software parts, pertaining to the Cloud computing, which will either be embedded in the device or installed in the Cloud (data management, broker, security, etc.) and their interfaces with the end user.

Cost of the platform and application in the Cloud

For the CAPEX part, starting at zero, to ensure the functional totality of the application software platform of a company (management of all the protocols such of HTTP, MQTP, etc., customer interface, user-friendliness of the sites, etc.), we must reckon with a charge of around one engineer per year, representing around €60k salary + managerial charge + administration costs + etc. = in short, a total of €100k ... and often this software part costs just as much as the hardware!

Then, for any new IoT project, on the basis of the calculation established above, only an adjustment of around 3-4 months per specific application project, i.e. around €30k, can suffice. It is up to you to run the calculations for all of this in order to charge your end customer an appropriate price.

19.1.1.8. *ROI*

Table 19.5 shows a simplified example of an initial estimation of the schedule of return on investment over the production of the same Thing for one and three years, with or without certain adjustments.

prod.	100k			100k			100k		
	year 1			year 2			year 3		
ROI over 1 year	BOM = €46/pieces = €4600k								
	assembly = €14/p = €1400k								
	NRE = €300k + 100k for software = €400k								
	COST PRICE = 6400/100 = 64								
ROI over 3 years	BOM = €46/piece × 300kp = €13,800k								
	assembly = €14/p × 300k = €4200k								
	NRE = €300k + 100k for software = €400k								
	COST PRICE = 61.33								
ROI over 3 years	BOM = €46/piece × 300kp = €13,800k								
	assembly = €14/p × 300k = €4200k								
	NRE = €300k + 100k for software + 30k for software updating = €430k								
	COST PRICE = 61.43								

Table 19.5. *Example of cost price facilitating ROI over 1 to 3 years*

To conclude, and so as to not leave readers with too negative an impression after these long series of numbers, in the face of such costs, we can look at all the benefits that can be drawn from such an operation:

– internal process benefits for the company, cost reductions, improved productivity, planning, measures, quality, reactivity and TTM (Time To Market), etc.

– benefits to services by improved products, added value, monetary profit, better positioning, improved image, customer satisfaction, etc.

Note that industrial examples of applications in IoT are the most profitable, because they always generate these two sets of benefits as a result.

19.1.2. *OPEX*

19.1.2.1. *How much will the operational expenditure be?*

Once again, IoT solutions need to be broken down in order to gain an idea of the OPEX (operational expenditure) of a product, a company or a system.

– what is the cost of the connection, with and without Internet?

– is the operator unique and/or does its own its network?

– what is the cost of renting its LPWA network?

– are the Things talkative (a great deal of bandwidth required), or not very?

– are the Things situated far from or near to the Cloud host?

– what are the impacts of these parameters on the costs of each of these communications?

– once we know the price of communications per Thing per month or per year, and have multiplied that by the millions of devices operating, is the sum to be paid per month, per year, all at once, etc.?

– if the network extends to other countries, what roaming charges are levied by the network provider to reintegrate the data locally?

– does the operator take a commission for uploading the information and transmitting it to the users? In what format would the data be? Raw data? Pre-treated data? From where?

– do we also need to pay the application host? On what conditions? At the price of the transaction? At the price of the API? etc.

– is the cost of all this low in relation to the price of the Thing? In relation to the price of the software to operate the application?

– etc.... and many other questions!

In fact, it is at this point that the work begins!

The paragraphs below informally present some examples of elements of responses to some of the points mentioned above.

Case of SIGFOX

SIGFOX, for its proprietary network, advertises a tariff of between €0.70 and €8 per Thing per year. Table 19.6 also shows, as at a given date, an example of the order of magnitude in Euros, excl. tax, of a tariff which decreases with an increase in number of Things to be connected.

level of subscription	volume of Things per contract	< 1k	< 10k				> 250k
	frames per Thing per day						
Platinum	101-140	15	-	-	-	-	5
Gold	51-100	10	-	-	-	-	-
Silver	3-50	20	-	-	-	-	-
One	1-2	8	-	-	-	-	0.8
plus a great many notes for all exemptions and conceivable situations							

Table 19.6. *Example for SIGFOX (illustrative purposes only)*

Case of LoRa

Three cases may arise: yes, maybe, and no (see Figure 19.2).

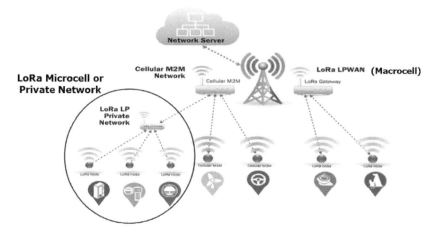

Figure 19.2. *Examples of the three specific cases for LoRa applications*

– you can choose to construct your network, purchasing and installing your own antennas. In this case, you need to take into account of the cost of installation of your own local network, with its 2, 3... *n* antennas;

– you wish to make use of an existing operator's network (e.g. Orange, Vodafone, etc.); for the same price, the operator offers you other services as well. Today, these operators' rates are somewhat obscure to the mere mortal, and we must wait until Bouygues, Orange, Qowisio and others unveil their commercial offers and their business approaches to be able to have a true debate about their price differences.

Case of Qowisio

The problem is different again, but fairly close to that of SIGFOX, because Qowisio's service, known as "device-to-you" [the user], ensures economic and security independence from a particular operator (to its own benefit!). Qowisio has its own network infrastructure, and can build any communication protocol into a device. In addition, based on the principle that the addition of connectivity is envisageable and financially viable only if the integration of the connectivity costs no more than a few Euros overall, and if we are billed no more than a few cents per month (per device, obviously, in both cases). With this aim in mind, the cost of Qowisio's concept is based on seeking out the lowest possible ARPU (the Average Revenue Per Unit is the mean monthly turnover per Thing generated by a company), based on a usage slot where data rates are very low (around 5 bits/s, so with very low energy consumption of the Thing) and where the ARPU is a few cents, meaning an average turnover generated per Thing over three years at around €5, including the cost of connection and data transport. Qowisio is not considered a competitor of other actors in the arena, but instead is held to provide a complementary service.

Cost of application platform in the Cloud

Once the operators and/or pseudo-operators have been paid, we need to create software applications for the end users and those for the broker, which can both be hosted in the Cloud, and of course, partially finance them as consumables, under OPEX.

For example, Amazon's AWS offers you, for your application, a secure transaction broker... charged at 5 dollars for a million exchanges.

Thus, it is up to you as designers to decide which services you wish to use.

19.1.3. Conclusions

In order to draw some semblance of a conclusion on CAPEX and especially on OPEX, sooner or later we need to discuss the true business and the real business needs that the various IoT networks can serve, because in general, end users are not electronics experts or radio experts, and are indifferent to the use of LoRa, SIGFOX, Qowisio, Ingenu, etc. In fact, the end users simply want the provider that they choose to offer them guaranteed connectivity over a given area, a global solution and a sensible cost! There is not one technology which is good while all others are bad (this has been known for a long time!), especially given that, as we have shown throughout this book, radiofrequency concepts have been in use since WWII, which is over 75 years at the time of writing! Thus, it is not particularly pertinent to try to set providers apart on the basis of technical and technological factors; such an attempt merely muddies the waters in IoT and blurs the perception of the public, future customers and future markets.

19.1.4. *Very important conclusions*

If we think, in accordance with the Marketing services of an IoT provider, that the final IoT application can serve five different customers, we need to be sure that for each of the target customers, the amount paid out in CAPEX for the company (even before the first sale is made) of $(100,000/5) \times €160$ excl. tax = €3200,000 = €3.2 million represents any interest at all, before embarking on any work!

We now come to the statement made earlier: "the 'sellable' sales price of the product must be in keeping with the 'buyable' price for the end customer to whom we hope to sell it"!!

First approach: switching from an existing solution to IoT

By switching from an existing solution whose price excl. tax is X, to an IoT solution offering technological "pluses", these customers will be able to sell their new products at a price of X+(10-15%) more than the old ones. On the other hand, to switch from one solution to another, they estimate that the cost of that switch to IoT must be such as to provide a minimum 30% gain in comparison to the existing situation, so X - 30% of X. Hence, we need to go find customers whose existing applications currently represent a turning excl. tax of around €4.5 million/year on the existing product... which is not bad to begin with! This is where truly high-quality IoT applications will gain ground, as opposed to those which are bandied about in the miasma of marketing.

Second approach: using IoT to acquire a strategic position

The second approach is based on the exploitation of a technological breakthrough (connectivity and IoT) which will have a considerable impact on the company's economic model. Let us look, in this instance, at the example of TESLA, the American electric car manufacturer, and consider a connected vehicle to be an IoT Thing like any other.

TESLA used the technological breakthrough of electrical propulsion, combined with connectivity, to acquire a strategic position which was entirely different to that of other car manufacturers, whose models have historically been based on shaping sheet metal (with no pejorative implication intended!). TESLA went about things in the opposite direction, adding four wheels to a connected computer, enabling the company to offer completely different services, such as, for example automatic driving, free recharges included in the sale price of the electric vehicle, etc.

In the latter case, the economic logic is based on the obtaining of a "position on the market" in automobile manufacture, rather than immediate profitability. At present, TESLA has been losing money every month since its creation, but its valuation is much higher than that of most car manufacturers having been in existence for over 100 years! Of course, the best thing to do in this case is to be Mr. Elon Musk, to have already made a success of several fruitful enterprises (PayPal, for example) in order to be able to raise considerable sums of money based simply on who you are, and maintain the trust of your shareholders… but in Musk's view, this represents the minimum cost to join the club of automobile manufacturers, and acquire a strategic position on the market, in the hope of ultimately controlling and steering it.

Now, all you need to do is to pick a side!

Conclusion

We have now come to the end of this book, the aim of which was to provide readers with a basic grounding so as to be able to begin to understand the complete chain of devices securely connected through the Internet, from the design ideas behind them to their concrete industrial creation.

Over the course of the foregoing chapters, we have sought to give as clear a view as possible of all the lengthy and varied stages of which one must be aware before boldly venturing into the jungle that is IoT. It is true that certain commercial services of certain IoT networks may seem to shorten that path, and give the impression that it is easy to establish an IoT network... but we need to be completely aware of what is often hidden behind such networks, in order to guard against future nasty surprises.

Our main ambition, therefore, was to enable you to constantly see both sides of an issue: hardware and software aspects; electronics and computing; economic and societal values, etc. etc. etc.

We hope we have fulfilled this purpose through this book and, if you have any questions, comments, remarks (constructive ones, of course!), you can contact the authors at the addresses shown below. You will always be more than welcome to do so: this kind of contact can only enrich everybody's knowledge!

Dominique PARET   dp-consulting@orange.fr

Jean-Paul HUON   jp.huon@gmail.com

Bibliography

Norms and Standards

ISO – International Organization for Standardization

ETSI – European Telecommunications Standards Institute
www.etsi.org/

FCC– Federal Communications Commission
https://www.fcc.gov/

IEEE – Institute of Electrical and Electronics Engineers
https://www.ieee.org/index.html

Regulations

ERO – ERC 7003 Recommendation
http://www.erodocdb.dk/docs/doc98/official/pdf/rec7003e.pdf

ICNIRP   International Commission on Non Ionizing Radiation Protection
http://www.icnirp.org/

GDPR – Official Journal of the European Union L119
http://eur-lex.europa.eu/legal-content/EN/TXT/?uri=OJ%3AL%3A2016%3A119%3ATOC

ANSSI – *Agence nationale de la sécurité des systèmes d'information*
https://www.ssi.gouv.fr/
https://www.ssi.gouv.fr/administration/produits-certifies/cc/

Radio Frequency Protocols

RFID (Radio Frequency IDentification)

Dominique Paret, *RFID and Contactless Smart Cards Applications*, John Wiley & Sons, 2005.
Dominique Paret, *RFID at Ultra and Super High Frequencies: Theory and Applications*, John Wiley & Sons, 2009.

NFC (Near Field Communication)

NFC Forum: http://nfc-forum.org/

Dominique Paret, *Design Constraints For NFC Devices*, ISTE Ltd, London and John Wiley & Sons, New York, 2016.
Dominique Paret, *NFC – Principles and Applications*, Dunod, 2012
Dominique Paret, *Antennas Designs for NFC Devices*, ISTE Ltd, London and John Wiley & Sons, New York, 2016.

Bluetooth: https://www.bluetooth.com/
DASH7: http://www.dash7-alliance.org/

LR LTN – Long Range Low Throughput Networks Protocols

LoRa: https://www.lora-alliance.org/

SIGFOX: https://www.sigfox.com/fr

Ingenu: http://www.ingenu.com/

LTE M NB IoT: http://www.gsma.com/connectedliving/mobile-iot-initiative/

Main Communication Protocols

AMQP: http://www.amqp.org/

MQTT: http://mqtt.org/

RFC – specifications:
https://www.rfc-editor.org
http://www.rfc-base.org/rfc-7252.html
RFC 793 – TCP Protocol
RFC 3261S – IP Protocol

RFC 2616 – HTTP/1.1 Protocol

RFC 7235 – Hypertext Transfer Protocol (HTTP/1.1): Authentication

RFC 7230 – Hypertext Transfer Protocol (HTTP/1.1): Message Syntax and Routing

RFC 7228 – Terminology for Constrained-Node Networks

RFC 7252 – Constrained Application Protocol

RFC 5321 – SMTP Protocol

RFC 959 – FTP Protocol

RFC 3550 – RTP Protocol

RFC 6690 – Constrained RESTful Environments (CoRE) Link Format

RFC 6282 – Compression Format for IPv6 Datagrams over IEEE 802.15.4-Based Networks

RFC 6961 – The Transport Layer Security (TLS) Multiple Certificate Status Request Extension

RFC 6655 – AES-CCM Cipher Suites for Transport Layer Security (TLS)

RFC 6347 – Datagram Transport Layer Security Version 1.2

RFC 5246 – Transport Layer Security Protocol

Press article: Antony Passemard, "From sensors to business value", available at: https://entrepreneurshiptalk.wordpress.com/2014/01/29/the-internet-of-thing-protocol-stack-from-sensors-to-business-value/, 2014.

Cloud Computing

Azure IoT: https://azure.microsoft.com/fr-fr/suites/iot-suite/

AWS IoT: https://aws.amazon.com/fr/iot/?hp=tile&so-exp=below

Slideware : Michael Garcia, "Traitement d'événements en temps réel", available at: http://www.slideshare.net/AmazonWebServices/apres-midi-track-2-s3-traitement-devenements?from_action=save, 2015.

Application (Example detailed in this book)

Z#BRE IoT: https://zbre.io/platform/

Index

Other titles from

in

Waves

2017

PARET Dominque, SIBONY Serge
Musical Techniques: Frequencies and Harmony

2016

ANSELMET Fabien, MATTEI Pierre-Olivier
Acoustics, Aeroacoustics and Vibrations

BAUDRAND Henri, TITAOUINE Mohammed, RAVEU Nathalie
The Wave Concept in Electromagnetism and Circuits: Theory and Applications

PARET Dominique
Antennas Designs for NFC Devices

PARET Dominique
Design Constraints for NFC Devices

WIART Joe
Radio-Frequency Human Exposure Assessment

GOURE Jean-Pierre
Optics in Instruments: Applications in Biology and Medicine

LAZAROV Andon, KOSTADINOV Todor Pavlov
Bistatic SAR/GISAR/FISAR Theory Algorithms and Program Implementation

LHEURETTE Eric
Metamaterials and Wave Control

PINEL Nicolas, BOURLIER Christophe
Electromagnetic Wave Scattering from Random Rough Surfaces: Asymptotic Models

SHINOHARA Naoki
Wireless Power Transfer via Radiowaves

TERRE Michel, PISCHELLA Mylène, VIVIER Emmanuelle
Wireless Telecommunication Systems

2012

LALAUZE René
Chemical Sensors and Biosensors

LE MENN Marc
Instrumentation and Metrology in Oceanography

LI Jun-chang, PICART Pascal
Digital Holography

2011

BECHERRAWY Tamer
Mechanical and Electromagnetic Vibrations and Waves

GOURE Jean-Pierre
Optics in Instruments

GROUS Ammar
Applied Metrology for Manufacturing Engineering

LE CHEVALIER François, LESSELIER Dominique, STARAJ Robert
Non-standard Antennas

2010

BEGAUD Xavier
Ultra Wide Band Antennas

MARAGE Jean-Paul, MORI Yvon
Sonar and Underwater Acoustics

2009

BOUDRIOUA Azzedine
Photonic Waveguides

BRUNEAU Michel, POTEL Catherine
Materials and Acoustics Handbook

DE FORNEL Frederique, FAVENNEC Pierre-Noël
Measurements using Optic and RF Waves

FRENCH COLLEGE OF METROLOGY
Transverse Disciplines in Metrology

2008

FILIPPI Paul J.T.
Vibrations and Acoustic Radiation of Thin Structures

LALAUZE René
Physical Chemistry of Solid-Gas Interfaces

2007

KUNDU Tribikram
Advanced Ultrasonic Methods for Material and Structure Inspection

PLACKO Dominique
Fundamentals of Instrumentation and Measurement

RIPKA Pavel, TIPEK Alois
Modern Sensors Handbook

2006

BALAGEAS Daniel *et al.*
Structural Health Monitoring

BOUCHET Olivier *et al.*
Free-Space Optics

BRUNEAU Michel, SCELO Thomas
Fundamentals of Acoustics

FRENCH COLLEGE OF METROLOGY
Metrology in Industry

GUILLAUME Philippe
Music and Acoustics

GUYADER Jean-Louis
Vibration in Continuous Media

Printed and bound by CPI Group (UK) Ltd, Croydon, CR0 4YY